THE
QUOTATIONARY
MANIFESTO

THE
QUOTATIONARY
MANIFESTO

A Positive Daily Dose of Inspiration
To Instill Motivation and Undergo Transformation

JOSEPH TURCHI

DEDICATION

I would like to dedicate this book to the following people.

My brothers and sisters,
Thank you for always being there through all our family highs and lows. You have been the examples and teachers of unconditional love, patience, tolerance, and acceptance. You have always had my back and supported me throughout my awesome journey. Thank you! Thank you! Thank you!

My many nieces and nephews,
I am so proud of each and every one of you. Your love for each other and genuine closeness is something special and certainly appreciated. But mostly I am grateful for each of you, and for your keeping our family traditions and values with your children. You all as a unit have decided to carry the family touch. Thank you!

To the lifelong learners,
The process of personal development is never-ending. Nobility to me is never thinking you are better than anyone else and always striving to remain conscious of just being better today than you were yesterday. I wrote this book for you. Be intentional in what you feed your brain; our thoughts become things. I challenge you to "own your morning" and take a daily dose of these powerful quotations. I am certain it will inspire, motivate, and transform your life for the better.

INTRODUCTION

GETTING THE MOST OUT OF THIS BOOK

This book was written to the reader with a desire to attain happiness, productivity, balance, peace, and fulfillment in their life. To the person who always has the chatter in their brain that says life should be better but has not discovered how to achieve it. The one who has been searching for meaning and purpose, which has been alluding you for years. In my lifetime, I have been a dreamer but never really believed my dreams would become a reality—until I changed my habits and my thinking. These quotes created belief and made a significant difference in my life.

After many years of trial and error, I discovered that if you put the right thoughts in your mind, your whole world could change. This book has the power to do just that. When you have the desire and ambition to change some things in your life and the will to acquire the skills necessary for personal growth, transformation will occur. This quotationary book was written to equip you for change. These quotations will captivate and inspire you as they have me to change your thought process on a daily basis.

Often, time is measured in minutes, and living is measured in moments. This book is about learning how to live in the moment. It will help you appreciate yourself and your worth through your daily routine of focusing on quiet mindfulness. In time, you will become fully alive again.

The creation of this resource book has been a collective journey of mine after personally reading and studying these quotes for over twenty-five years. It has always been my intention to create a comprehensive resourceful book to help anyone with a desire to create their own positive mindset.

For this book to be effective, it is not meant to function like a dictionary. This book, if used correctly, is a daily dose of mental power and energy. Just as we know our body needs nutrition, hydration, supplements, and a daily exercise regiment, we know the same routine is needed for the brain.

Introduction

When you feed your brain with daily quotations from this book, your thinking will change dramatically. Throughout my years as an educator, a business owner, life coach, and motivational speaker, I have discovered that what we feed into our brains will be the result of what our reality becomes. Research has demonstrated that the answers to our daily challenges and struggles we face can be solved with the power of our thoughts. There is a constant voice, a dialogue you might say, that never stops in our brains. These thoughts on many occasions create melodrama within the chatter to remind us of fear. Fear of failure, fear of not having enough, fear of not being good enough. Only you know what fears are in your daily internal chatter. The only way to address these fears is through awareness. Your unconscious mind is always at work reminding us of the past. To address our internal chatterbox, we must practice the power of awareness and consciously release the failure thoughts by proactively feeding our brain with these daily quotes to nourish the positivity of our lives.

Our world as we live it today is on a constant negative merry-go-round, and the only way to get off is to start every day with something affirming and positive. An intentional, driven quiet time with positive quotes may be the perfect solution.

It is my intention that within three to six months of instilling a daily dose of this prescription, your life will be happier, have increased feelings of achievement and boost your overall confidence personally and professionally. Your life will feel happier with increased feelings of achievement, confidence, self-esteem, peace, and well-being. You will handle adversity, struggles, and even challenges in work or in your relationship with a much better perspective.

So if you desire to experience personal growth, productivity, happiness, balance, and security, this is my recommendation for you. Find your secret place, your quiet spot, and take time as to what topic in The Quotationary Book you might need for your day. Pick two or three quotes each morning, read them twice, allow them to sink in, and then carry it through your day. When you own your morning, you will own your entire day.

THE QUOTES

Ability

Ability may get you to the top, but it takes character to keep you there.
                                                    ~John Wooden

They are able who think they are able.
                                                    ~Virgil

We are often imprisoned in the cage of our own abilities and routines, which provides us with a sense of security.
                                                    ~Alice Miller

Knowing what you can not do is more important than knowing what you can do. In fact, that's good taste.
                                                    ~Lucille Ball

If you have great talents, industry will improve them: if you have but moderate abilities, industry will supply their deficiency.
                                                    ~Sir Joshua Reynolds

We judge ourselves by what we feel capable of doing, while others judge us by what we have already done.
                                                    ~Henry Wadsworth Longfellow

I choose . . . to live so that which came to me as seed goes to the next as blossom, and that which came to me as blossom, goes on as fruit.
                                                    ~Dawna Markova

Man seems to be capable of great virtues but not of small virtues; capable of defying his torturer but not of keeping his temper.
                                                    ~G. K. Chesterton

Intelligence is quickness to apprehend as distinct from ability, which is capacity to act wisely on the thing apprehended.
                                                    ~Alfred North Whitehead

People are capable of doing an awful lot when they have no choice and I had no choice. Courage is when you have choices.

~Terry Anderson

A pint can't hold a quart—if it holds a pint it is doing all that can be expected of it.

~Margaret Deland

A man must not deny his manifest abilities, for that is to evade his obligations.

~William Feather

What one has to do usually can be done.

~Eleanor Roosevelt

Only the mediocre are always at their best.

~Jean Giraudoux

Talent wins games, but teamwork and intelligence win championships.

~Michael Jordan

Natural ability without education has more often raised a man to glory and virtue than education without natural ability.

~Marcus Aurelius

I found that there were these incredibly great people at doing certain things, and that you couldn't replace one of these people with 50 average people. They could just do things that no number of average people could do.

~Steve Jobs

Ability is what you're capable of doing. Motivation determines what you do. Attitude determines how well you do it.

~Lou Holtz

Can't usually means won't. We can . . . if we will.

~Don Ward

They can say you can't do it, but sometimes it doesn't always work.

~Casey Stengel

Great ability develops and reveals itself increasingly with every new assignment.

~Baltasar Gracián y Morales

Let not thy will roar, when thy power can but whisper.

~Thomas Fuller

Absurdity

The absurd man is he who never changes.

~Auguste-Marseille Barthélémy

Acceptance

Our entire life—consists ultimately in accepting ourselves as we are.

~Jean Anouilh

Acceptance is not submission; it is acknowledgment of the facts of a situation. Then deciding what you're going to do about it.

~Kathleen Casey Theisen

Any man who does not accept the conditions of life sells his soul.

~Charles Baudelaire

Accidents

I don't believe in accidents. There are only encounters in history. There are no accidents.

~Pablo Picasso

Accomplishments

If what you did yesterday seems big, you haven't done anything today.

~Lou Holtz

We may go to the moon, but that's not very far. The greatest distance we have to cover still lies within us.

~Charles de Gaulle

Life is not easy for any of us. But what of that? We must have perseverance and, above all, confidence in ourselves. We must believe that we are gifted for something, and that this thing must be attained.

~Marie Curie

To be yourself in a world that is constantly trying to make you something else is the greatest accomplishment.

~Ralph Waldo Emerson

The whole point of getting things done is knowing what to leave undone.

~Oswald Chambers

The starting point of all achievement is desire.

~Napoleon Hill

Too many of us, when we accomplish what we set out to do, exclaim, "See what I have done!" instead of saying, "See where I have been led."

~Henry Ford

I love the challenge of starting at zero every day and seeing how much I can accomplish.

~Martha Stewart

I am only one, but still I am one. I cannot do everything, but still I can do something. And because I cannot do everything I will not refuse to do the something that I can do.

~Edward Everette Hale

People with clear, written goals, accomplish more in a shorter period of time than people without them could ever imagine.

~Brian Tracy

Great things are done by a series of small things brought together.

~Vincent van Gogh

Do not let time pass without accomplishing something. Otherwise you will regret it when your hair turns gray.

~Yue Fei

It is amazing what you can accomplish if you do not care who gets the credit.

~Harry S. Truman

The height of your accomplishments will equal the depth of your convictions.

~William F. Scolavino

The man who has accomplished all that he thinks worthwhile has begun to die.

~E. T. Trigg

Accountability

We should every night call ourselves to an account: What infirmity have I mastered today? What passions opposed? What temptation resisted? What virtue acquired?

~Lucius Annaeus Seneca

The only thing necessary for the triumph of evil is for good men to do nothing.

~Edmund Burke

Achieve

Happiness lies in the joy of achievement, in the thrill of creative effort.

~Franklin D. Roosevelt

Those who dare to fail miserably can achieve greatly.

~John F. Kennedy

No man ever got very high by pulling other people down.

~Alfred Lord Tennyson

Optimism is the faith that leads to achievement. Nothing can be done without hope and confidence.

~Helen Keller

I have climbed to the top of the greasy pole!

~Benjamin Disraeli

There are countless ways of achieving greatness, but any road to achieving one's maximum potential must be built on a bedrock of respect for the individual, a commitment to excellence, and a rejection of mediocrity.

~Buck Rodgers

There are no gold medals for the 95-yard dash.

~Max De Pree

There is no penalty for overachievement.

~George W. Miller

No matter what accomplishments you achieve, somebody helped you.

~Althea Gibson

I used to want the words "She tried" on my tombstone. Now I want "She did it."

~Katherine Dunham

The greatest achievement of the human spirit is to live up to one's opportunities and make the most of one's resources.

~Luc de Clapiers

High achievement always takes place in the framework of high expectation.

~Charles F. Kettering

Action

And of all glad words of prose or rhyme, The gladdest are Act while there yet is time.

~Franklin P. Adams

The ordinary acts we practice every day at home are of more importance to the soul than their simplicity might suggest.

~Thomas Moore

What you do today can improve all your tomorrows.

~Ralph Marston

Don't let ideas die of neglect.

~Harold R. McAlindon

The way to get things done is not to mind who gets the credit of doing them.
~Benjamin Jowett

If it's not illegal, immoral, or fattening . . . go for it!
~Harold R. McAlindon

I have always thought the actions of men the best interpreters of their thoughts.
~John Locke

Either move or be moved.
~Ezra Pound

How wonderful it is that nobody need wait a single moment before starting to improve the world.
~Anne Frank

Be a "go-giver" as well as a "go-getter."
~Leonard Hudson

The superior man is modest in his speech, but exceeds in his actions.
~Confucius

The way to get started is to quit talking and begin doing.
~Walt Disney

'Tis the motive exalts the action; 'Tis the doing, and not the deed.
~Margaret Preston

Act as if it were impossible to fail.
~Dorothea Brande

Man is born a predestined idealist, for he is born to act. To act is to affirm the worth of an end, and to persist in affirming the worth of an end is to make an ideal.
~Oliver Wendell Holmes Sr.

The most decisive actions of our life—I mean those that are most likely to decide the whole course of our future—are, more often than not, unconsidered.
~André Gide

A thought which does not result in an action is nothing much, and an action which does not proceed from a thought is nothing at all.
~Georges Bernanos

I was brought up to believe that the only thing worth doing was to add to the sum of accurate information in the world.
~Margaret Mead

A ship in harbor is safe, but it is not what ships are built for.
~John A. Shedd

Happy people plan actions, they don't plan results.
~Denis Waitley

Doubt, of whatever kind, can be ended by action alone.
~Thomas Carlyle

Great thoughts speak only to the thoughtful mind, but great actions speak to all mankind.
~Theodore Roosevelt

So here hath been dawning. Another blue day: Think, wilt thou let it. Slip useless away.
~Thomas Carlyle

Don't let the fear of the time it will take to accomplish something stand in the way of your doing it.
~Earl Nightingale

Put your heart, mind, and soul into even your smallest acts. This is the secret of success.
~Swami Sivananda

The amount of good luck coming your way depends on your willingness to act.
~Barbara Sher

Say what you know, do what you must, come what may.
~Sofia Kovalevskaya

Don't be afraid to take a big step. You can't cross a chasm in two small jumps.
~David Lloyd George

Let us, then, be up and doing, With a heart for any fate; Still achieving, still pursuing, Learn to labor and to wait.

~Henry Wadsworth Longfellow

The quality of our expectations determines the quality of our actions.

~André Godin

We should be taught not to wait for inspiration to start a thing. Action always generates inspiration. Inspiration seldom generates action.

~Frank Tibolt

Our real problem, then, is not our strength today; it is the vital necessity of action today to ensure our strength tomorrow.

~Dwight D. Eisenhower

Self-knowledge is best learned, not by contemplation, but by action. Strive to do your duty and you will soon discover of what stuff you are made.

~Johann Wolfgang von Goethe

We know what a person thinks not when he tells us what he thinks, but by his actions.

~Isaac Bashevis Singer

It's wonderful what we can do if we're always doing.

~George Washington

He rises on the toe: that spirit of his. In aspiration lifts him from the earth.

~William Shakespeare

What you are will show in what you do.

~Thomas A. Edison

Knowledge must come through action.

~Sophocles

Words are nothing but words; power lies in deeds. Be a person of action.

~Mali Oriot Mamadu Konyate

Who are the learned? Those who practice what they know.
~Elijah Muhammad

The more often [a man] feels without acting, the less he will ever be able to act, and, in the long run, the less he will be able to feel.
~C. S. Lewis

The secret of getting things done is to act.
~Dante Alighieri

Let us take our proper station; We, the rising generation, Let us stamp the age as ours!
~Mary Howitt

People do not decide to become extraordinary. They decide to accomplish extraordinary things.
~Edmund Hillary

In the arena of human life the honors and rewards fall to those who show their good qualities.
~Aristotle

Nobody made a greater mistake than he who did nothing because he could do only a little.
~Edmund Burke

Whatever you can do or dream you can, begin it. Boldness has genius, power, and magic in it. Begin it now.
~Johann Wolfgang von Goethe

The best way to make your dreams come true is to wake up.
~Paul Valéry

We must sail sometimes with the wind and sometimes against it — but we must sail, and not drift, nor lie at anchor.
~Oliver Wendell Holmes

Anything you can do needs to be done, so pick up the tool of your choice and get started.
~Ben Linder

An acre of performance is worth a whole world of promise.
~William Dean Howells

Don't let the possibilities be suffocated by procrastination. Go! Now!

~Robert H. Schuller

To be is to do.

~Kurt Vonnegut

Everyone can do something that makes a difference.

~Todd R. Wagner

People may doubt what you say, but they will believe what you do.

~Lewis Cass

In theory, there is no difference between theory and practice. But in practice, there is.

~Yogi Berra

You can outdo you—if you really want to.

~Paul Harvey

There ain't no rules around here. We're trying to accomplish something.

~Thomas Edison

So what do we do? Anything. Something. So long as we just don't sit there. . . . If we wait until we've satisfied all the uncertainties, it may be too late.

~Lee Iacocca

One of these days is none of these days.

~English Proverb

Reappraise the past, reevaluate where we've been, clarify where we are, and predict or anticipate where we are headed. Then go.

~Toni Cade Bambara

What is it going to be—reasons or results?

~Art Turock

Focused action beats brilliance every time.

~Art Turock

If you want to do something, you'll find a way. If you don't, you'll find an excuse.

~Jim Rohn

Act like you expect to get into the end zone.

~Christopher Morley

Do not delay: the golden moments fly!

~Henry Wadsworth Longfellow

If you don't execute your ideas, they die.

~Roger von Oech

You can't wring your hands and roll up your sleeves at the same time.

~Patricia Schroeder

To love what you are doing. To believe in what you are doing. To know what you are doing. These are the three essentials.

~Steve Musseau

The greatest happiness is to transform one's feelings into actions.

~Germaine de Staël

The question is: Who will get to heaven first; the man who talks or the man who acts?

~Melvin B. Tolson

No matter what we feel or know, no matter what our potential gifts or talents, only action brings them to life.

~Dan Millman

Let no one be deluded that a knowledge of the path can substitute for putting one foot in front of the other.

~Mary Caroline Richards

Begin somewhere; you cannot build a reputation on what you intend to do.

~Liz Smith

The future cannot be predicted, but futures can be invented.

~Dennis Gabor

Action is the foundational key to all success.
~Pablo Picasso

To do anything in this world worth doing, we must not stand back shivering and thinking of the cold and danger, but jump in, and scramble through as well as we can.
~Sydney Smith

The greatest happiness is to transform one's feelings into actions.
~Germaine de Staël

Don't sit down and wait for the opportunities to come. Get up and make them.
~Madame C. J. Walker

What is right to be done cannot be done too soon.
~Jane Austen

One should always act from one's inner sense of rhythm.
~Rosamond Lehmann

To always be intending to live a new life, but never to find time to set about it; this is as if a man should put off eating and drinking and sleeping from one day and night to another, till he is starved and destroyed.
~John Tillotson

An ounce of action is worth a ton of theory.
~Friedrich Engels

Things won are done; joy's soul lies in the doing.
~William Shakespeare

I say if it's going to be done, let's do it. Let's not put it in the hands of fate. Let's not put it in the hands of someone who doesn't know me. I know me best. Then take a breath and go ahead.
~Anita Baker

You will learn and grow according to the nature and consequences of your actions.
~Robert Anthony

Good will, like a good name, is got by many actions and lost by one.

~Francis Jeffrey

Never leave well enough alone.

~Raymond Lowey

The essential conditions of everything you do must be choice, love, passion.

~Nadia Boulanger

The woods are lovely, dark and deep, But I have promises to keep, And miles to go before I sleep, And miles to go before I sleep.

~Robert Frost

Reappraise the past, reevaluate where we've been, clarify where we are, and predict or anticipate where we are headed. Then go.

~Toni Cade Bambara

Either move or be moved.

~Ezra Pound

Life takes on meaning when you become motivated, set goals and charge after them in an unstoppable manner.

~Les Brown

The vitality of thought is in adventure. Ideas won't keep. Something must be done about them.

~Alfred North Whitehead

Determine never to be idle. No person will have occasion to complain of the want of time who never loses any. It is wonderful how much may be done if we are always doing.

~Thomas Jefferson

Adventure

Adventure is worthwhile.

~Amelia Earhart

One way to get the most out of life is to look upon it as an adventure.

~William Feather

Twenty years from now you will be more disappointed by the things that you didn't do than by the ones you did do. So throw off the bowlines. Sail away from the safe harbor. Catch the trade winds in your sails. Explore. Dream. Discover.
~Mark Twain

All adventures, especially into new territory, are scary.
~Sally Ride

I know absolutely nothing. That is why each new day, each new moment, is truly an adventure.
~Ross Fields

This is the only chance you will ever have on earth with this exciting adventure called life. So why not plan it, and try to live it as richly, as happily as possible?
~Dale Carnegie

Where the old tracks are lost, new country is revealed with its wonders.
~Rabindranath Tagore

No, you never get any fun out of the things you haven't done.
~Ogden Nash

Adversity

Prosperity proves the fortunate, adversity the great.
~Rose Kennedy

Adversity is the diamond dust that Heaven polishes its jewels with.
~Thomas Carlyle

If we had no winter, the spring would not be so pleasant: if we did not sometimes taste of adversity, prosperity would not be so welcome.
~Anne Bradstreet

Fire is the test of gold; adversity, of strong men.
~Lucius Annaeus Seneca

Sweet are the uses of adversity, which, like the toad, ugly and venomous, wears yet a precious jewel in his head.

~William Shakespeare

Prosperity doth best discover vice, but adversity doth best discover virtue.

~Francis Bacon

In adversity, remember to keep an even mind.

~Horace

Adversity, if a man is set down to it by degrees, is more supportable with equanimity by most people than any great prosperity arrived at in a single lifetime.

~Samuel Butler

It is courage, courage, courage, that raises the blood of life to crimson splendor. Live bravely and present a brave front to adversity.

~Horace

All adverse and depressing influences can be overcome, not by fighting, but by rising above them.

~Charles Caleb Colton

Adversity is the trial of principle. Without it, a man hardly knows whether he is honest or not.

~Henry Fielding

If you watch how nature deals with adversity, continually renewing itself, you can't help but learn.

~Bernie Siegel

Adversities do not make the man either weak or strong, but they reveal what he is.

~Faith Forsyte

When life is too easy for us, we must beware or we may not be ready to meet the blows which sooner or later come to everyone, rich or poor.

~Eleanor Roosevelt

Our real blessings often appear to us in the shape of pains, losses and disappointments; but let us have patience and we soon shall see them in their proper figures.

~Joseph Addison

Revel in the ordinary.

~M. J. Ryan

When you choose your fields of labor go where nobody else is willing to go.

~Mary Lyon

Advice

There are two types of people who will tell you that you cannot make a difference in this world: those who are afraid to try and those who are afraid you will succeed.

~Ray Goforth

Fear less, hope more; eat less, chew more; whine less, breathe more; talk less, say more; hate less, love more; and all good things are yours.

~Swedish Proverb

Advice is what we ask for when we already know the answer but wish we didn't.

~Erica Jong

Advice is like snow; the softer it falls, and the longer it dwells upon, and the deeper it sinks into the mind.

~Samuel Taylor Coleridge

Affirmation

It is far more impressive when others discover your good qualities without your help.

~Judith Martin

Age

The older I get, the greater power I seem to have to help the world; I am like a snowball—the further I am rolled the more I gain.
~Susan B. Anthony

Never suffer youth to be an excuse for inadequacy, nor age and fame to be an excuse for indolence.
~Benjamin Hayden

In the end, it's not the years in your life that count. It's the life in your years.
~Abraham Lincoln

Aging is not lost youth but a new stage of opportunity and strength.
~Betty Friedan

Youth is the gift of nature, but age is a work of art.
~Stanisław Jerzy Lec

Let age, not envy, draw wrinkles on thy cheeks.
~Thomas Browne

Age is opportunity no less than youth itself, though in another dress, and as the evening twilight fades away the sky is filled with stars, invisible by day.
~Henry Wadsworth Longfellow

I think your whole life shows in your face and you should be proud of that.
~Lauren Bacall

Nobody grows old by merely living a number of years. People grow old by deserting their ideals . . . You are as young as your faith, as old as your doubts; as young as your self-confidence, as old as your fear; as young as your hope, as old as your despair.
~James E. Faust

The measure of a man's life is the well spending of it, and not the length.
~Plutarch

Youth is a circumstance you can't do anything about. The trick is to grow up without getting old.

~Frank Lloyd Wright

The older I grow the more I distrust the familiar doctrine that age brings wisdom.

~H. L. Mencken

For the unlearned, old age is winter; for the learned, it is the season of the harvest.

~Hasidic Proverb

The old believe everything; the middle-aged suspect everything; the young know everything.

~Oscar Wilde

The secret of staying young is to live honestly, eat slowly, and lie about your age.

~Lucille Ball

The world ages us too fast. We grow up too quickly, we stop dreaming too early, and we develop the ability to worry at far too young an age.

~Doug Wecker

There's no such thing as old age, there is only sorrow.

~Edith Wharton

Old age has deformities enough of its own. It should never add to them the deformity of vice.

~Eleanor Roosevelt

Cherish all your happy moments: they make a fine cushion for old age.

~Christopher Morley

Agony

There is no greater agony than bearing an untold story inside you.
~Maya Angelou

Agree

Unless both sides win, no agreement can be permanent.
~Jimmy Carter

When men and women agree, it is only in their conclusions; their reasons are always different.
~George Santayana

Always fall in with what you're asked to accept. Take what is given, and make it over your way. My aim in life has always been to hold my own with whatever's going. Not against: with.
~Robert Frost

Aims

When I was young, my ambition was to be one of the people who made a difference in this world.
~Jim Henson

An ambitious man can never know peace.
~J. Krishnamurti

Make no little plans. They have no magic to stir men's blood . . . Make big plans, aim high in hope and work.
~Daniel H. Burnham

If I had not had so much ambition and had not tried to do so many things, I probably would have been happier, but less useful.
~Thomas Edison

Keep your eyes on the stars, and your feet on the ground.
~Theodore Roosevelt

A man's worth is no greater than his ambitions.
~Marcus Aurelius

Fire above the mark you intend to hit. Energy, invincible determination, with the right motive, are the levers that move the world.
~Noah Porter

If you would hit the mark, you must aim a little above it; every arrow that flies feels the attraction of earth.
~Henry Wadsworth Longfellow

As wise people often defeat their aims by too great caution, cunning also frequently overshoots the mark by too much craft.
~Jane West

Never measure the height of a mountain, until you have reached the top. Then you will see how low it was.
~Dag Hammarskjöld

I would rather lose in a cause that will someday win, than win in a cause that will someday lose!
~Woodrow Wilson

Winning isn't everything—but wanting to win is.
~Vince Lombardi

What would you attempt to do if you knew you would not fail?
~Robert H. Schuller

Life is a mission. Every other definition of life is false, and leads all who accept it astray. Religion, science, philosophy, though still at variance upon many points, all agree in this, that every existence is an aim.
~Giuseppe Mazzini

No one rises to low expectations.
~Les Brown

Most people fail not because they aim too high and miss, but because they aim too low and hit.
~Les Brown

Once you say you're going to settle for second, that's what happens to you in life, I find.
~John F. Kennedy

Aim so high you'll never be bored.
~Linda Gibbons

Ambition leads me not only farther than any other man has been before me, but as far as I think it possible for man to go.

~Captain James Cook

Love the moment, and the energy of that moment will spread beyond all boundaries.

~Corita Kent

I want to be able to say in the last four seconds of my life that I tried to do my best.

~Rubén Blades

There are two things to aim at in life: first, to get what you want, and after that to enjoy it. Only the wisest of mankind achieve the second.

~Logan Pearsall Smith

If you seek what is honorable, what is good, what is the truth of your life, all the other things you could not imagine come as a matter of course.

~Oprah Winfrey

The aim, if reached or not, makes great the life: Try to be Shakespeare, leave the rest to fate.

~Robert Browning

Reach high, for stars lie hidden in your soul. Dream deep, for every dream precedes the goal.

~Pamela Vaull Starr

Ambition is a commendable attribute, without which no man succeeds. Only inconsiderate ambition imperils.

~Warren G. Harding

Intelligence without ambition is a bird without wings.

~C. Archie Danielson

Alone

We allow our ignorance to prevail upon us and make us think we can survive alone, alone in patches, alone in groups, alone in races, even alone in genders.

~Maya Angelou

Associate yourself with men of good quality, if you esteem your own reputation; for 'tis better to be alone than in bad company.
~George Washington

It's like magic. When you live by yourself, all your annoying habits are gone!
~Merrill Markoe

Ambition

Ambition is the last refuge of the failure.
~Oscar Wilde

Never measure the height of a mountain until you have reached the top. Then you will see how low it was.
~Dag Hammarskjöld

An ambitious man can never know peace.
~J. Krishnamurti

If I had not had so much ambition and had not tried to do so many things, I probably would have been happier, but less useful.
~Thomas Edison

Make no little plans. They have no magic to stir men's blood . . . Make big plans, aim high in hope and work.
~Daniel H. Burnham

America

America—it is a fabulous country, the only fabulous country; it is the only place where miracles not only happen, but where they happen all the time.
~Thomas Wolfe

The strength of a nation derives from the integrity of the home.
~Confucius

The first requisite of a good citizen in this Republic of ours is that he shall be able and willing to pull his weight.
~Theodore Roosevelt

There is a mysterious cycle in human events. To some generations much is given. Of other generations much is expected. This generation of Americans has a rendezvous with destiny.

~Franklin D. Roosevelt

The American flag is the symbol of our freedom, national pride and history.

~Mike Fitzpatrick

Our flag honors those who have fought to protect it, and is a reminder of the sacrifice of our nation's founders and heroes. As the ultimate icon of America's storied history, the Stars and Stripes represents the very best of this nation.

~Joe Barton

All great change in America begins at the dinner table.

~Ronald Reagan

I always consider the settlement of America with reverence and wonder, as the opening of a grand scene and design in providence, for the illumination of the ignorant and the emancipation of the slavish part of mankind all over the earth.

~John Adams

Ancestry

We inherit from our ancestors gifts so often taken for granted. Each of us contains within us this inheritance of soul. We are links between the ages, containing past and present expectations, sacred memories and future promise.

~Edward Sellner

I believe that what we become depends on what our fathers teach us at odd moments, when they aren't trying to teach us.

~Umberto Eco

Angels

We shall find peace. We shall hear the angels, we shall see the sky sparkling with diamonds.

~Anton Chekhov

Anger

What I've learned about being angry with people is that it generally hurts you more than it hurts them.

~Oprah Winfrey

Anger is like milk, it should not be kept too long.

~Phyllis Bottome

Anger is never without a reason, but seldom with a good one.

~Benjamin Franklin

Human pain does not let go of its grip at one point in time. Rather, it works its way out of our consciousness over time. There is a season of sadness. A season of anger. A season of tranquility. A season of hope.

~Robert Veninga

For every minute you are angry you lose sixty seconds of happiness.

~Ralph Waldo Emerson

Anger repressed can poison a relationship as surely as the cruelest words.

~Joyce Brothers

Whatever is begun in anger, ends in shame.

~Benjamin Franklin

Two things a man should never be angry at: what he can help, and what he cannot help.

~Thomas Fuller

Anger dwells only in the bosom of fools.

~Albert Einstein

No man can think clearly when his fists are clenched.

~George Jean Nathan

Anybody can become angry — that is easy, but to be angry with the right person and to the right degree and at the right time and for the right purpose, and in the right way — that is not within everybody's power and is not easy.

~Aristotle

Annoyance

Few things are harder to put up with than the annoyance of a good example.

~Mark Twain

Answer

Don't dwell on what went wrong. Instead, focus on what to do next. Spend your energies on moving forward toward finding the answer.

~Denis Waitley

Judge a man by his questions rather than his answers.

~Voltaire

Anticipation

Not many sounds in life . . . exceed in interest a knock at the door.
~Charles Lamb

Anxiety

Better to be despised for too anxious apprehensions, than ruined by too confident security.

~Edmund Burke

Apathy

The world is a dangerous place, not because of those who do evil, but because of those who look on and do anything.
~Albert Einstein

Apology

Apology is a lovely perfume; it can transform the clumsiest moment into a gracious gift.

~Margaret Lee Runbeck

Never ruin an apology with an excuse.

~Benjamin Franklin

Appreciation

It is the appreciation of beauty and truth, the striving for knowledge which makes life worth living.

~Morris Ralphael Cohen

Truly appreciate those around you, and you'll soon find many others around you. Truly appreciate life, and you'll find that you have more of it.

~Ralph Marston

As we express our gratitude, we must never forget that the highest appreciation is not to utter words, but to live by them.

~John F. Kennedy

Blessed is the man who has some congenial work, some occupation in which he can put his heart.

~John Burroughs

And he just stared out at the ocean and said, "Look at the view, young lady. Look at the view." And every day, in some little way, I try to do what he said.

~Shaun Usher

Arise

Work hard, stay positive, and get up early. It's the best part of the day.

~George Allen

One who looks outside, dreams. One who looks inside, awakes.

~Carl Jung

Art

The arts must be considered an essential element of education . . . . They are tools for living life reflectively, joyfully and with the ability to shape the future.

~Shirley Trusty Corey

Art is anything people do with distinction.

~Louis Dudek

To create one's world, in any of the arts, takes courage.
~Georgia O'Keeffe

Art consists of reshaping life but it does not create life, nor cause life.
~Stanley Kubrick

Give me a museum and I'll fill it.
~Pablo Picasso

The purpose of art is washing the dust of daily life off our souls.
~Pablo Picasso

Painting is a poetry that is seen rather than felt, and poetry is painting that is felt rather than seen.
~Leonardo da Vinci

Being an artist means ceasing to take seriously that very serious person we are when we are not an artist.
~José Ortega y Gasset

Art does not reproduce the visible; rather, it makes visible.
~Paul Klee

Aspiration

Far away there in the sunshine are my highest aspirations. I may not reach them, but I can look up and see their beauty, believe in them, and try to follow where they lead.
~Louisa May Alcott

You can judge the height of someone's talent by what he aspires to. Only a great thing can satisfy a great talent.
~Baltasar Gracián y Morales

If you have built castles in the air, your work need not be lost. That is where they should be. Now put foundations under them.
~Henry David Thoreau

Let me be a little kinder, Let me be a little blinder, To the faults of those around me, Let me praise a little more.
~Edgar A. Guest

Peace and friendship with all mankind is our wisest policy; and I wish we may be permitted to pursue it.

~Thomas Jefferson

You can't live a perfect day without doing something for someone who will never be able to repay you.

~John Wooden

Attitude

Your attitude, not your aptitude, will determine your altitude.

~Zig Ziglar

Could we change our attitude, we should not only see life differently, but life itself would come to be different. Life would undergo a change of appearance because we ourselves had undergone a change of attitude.

~Katherine Mansfield

You may not be able to change a situation, but with humor you can change your attitude about it.

~Allen Klein

If you don't like something, change it. If you can't change it, change your attitude.

~Maya Angelou

The trick is in what one emphasizes. We either make ourselves miserable, or we make ourselves happy. The amount of work is the same.

~Carlos Castaneda

Life is 10% what happens to you and 90% how you react to it.

~Charles R. Swindoll

You cannot have a positive life and a negative mind.

~Joyce Meyer

A positive attitude is something everyone can work on, and everyone can learn how to employ it.

~Joan Lunden

Keep your face always toward the sunshine — and shadows will fall behind you.

~Walt Whitman

Nobody grows old by merely living a number of years. People grow old by deserting their ideals . . . You are as young as your faith, as old as your doubts; as young as your self-confidence, as old as your fear; as young as your hope, as old as your despair.

~James E. Faust

Ability is what you're capable of doing. Motivation determines what you do. Attitude determines how well you do it.

~Lou Holtz

'Tis easy enough to be pleasant when life flows along like a song, but the man worth while is the one who will smile when everything goes dead wrong.

~Ella Wheeler Wilcox

Everything can be taken from a man but one thing: the last of the human freedoms — to choose one's attitude in any given set of circumstances, to choose one's own way.

~Viktor E. Frankl

It is our attitude at the beginning of a difficult task which, more than anything else, will affect its successful outcome.

~William James

A willing heart adds feather to the heel.

~Joanna Baillie

No life is so hard that you can't make it easier by the way you take it.

~Ellen Glasgow

Act as if you were already happy and that will tend to make you happy.

~Dale Carnegie

Cheerfulness, sir, is the principal ingredient in the composition of health.

~Arthur Murphy

Man's rise or fall, success or failure, happiness or unhappiness depends on his attitude . . . a man's attitude will create the situation he imagines.

~James Lane Allen

Flight is nothing but an attitude in motion.

~Diane Ackerman

Thinking a smile all the time will keep your face youthful.

~Gelett Burgess

Be willing to take the first step, no matter how small it is. Concentrate on the fact that you are willing to learn. Absolute miracles will happen.

~Louise L. Hay

A healthy attitude is contagious, but don't wait to catch it from others. Be a carrier.

~Tom Stoppard

Act as if what you do makes a difference. It does.

~William James

Authority

Authority without wisdom is like a heavy axe without an edge, fitter to bruise than polish.

~Anne Bradstreet

What I wanted to be when I grew up was—in charge.

~Wilma Vaught

When in doubt, mumble; when in trouble, delegate; when in charge, ponder.

~James H. Boren

Balance

There is a very real relationship, both quantitatively and qualitatively, between what you contribute and what you get out of this world.

~Oscar Hammerstein II

If passion drives you, let reason hold the reins.
~Benjamin Franklin

Whatever you do, don't congratulate yourself too much, or berate yourself either. Your choices are half chance. So are everybody else's.
~Mary Schmich

We can be sure that the greatest hope for maintaining equilibrium in the face of any situation rests within ourselves.
~Francis J. Braceland

I feel that sin and evil are the negative part of you, and I think it's like a battery: you've got to have the negative and the positive in order to be a complete person.
~Dolly Parton

Everything is changing. People are taking their comedians seriously and the politicians as a joke.
~Will Rogers

The rose and the thorn, and sorrow and gladness are linked together.
~Moslih Eddin Saadi

People . . . sometimes think that a thing cannot be good and terrible at the same time.
~C. S. Lewis

The secret of life is to know when enough is enough.
~Vincent Ryan

I don't believe that life is supposed to make you feel good, or to make you feel miserable either. Life is just supposed to make you feel.
~Gloria Naylor

Often the wisdom of the body clarifies the despair of the spirit.
~Marion Woodman

As wise people often defeat their aims by too great caution, cunning also frequently overshoots the mark by too much craft.
~Jane West

Work is not always required . . . there is such a thing as sacred idleness, the cultivation of which is now fearfully neglected.
~George MacDonald

Battle

I will write of him who fights and vanquishes his sins, who struggles on through weary years against himself . . . and wins.
~Caroline Begelow LeRow

In every battle there comes a time when both sides consider themselves beaten, then he who continues the attack win.
~Ulysses S. Grant

Beauty

Everything has beauty, but not everyone sees it.
~Confucius

Character contributes to beauty. It fortifies a woman as her youth fades. A mode of conduct, a standard of courage, discipline, fortitude, and integrity can do a great deal to make a woman beautiful.
~Jacqueline Bisset

Who walks with Beauty has no need to fear: The sun and moon and stars keep pace with him; Invisible hands restore the ruined year, And time itself grows beautifully dim.
~David Morton

Beauty is no quality in things themselves: it exists merely in the mind which contemplates them.
~David Hume

What is beautiful is good, and who is good will soon also be beautiful.
~Sappho

The kind of beauty I want most is the hard-to-get kind that comes from within—strength, courage, dignity.
~Ruby Dee

The best and most beautiful things in the world cannot be seen or even touched, but just felt in the heart.
~Helen Keller

Art produces ugly things which frequently become more beautiful with time. Fashion, on the other hand, produces beautiful things which always become ugly with time.
~Jean Cocteau

The absence of flaw in beauty is itself a flaw.
~Havelock Ellis

Beauty, like truth, never is so glorious as when it goes the plainest.
~Laurence Sterne

There is nothing ugly; I never saw an ugly thing in my life: for let the form of an object be what it may —light, shade, and perspective will always make it beautiful.
~John Constable

At some point in life the world's beauty becomes enough. You don't need to photograph, paint, or even remember it. It is enough.
~Toni Morrison

We are cups, constantly and quietly being filled. The trick is, knowing how to tip ourselves over and let the beautiful stuff out.
~Ray Bradbury

Believe

A man is shaped to beliefs long held however uncritically —as the roots of a tree that have grown in the crevices of a rock.
~Oliver Wendell Holmes

Believe that life is worth living, and your belief will help create the fact.
~William James

We do not believe if we do not live and work according to our belief.
~Heidi Wills

It is your own assent to yourself, and the constant voice of your own reason, and not of others, that should make you believe.
~Blaise Pascal

Whatever you want in life, other people are going to want it too. Believe in yourself enough to accept the idea that you have an equal right to it.
~Diane Sawyer

After observation and analysis, when you find that anything agrees with reason and is conducive to the good and benefit of one and all, then accept it and live up to it.
~Buddha Siddhartha Guatama Shakyamuni

One person with a belief is equal to ninety-nine who have only interests.
~John Stuart Mill

Our beliefs in a rich future life are of little importance unless we coin them into a rich present life.
~Thomas Dreier

The old believe everything; the middle-aged suspect everything; the young know everything.
~Oscar Wilde

Believe that you have received it, and it will be yours.
~Mark 11:24 New International Version

He that will believe only what he can fully comprehend must have a very long head or a very short creed.
~Pierre Teilhard de Chardin

A belief is not true because it is useful.
~Henri-Frédéric Amiel

Believe it is possible to solve your problem. Tremendous things happen to the believer. So believe the answer will come. It will.
~Norman Vincent Peale

Whether you think you can or you can't—you're right.
~Henry Ford

People may doubt what you say, but they will believe what you do.
~Lewis Cass

When you believe in a thing, believe in it all the way, implicitly and unquestionable.

~Walt Disney

Hope unbelieved is always considered nonsense. But hope believed is history in the process of being changed.

~Jim Wallis

A belief is not merely an idea that the mind possesses; it is an idea that possesses the mind.

~Robert Oxton Bolton

All things are possible for the one who believes.
~Mark 9:23 English Standard Version

Begin challenging your own assumptions. Your assumptions are your windows on the world. Scrub them off every once in a while, or the light won't come in.

~Alan Alda

Belonging

A true man never frets about his place in the world, but just slides into it by the gravitations of his nature, and swings there as easily as a star.

~Edwin Hubbell Chapin

There is no house like the house of belonging.

~David Whyte

Best

I strive for the best and I do the possible.

~Lyndon B. Johnson

Good, better, best. Never let it rest. 'Til your good is better and your better is best.

~St. Jerome

Always do your best. What you plant now, you will harvest later.
~Og Mandino

A person always doing his or her best becomes a natural leader, just by example.

~Joe DiMaggio

Don't let the good things of life rob you of the best things.
~Maltbie D. Babcock

The good is the greatest rival of the best.
~Nellie L. McClung

Half of success is thinking that what we are doing has got to be done the best anybody ever did it.
~Helen Gurley Brown

Do your best every day and your life will gradually expand into satisfying fullness.
~Horatio W. Dresser

Birth

We are ever dying to one world and being born into another.
~Henry David Thoreau

Blame

The best years of your life are the ones in which you decide your problems are your own. You don't blame them on your mother, the ecology, or the president. You realize that you control your own destiny.
~Albert Ellis

You are responsible for your life. You can't keep blaming somebody else for your dysfunction. Life is really about moving on.
~Oprah Winfrey

Blessings

Over and over I marvel at the blessings of my life: each year has grown better than the last.
~Lawrence Welk

Reflect upon your present blessings—of which every man has many—not on your past misfortunes, of which all men have some.

~Charles Dickens

Body

The body is the soul's house. Shouldn't we therefore take care of our house so that it doesn't fall into ruin?

~Philo Judaeus

A healthy body is guest chamber for the soul: a sick body is a prison.

~Francis Bacon

The body is the instrument of the soul.

~Gary Zukav

Bold

Freedom lies in being bold.

~Robert Frost

Boldness be my friend.

~William Shakespeare

Whatever you can do or dream you can, begin it. Boldness has genius, power, and magic in it. Begin it now.

~Johann Wolfgang von Goethe

Books

A room without books is like a body without a soul.

~Marcus Tullius Cicero

If you have a garden and a library, you have everything you need.

~Marcus Tullius Cicero

Someday you will be old enough to start reading fairy tales again.

~C. S. Lewis

Books are the quietest and most constant of friends; they are the most accessible and wisest of counselors, and the most patient of teachers.

~Charles W. Eliot

Boredom

In order to live free and happily you must sacrifice boredom. It is not always an easy sacrifice.

~Richard Bach

It is the dull man who is always sure, and the sure man who is always dull.

~H. L. Mencken

Punctuality is the virtue of the bored.

~Evelyn Waugh

Boundaries

Walls turned sideways are bridges.

~Angela Davis

It's not trespassing when you cross your own boundaries.
~Johnnie Walker

Bravery

I count him braver who overcomes his desires than him who overcomes his enemies.

~Aristotle

Be brave. Take risks. Nothing can substitute experience.
~Paulo Coelho

There is, in addition to a courage with which men die, a courage by which men must live.

~John F. Kennedy

There is a certain enthusiasm in liberty, that makes human nature rise above itself, in acts of bravery and heroism.
~Alexander Hamilton

Bravery is the capacity to perform properly even when scared half to death.

~General Omar Nelson Bradley

You're braver than you believe, stronger than you seem, and smarter than you think.

~A. A. Milne

Take chances, make mistakes. That's how you grow. Pain nourishes your courage. You have to fail in order to practice being brave.

~Mary Tyler Moore

It is easy to be brave at a safe distance.

~Aesop

Strength of numbers is the delight of the timid. The valiant in spirit glory in fighting alone.

~Mohandas Gandhi

Those who face that which is actually before them, unburdened by the past, undistracted by the future, these are they who live, who make the best use of their lives; these are those who have found the secret of contentment.

~Alban Goodier

Forgiveness is a virtue of the brave.

~Indira Gandhi

Be scared. You can't help that. But don't be afraid. Ain't nothing in the woods going to hurt you if you don't corner it, or it don't smell that you are afraid. A bear or a deer has got to be scared of a coward the same as a brave man has got to be.

~William Faulkner

It is the character of a brave and resolute man not to be ruffled by adversity and not to desert his post.

~Marcus Tullius Cicero

The brave man is not he who feels no fear, For that were stupid and irrational; But he, whose noble soul its fears subdues, And bravely dares the danger nature shrinks from.

~Joanna Baillie

Burden

People become attached to their burdens sometimes more than the burdens are attached to them.

~George Bernard Shaw

Money and time are the heaviest burdens of life, and . . . the unhappiest of all mortals are those who have more of either than they know how to use.

~Samuel Johnson

Very few burdens are heavy if everyone lifts.

~Sy Wise

Business

If you don't drive your business, you will be driven out of business.
~B. C. Forbes

A friendship founded on business is a good deal better than a business founded on friendship.

~John D. Rockefeller

The conduct of a successful business merely consists in doing things in a very simple way, doing them regularly, and never neglecting to do them.

~William Hesketh Lever

All lasting business is built on friendship.
~Alfred A. Montapert

Busy

If you observe a really happy man, you will find . . . that he is happy in the course of living life twenty-four crowded hours each day.
~W. Beran Wolfe

Being busy does not always mean real work. The object of all work is production or accomplishment and to either of these ends there must be forethought, system, planning, intelligence, and honest purpose, as well as perspiration. Seeming to do is not doing.
~Thomas Edison

Most of us are so busy doing what we think we have to do, that we do not think about what we really want to do.

~Robert Percival

Calm

Nothing gives one person so much advantage over another as to remain always cool and unruffled under all circumstances.

~Thomas Jefferson

The beauty of the soul shines out when a man bears with composure one heavy mischance after another, not because he does not feel them, but because he is a man of high and heroic temper.

~Aristotle

Go placidly amid the noise and the haste, and remember what peace there may be in silence.

~Desiderata

Quiet minds cannot be perplexed or frightened but go on in fortune or misfortune at their own private pace, like a clock during a thunderstorm.

~Robert Louis Stevenson

Capability

If we did all the things we are capable of, we would literally astound ourselves.

~Thomas Edison

A pint can't hold a quart—if it holds a pint it is doing all that can be expected of it.

~Margaret Deland

We must make the choices that enable us to fulfill the deepest capacities of our real selves.

~Thomas Merton

We are not all capable of everything.

~Virgil

When you know that you're capable of dealing with whatever comes, you have the only security the world has to offer.

~Harry Browne

Care

Care and diligence bring luck.

~Thomas Fuller

If you care enough for a result, you will most certainly attain it.

~William James

If we win, nobody will care. If we lose, there will be nobody to care.

~Winston Churchill

Caring is the ultimate competitive advantage.

~Ron Kendrick

Caution

My own experience has taught me this: if you wait for the perfect moment when all is safe and assured it may never arrive.

~Maurice Chevalier

The policy of being too cautious is the greatest risk of all.

~Jawaharlal Nehru

Better to be despised for too anxious apprehensions, than ruined by too confident security.

~Edmund Burke

In skating over thin ice, our safety is in our speed.

~Ralph Waldo Emerson

Challenge

The ultimate measure of a man is not where he stands in moments of convenience and comfort, but where he stands at times of challenge and controversy.

~Martin Luther King Jr.

Accept the challenges so that you can feel the exhilaration of victory.

~George S. Patton

Nothing happens to anybody which he is not fitted by nature to bear.

~Marcus Aurelius

Champion

Champions do not believe in chance.

~Rob Gilbert

As strong as my legs are, it is my mind that has made me a champion.

~Michael Johnson

Chance

I like second chances. I've given people second chances. You have fall-outs with friends, and forgiveness is a great thing to have. It's not easy to forgive. I definitely don't forget, but I do forgive.

~Odette Annable

Your life does not get better by chance, it gets better by change.

~Jim Rohn

Champions do not believe in chance.

~Rob Gilbert

Take chances, make mistakes. That's how you grow. Pain nourishes your courage. You have to fail in order to practice being brave.

~Mary Tyler Moore

I have always been delighted at the prospect of a new day, a fresh try, one more start, with perhaps a bit of magic waiting somewhere behind the morning.

~J. B. Priestley

Whatever you do, don't congratulate yourself too much, or berate yourself either. Your choices are half chance. So are everybody else's.

~Mary Schmich

Change

The absurd man is he who never changes.
~Auguste-Marseille Barthélémy

A state without the means of some change is without the means of its conservation.
~Edmund Burke

A competitive world offers two possibilities. You can lose. Or, if you want to win, you can change.
~Lester Thurow

Change your life today. Don't gamble on the future, act now, without delay.
~Simone de Beauvoir

No man ever steps in the same river twice, for it's not the same river and he's not the same man.
~Heraclitus

Our being is continually undergoing and entering upon changes . . . We must, strictly speaking, at every moment give each other up and let each other go and not hold each other back.
~Rainer Maria Rilke

Change is the process by which the future invades our lives.
~Alvin Toffler

We must always change, renew, rejuvenate ourselves; otherwise, we harden.
~Johann Wolfgang von Goethe

Person to person, moment to moment, as we love, we change the world.
~Samahria Lyte Kaufman

Could we change our attitude, we should not only see life differently, but life itself would come to be different. Life would undergo a change of appearance because we ourselves had undergone a change of attitude.
~Katherine Mansfield

In a time of drastic change it is the learners who inherit the future. The learned usually find themselves equipped to live in a world that no longer exists.

~Eric Hoffer

We cannot change anything unless we accept it. Condemnation does not liberate; it oppresses.

~Carl Jung

Your life does not get better by chance, it gets better by change.

~Jim Rohn

We cannot become what we need to be, by remaining what we are.

~Max De Pree

Open your arms to change, but don't let go of your values.

~Dalai Lama

Never doubt that you can change history. You already have.

~Marge Piercy

If you don't like something, change it. If you can't change it, change your attitude.

~Maya Angelou

The most powerful agent of growth and transformation is something much more basic than any technique: a change of heart.

~John Welwood

They always say time changes things, but you actually have to change them yourself.

~Andy Warhol

They must often change who would remain constant in happiness or wisdom.

~Confucius

I fear there will be no future for those who do not change.

~Louis L'Amour

To live is to change, and to be perfect is to have changed often.

~John Henry Newman

To some will come a time when change itself is beauty, if not heaven.

~Edwin Arlington Robinson

In a progressive country change is constant . . . change . . . is inevitable.

~Benjamin Disraeli

It's the most unhappy people who most fear change.
~Mignon McLaughlin

Intelligence is the ability to adapt to change.
~Stephen Hawking

Observe constantly that all things take place by change.
~Marcus Aurelius

Continuity gives us roots; change gives us branches, letting us stretch and grow and reach new heights.

~Pauline R. Kezer

Man needs, for his happiness, not only the enjoyment of this or that, but hope and enterprise and change.

~Bertrand Russell

To keep our faces toward change and behave like free spirits in the presence of fate is strength undefeatable.

~Helen Keller

Not everything that is faced can be changed, but nothing can be changed until it is faced.

~James Arthur Baldwin

The art of progress is to preserve order amid change and to preserve change amid order.

~Alfred North Whitehead

The dinosaurs disappeared because they could not adapt to their changing environment. We shall disappear if we cannot adapt to an environment that now contains spaceships, computers—and thermonuclear weapons.

~Arthur C. Clarke

We have it in our power to begin the world over again.

~Thomas Paine

A change in bad habits leads to a change in life.

~Jenny Craig

The first step towards getting somewhere is to decide that you are not going to stay where you are.

~J. P. Morgan

When you're through changing, you're through.

~Bruce Barton

The main dangers in this life are the people who want to change everything . . . or nothing.

~Nancy Astor

The progression or emancipation of any class usually, if not always, takes place through the efforts of individuals of that class.

~Harriet Martineau

Just when I discovered the meaning of life, they changed it.

~George Carlin

Change is not made without inconvenience, even from worse to better.

~Richard Hooker

Change brings opportunities when people have been planning for it, are ready for it, and have just the thing in mind to do when the new state comes into being.

~Rosabeth Moss Kanter

Take your mind out every now and then and dance on it. It is getting all caked up.

~Mark Twain

Without accepting the fact that everything changes, we cannot find perfect composure. But unfortunately, although it is true, it is difficult for us to accept it. Because we cannot accept the truth of transience, we suffer.

~Shunryu Suzuki

Any change, even a change for the better, is always accompanied by drawbacks and discomforts.

~Arnold Bennett

Character

Character is the architecture of the being.

~Louise Nevelson

Ability may get you to the top, but it takes character to keep you there.

~John Wooden

It is fortunate to be of high birth, but it is no less to be of such character that people do not care to know whether you are or are not.

~Jean de la Bruyère

Character contributes to beauty. It fortifies a woman as her youth fades. A mode of conduct, a standard of courage, discipline, fortitude, and integrity can do a great deal to make a woman beautiful.

~Jacqueline Bisset

Sincerity is impossible, unless it pervades the whole being, and the pretence of it saps the very foundation of character.

~James Russell Lowell

Character is the architecture of the being.

~Louise Nevelson

The best index to a person's character is how he treats people who can't do him any good, and how he treats people who can't fight back.

~Abigail Van Buren

Difficulty shows what men are.

~Epictetus

Instead of developing your personality, charm, or intellect, try exercising your character today.

~Stephanie Goddard Davidson

People do not seem to realize that their opinion of the world is also a confession of character.

~Ralph Waldo Emerson

The majority of people perform well in a crisis and when the spotlight is on them; it's on the Sunday afternoons of this life, when the nobody is looking, that the spirit falters.

~Alan Bennett

The final forming of a person's character lies in their own hands.

~Anne Frank

Knowledge will give you power, but character respect.

~Bruce Lee

What you are will show in what you do.

~Thomas A. Edison

People do not seem to realize that their opinion of the world is also a confession of character.

~Ralph Waldo Emerson

Character is the basis of happiness, and happiness the sanction of character.

~George Santayana

'Tis easy enough to be pleasant when life flows along like a song, but the man worth while is the one who will smile when everything goes dead wrong.

~Ella Wheeler Wilcox

Adversity is the trial of principle. Without it, a man hardly knows whether he is honest or not.

~Henry Fielding

Difficulty shows what men are.

~Epictetus

It is not what he has, or even what he does which expresses the worth of a man, but what he is.

~Henri-Frédéric Amiel

A man's character is like a tree and reputation like its shadow. The shadow is what we think of it; the tree is the real thing.

~Abraham Lincoln

How far you go in life depends on your being tender with the young, compassionate with the aged, sympathetic with the striving, and tolerant of the weak and the strong. Because someday in life you will have been all of these.

~George Washington Carver

The altar of sacrifice is the touchstone of character.

~O. P. Gifford

My great concern is not whether you have failed, but whether you are content with your failure.

~Abraham Lincoln

I hope I shall always possess firmness and virtue enough to maintain what I consider the most enviable of all titles, the character of an honest man.

~George Washington

Adversities do not make the man either weak or strong, but they reveal what he is.

~Faith Forsyte

Character is what emerges from all the little things you were too busy to do yesterday, but did anyway.

~Mignon McLaughlin

The best thing to give to your enemy is forgiveness; to an opponent, tolerance; to a friend, your heart; to your child, a good example; to a father, deference; to your mother, conduct that will make her proud of you; to yourself, respect; to all others, charity.

~Benjamin Franklin

When a man speaks the truth in the spirit of truth, his eye is as clear as the heavens. When he has base ends, and speaks falsely, the eye is muddy, and sometimes asquint.

~Ralph Waldo Emerson

I don't have to be what you want me to be.

~Muhammad Ali

The ideal man bears the accidents of life with dignity and grace, making the best of circumstances.

~Aristotle

Simplicity of character is the natural result of profound thought.
~William Hazlitt

What helps luck is a habit of watching for opportunities, of having a patient but restless mind, of sacrificing one's ease or vanity, or uniting a love of detail to foresight, and of passing through hard times bravely and cheerfully.
~Victor Cherbuliez

One isn't necessarily born with courage, but one is born with potential. Without courage, we cannot practice any other virtue with consistency. We can't be kind, true, merciful, generous, or honest.
~Maya Angelou

The important thing in life is . . . not victory but the combat; the essential thing is not to have won, but to have fought well.
~Pierre de Coubertin

The spirit, the will to win, and the will to excel, are the things that endure. These qualities are so much more important than the events that occur.
~Vince Lombardi

It is not genius, nor glory, nor love that reflects the greatness of the human soul; it is kindness.
~Jean-Baptiste Henri Lacordaire

Your net worth to the world is usually determined by what remains after your bad habits are subtracted from your good ones.
~Benjamin Franklin

It is in the character of very few men to honor without envy a friend who has prospered.
~Aeschylus

Nearly all men can stand adversity, but if you want to test a man's character, give him power.
~Abraham Lincoln

Charity

Charity is a virtue of the heart, and not of the hands.
~Joseph Addison

This only is charity, to do all, all that we can.

~John Donne

In charity there is no excess.

~Francis Bacon

True charity is the desire to be useful to others without the thought of recompense.

~Emanuel Swedenborg

This only is charity, to do all, all that we can.

~John Donne

Christmas is a season for kindling the fire of hospitality in the hall, the genial flame of charity in the heart.

~Washington Irving

Unless we think of others and do something for them, we miss one of the greatest sources of happiness.

~Ray Lyman Wilbur

Provision for others is a fundamental responsibility of human life.
~Woodrow Wilson

Cheerful

You find yourself refreshed by the presence of cheerful people. Why not make an honest effort to confer that pleasure on others? Half the battle is gained if you never allow yourself to say anything gloomy.

~Lydia Marie Child

Be of good cheer. Do not think of today's failures, but of the success that may come tomorrow.

~Helen Keller

Mirth is like a flash of lightning that breaks through a gloom of clouds and glitters for a moment. Cheerfulness keeps up a daylight in the mind, filling it with a steady and perpetual serenity.
~Samuel Johnson

Children

Childhood is never troubled with foresight.

~Fanny Burney

Our children give us the opportunity to become the parents we always wished we'd had.

~Louise Hart

It is my pleasure that my children are free and happy, and unrestrained by parental tyranny. Love is the chain whereby to bind a child to its parents.

~Abraham Lincoln

It's frightening to think that you mark your children merely by being yourself.

~Simone de Beauvoir

We find delight in the beauty and happiness of children that makes the heart too big for the body.

~Ralph Waldo Emerson

Blessed indeed is the man who hears many gentle voices call him father.

~Lydia Maria Child

What we forgot as children is that our parents are children, also. The child in them has not been satisfied or met or loved, often.

~Edna O'Brien

Children are made of eyes and ears, and nothing, however minute, escapes their microscopic observation.

~Fanny Kemble

In a world as empirical as ours, a youngster who does not know what he is good at will not be sure what he is good for.

~Edgar Z. Friedenberg

If help and salvation are to come they can only come from the children, for the children are the makers of men.

~Maria Montessori

Since it is so likely that [children] will meet cruel enemies, let them at least have heard of brave knights and heroic courage. Otherwise you are making their destiny not brighter but darker.

~C. S. Lewis

One of the most obvious facts about grown-ups, to a child, is that they have forgotten what it is like to be a child.

~Randall Jarrell

Choices

It is our choices . . . that show what we truly are, far more than our abilities.

~J. K. Rowling

When you have to make a choice and don't make it, that is in itself a choice.

~William James

It is your own conviction which compels you; that is, choice compels choice.

~Epictetus

Oh, how easy it must be to be good when one has the power of doing good!

~Susan Edmonstone Ferrier

Be miserable. Or motivate yourself. Whatever has to be done, it's always your choice.

~Wayne Dyer

The luxury of doing good surpasses every other personal enjoyment.

~John Gay

All problems boil down to limited choices, and the choice we often forget is love.

~Tom Daly

Sow good services: sweet remembrances will grow from them.
~Madame de Staël

I choose . . . to live so that which came to me as seed goes to the next as blossom, and that which came to me as blossom, goes on as fruit.

~Dawna Markova

We must make the choices that enable us to fulfill the deepest capacities of our real selves.

~Thomas Merton

All your life, you will be faced with a choice. You can choose love or hate . . . I choose love.

~Johnny Cash

Whatever you do, don't congratulate yourself too much, or berate yourself either. Your choices are half chance. So are everybody else's.

~Mary Schmich

People are capable of doing an awful lot when they have no choice and I had no choice. Courage is when you have choices.

~Terry Anderson

The more decisions that you are forced to make alone, the more you are aware of your freedom to choose.

~Thornton Wilder

You can't make someone else's choices. You shouldn't let someone else make yours.

~Colin Powell

One's philosophy is not best expressed in words; it is expressed in the choices one makes. In the long run, we shape our lives, and we shape ourselves. The process never ends until we die. And the choices we make are ultimately our own responsibility.

~Eleanor Roosevelt

The key word is paradox. As a fool I sidestep the either/or choices of logic and choose both.

~Ken Feit

One's philosophy is not best expressed in words; it is expressed in the choices one makes.

~Eleanor Roosevelt

What is it going to be—reasons or results?

~Art Turock

If things go wrong, don't go with them.

~Roger Babson

Others can stop you temporarily—you are the only one who can do it permanently.

~Zig Ziglar

The choice is ours, in every moment.

~M. J. Ryan

There is a sacred realm of privacy for every man and woman where he makes his choices and decisions—a realm of his own essential rights and liberties into which the law, generally speaking, must not intrude.

~Geoffrey Fisher

You have brains in your head. You have feet in your shoes. You can steer yourself any direction you choose.

~Theodor Seuss Geisel (Dr. Seuss)

The way you think, the way you behave, the way you eat, can influence your life by 30-50 years.

~Deepak Chopra

Life is raw material. We are artisans. We can sculpt our existence into something beautiful, or debase it into ugliness. It's in our hands.

~Cathy Better

The self is not something ready-made, but something in continuous formation through choice of action.

~John Dewey

You and I are essentially infinite choice-makers. In every moment of our existence, we are in that field of all possibilities where we have access to an infinity of choices.

~Deepak Chopra

The greatest power that a person possesses is the power to choose.
~J. Martin Kohe

But today is ours to live Its treasures now to use, And it can be our best day We alone can choose.

~Helen Gleason

Sometimes the most proactive thing we can do is to be happy, just to genuinely smile. Happiness, like unhappiness, is a proactive choice.

~Stephen R. Covey

Christmas

Christmas waves a magic wand over this world, and behold, every-thing is softer and more beautiful.

~Norman Vincent Peale

Some people are born for Halloween, and some are just counting the days until Christmas.

~Stephen Graham Jones

Christmas isn't a season. It's a feeling.

~Edna Ferber

Christmas is a season for kindling the fire for hospitality in the hall, the genial flame of charity in the heart.

~Washington Irving

There are no strangers on Christmas Eve.

~Adele Comandini

I sometimes think we expect too much of Christmas Day. We try to crowd into it the long arrears of kindliness and humanity of the whole year. As for me, I like to take Christmas a little at a time, all through the year.

~David Grayson

Yes, Virginia, there is a Santa Claus. He exists as certainly as love and generosity and devotion exist, and you know that they abound and give to your life its highest beauty and joy.

~Francis P. Church

Christmas is a bridge. We need bridges as the river of time flows past. Today's Christmas should mean creating happy hours for tomorrow and reliving those of yesterday.

~Gladys Taber

My idea of Christmas, whether old-fashioned or modern, is very simple: loving others. Come to think of it, why do we have to wait for Christmas to do that?

~Bob Hope

Christmas, my child, is love in action. Every time we love, every time we give, it's Christmas.

~Dale Evans Rogers

Circumstances

Your present circumstances don't determine where you can go they merely determine where you start.

~Nido Qubein

The ideal man bears the accidents of life with dignity and grace, making the best of circumstances.

~Aristotle

You may not be able to change a situation, but with humor you can change your attitude about it.

~Allen Klein

You cannot always control your circumstances. But you can control your own thoughts.

~Charles E. Popplestone

Do not wait for ideal circumstances, nor the best opportunities; they will never come.

~Janet Erskine Stuart

Youth is a circumstance you can't do anything about. The trick is to grow up without getting old.

~Frank Lloyd Wright

What we actually learn, from any given set of circumstances, determines whether we become increasingly powerless or more powerful.

~Blaine Lee

It's not what happens to you, but how you react to it that matters.

~Epictetus

There is nothing we cannot live down, rise above or overcome.
~Ella Wheeler Wilcox

You are the embodiment of the information you choose to accept and act upon. To change your circumstances you need to change your thinking and subsequent actions.
~Aldin Sinclair

Civil

Civility costs nothing, and buys everything.
~Mary Wortley Montagu

We must remember that any oppression, any injustice, any hatred, is a wedge designed to attack our civilization.
~Franklin D. Roosevelt

The exact measure of the progress of civilization is the degree in which the intelligence of the common mind has prevailed over wealth and brute force.
~George Bancroft

Civility is not a sign of weakness, and sincerity is always subject to proof.
~John F. Kennedy

Clarity

The more sand that has escaped from the hourglass of our life, the clearer we should see through it.
~Jean-Paul Sartre

Clever

A clever person solves a problem. A wise person avoids it.
~Albert Einstein

The next best thing to being clever is being able to quote someone who is.
~Mary Pettibone Poole

Comfort

Do not believe that he who seeks to comfort you lives untroubled among the simple and quiet words that sometimes do you good. His life has much difficulty . . . Were it otherwise he would never have been able to find those words.

~Rainer Marie Rilke

To ease another's heartache is to forget one's own.

~Abraham Lincoln

Commitment

A total commitment is paramount to reaching the ultimate in performance.

~Tom Flores

The achievement of your goal is assured the moment you commit yourself to it.

~Mack R. Douglas

Common Sense

Common sense is not so common.

~Voltaire

All truth, in the long run, is only common sense clarified.

~Thomas Henry Huxley

The greatest results in life are usually attained by simple means and the exercise of ordinary qualities. These may for the most part be summed in these two—common sense and perseverance.

~Owen Feltham

Communication

Occasionally in life there are those moments of unutterable fulfillment which cannot be completely explained by those symbols called words. Their meanings can only be articulated by the inaudible language of the heart.

~Martin Luther King Jr.

Thanks . . . Small word . . . Big meaning.
~Barbara Bartocci

Take advantage of every opportunity to practice your communication skills so that when important occasions arise, you will have the gift, the style, the sharpness, the clarity, and the emotions to affect other people.
~Jim Rohn

What comes from the heart, goes to the heart.
~Samuel Taylor Coleridge

The most beautiful thought runs the risk of being irrevocably forgotten if it is not written down.
~Arthur S. Schopenhauer

Companions

Associate yourself with men of good quality, if you esteem your own reputation; for 'tis better to be alone than in bad company.
~George Washington

Compassion

Compassion will cure more sins than condemnation.
~Henry Ward Beecher

Compassion means to lay a bridge over to the other without knowing whether he wants to be reached.
~Henri J. M. Nouwen

Compassion is the basis of all morality.
~Arthur Schopenhauer

Competition

A competitive world offers two possibilities. You can lose. Or, if you want to win, you can change.
~Lester Thurow

The only competition worthy a wise man is with himself.
~Anna Brownell Jameson

Complain

Singular indeed that the people should be writhing under oppression and injury, and yet not one among them to be found, to raise the voice of complaint.

~Abraham Lincoln

Noise proves nothing. Often a hen who has merely laid an egg cackles as if she had laid an asteroid.

~Mark Twain

Condemn

We cannot change anything unless we accept it. Condemnation does not liberate; it oppresses.

~Carl Jung

Conduct

You can preach a better sermon with your life than with your lips.
~Oliver Goldsmith

Character contributes to beauty. It fortifies a woman as her youth fades. A mode of conduct, a standard of courage, discipline, fortitude, and integrity can do a great deal to make a woman beautiful.
~Jacqueline Bisset

Patience is not simply the ability to wait—it's how we behave while we're waiting.

~Joyce Meyer

Patience and goodness will ever in the end conciliate the goodwill of others.

~Josephine

[Only by] the good influence of our conduct may we bring salvation in human affairs.

~Desiderius Erasmus

Almost all our faults are more pardonable than the methods we resort to to hide them.
~François Duc de La Rochefoucauld

Confidence

Life is not easy for any of us. But what of that? We must have perseverance and, above all, confidence in ourselves. We must believe that we are gifted for something, and that this thing must be attained.

~Marie Curie

When enthusiasm is driven by confidence, any goal can be attained.
~Robert E. Regent

Have confidence that if you have done a little thing well, you can do a bigger thing well, too.

~David Storey

When you have confidence, you can have a lot of fun. And when you have fun, you can do amazing things.

~Joe Namath

It is the dull man who is always sure, and the sure man who is always dull.

~H. L. Mencken

Some men are just as firmly convinced of what they think as others are of what they know.

~Aristotle

You've got to take the initiative and play your game. . . . Confidence makes the difference.

~Chris Evert

He that respects himself is safe from others. He wears a coat of mail that none can pierce.

~Henry Wadsworth Longfellow

Conflict

Men are afraid to rock the boat in which they hope to drift safely through life's currents, when, actually, the boat is stuck on a sandbar. They would be better off to rock the boat and try to shake it loose.

~Thomas Szasz

Peace is not absence of conflict, but the ability to cope with conflict by peaceful means.

~Ronald Reagan

The worst loneliness is not to be comfortable with yourself.

~Mark Twain

Confront

Men are afraid to rock the boat in which they hope to drift safely through life's currents, when, actually, the boat is stuck on a sandbar. They would be better off to rock the boat and try to shake it loose.

~Thomas Szasz

Great spirits have always encountered violent opposition from mediocre minds.

~Albert Einstein

Connected

We inherit from our ancestors gifts so often taken for granted. Each of us contains within us this inheritance of soul. We are links between the ages, containing past and present expectations, sacred memories and future promise.

~Edward Sellner

We cannot live only for ourselves. A thousand fibers connect us with our fellow man.

~Herman Melville

Conquer

To conquer without risk is to triumph without glory.

~Pierre Corneille

I learned that courage was not the absence of fear, but the triumph over it. The brave man is not he who does not feel afraid, but he who conquers that fear.

~Nelson Mandela

It's not the mountain we conquer, but ourselves.

~Edmund Hillary

Consciousness

In forming a bridge between body and mind, dreams may be used as a springboard from which man can leap to new realms of experience lying outside his normal state of consciousness and enlarge his vision.

~Ann Faraday

The needle of our conscience is as good a compass as any.

~Ruth Wolff

Everything that exalts and expands consciousness is good, while that which depresses and diminishes it is evil.

~Miguel de Unamuno

Every judgment of conscience, be it right or wrong, be it about things evil in themselves or morally indifferent, is obligatory, in such wise that he who acts against his conscience always sins.

~Thomas Aquinas

There is one thing alone that stands the brunt of life throughout its course: a quiet conscience.

~Euripides

The highest purpose of intellectual cultivation is to give a man a perfect knowledge and mastery of his own inner self.

~Novalis

I desire to so conduct the affairs of this administration that if at the end, when I come to lay down the reins of power, I have lost every friend on earth, I shall at least have one friend left and that friend shall be down inside of me.

~Abraham Lincoln

Vanity asks the question, "Is it popular?" But, conscience asks the question, "Is it right?"

~Martin Luther King Jr.

The needle of our conscience is as good a compass as any.
~Ruth Wolff

Labor to keep alive in your breast that little spark of celestial fire called conscience.
~George Washington

Consequence

You can avoid reality, but you cannot avoid the consequences of avoiding reality.
~Ayn Rand

By polluting clear water with slime you will never find good drinking water.
~Aeschylus

Consistent

The conduct of a successful business merely consists in doing things in a very simple way, doing them regularly, and never neglecting to do them.
~William Hesketh Lever

True consistency, that of the prudent and the wise, is to act in conformity with circumstances.
~John C. Calhoun

Contentment

When you are content to be simply yourself and don't compare or compete, everybody will respect you.
~Lao Tzu

The hardest thing is to take less when you can get more.
~Kin Hubbard

My great concern is not whether you have failed, but whether you are content with your failure.
~Abraham Lincoln

When we are unable to find tranquility within ourselves, it is useless to seek it elsewhere.

~François de La Rochefoucauld

Contentment is a pearl of great price, and whoever procures it at the expense of ten thousand desires makes a wise and a happy purchase.

~John Balguy

Who is wise? He that learns from everyone. Who is powerful? He that governs his passions. Who is rich? He that is content.

~Benjamin Franklin

Beware of undertaking too much at the start. Be content with quite a little. Allow for accidents. Allow for human nature, especially your own.

~Arnold Bennett

To be satisfied with little is hard, to be satisfied with a lot is impossible.

~Marie von Ebner-Eschenbach

Do not dwell in the past, do not dream of the future, concentrate the mind on the present moment.

~Buddha

You can never get enough of what you don't need, because what you don't need won't satisfy you.

~Dallin H. Oaks

All of us tend to put off living. We are all dreaming of some magical rose garden over the horizon—instead of enjoying the roses that are blooming outside our windows today.

~Dale Carnegie

Contribution

There is a very real relationship, both quantitatively and qualitatively, between what you contribute and what you get out of this world.

~Oscar Hammerstein II

Controversy

The ultimate measure of a man is not where he stands in moments of convenience and comfort, but where he stands at times of challenge and controversy.

~Martin Luther King Jr.

Conversation

If a man is often the subject of conversation, he soon becomes the subject of criticism.

~Immanuel Kant

Good, the more communicated, more abundant grows.

~John Milton

When people talk, listen completely . . . Most people never listen.

~Ernest Hemingway

For good or ill, your conversation is your advertisement. Every time you open your mouth, you let me look into your mind. Do they see it well clothed, neat, business wise?

~Bruce Burton

There are times when silence has the loudest voice.

~Leroy Brownlow

Discussing how old you are is the temple of boredom.

~Ruth Gordon

Conversation may be compared to a lyre with seven cords — philosophy, art, poetry, politics, love, scandal, and the weather.

~Anna Brownell Jameson

It's a toss-up as to which are finally the most exasperating — the dull people who never talk, or the bright people who never listen.

~Sydney J. Harris

I never make the mistake of arguing with people for whose opinions I have no respect.

~Edward Gibbon

Convictions

It is your own conviction which compels you; that is, choice compels choice.

~Epictetus

Never, for the sake of peace and quiet, deny your own experience and convictions.

~Dag Hammarskjöld

One's belief that one is sincere is not so dangerous as one's conviction that one is right. We all feel we are right; but we felt the same twenty years ago and today we know we weren't always right.

~Igor Stravinsky

The height of your accomplishments will equal the depth of your convictions.

~William F. Scolavino

Cooperation

Getting along with others is the essence of getting ahead, success being linked with cooperation.

~William Feather

Great discoveries and improvement invariably involve the cooperation of many minds. I may be given credit for having blazed the trail, but when I look at the subsequent developments I feel the credit is due to others rather than to myself.

~Alexander Graham Bell

Cope

Accept the diagnosis; defy the prognosis.

~Norman Cousins

Humor can alter any situation and help us cope at the very instant we are laughing.

~Allen Klein

Courage

Bravery is the capacity to perform properly even when scared half to death.
~General Omar Nelson Bradley

Character contributes to beauty. It fortifies a woman as her youth fades. A mode of conduct, a standard of courage, discipline, fortitude, and integrity can do a great deal to make a woman beautiful.
~Jacqueline Bisset

Strength of numbers is the delight of the timid. The valiant in spirit glory in fighting alone.
~Mohandas Gandhi

Great crises produce great men and great deeds of courage.
~John F. Kennedy

You're braver than you believe, stronger than you seem, and smarter than you think.
~A. A. Milne

The most courageous act is still to think for yourself. Aloud.
~Coco Chanel

Success is never final. Failure is never fatal. It's courage that counts.
~Winston Churchill

Life shrinks or expands in proportion to one's courage.
~Anaïs Nin

Because of a great love, one is courageous.
~Lao Tzu

Courage is resistance to fear, mastery of fear—not absence of fear.
~Mark Twain

I learned that courage was not the absence of fear, but the triumph over it. The brave man is not he who does not feel afraid, but he who conquers that fear.
~Nelson Mandela

Take chances, make mistakes. That's how you grow. Pain nourishes your courage. You have to fail in order to practice being brave.
~Mary Tyler Moore

All serious daring starts from within.

~Eudora Welty

Everyone has talent. What is rare is the courage to follow the talent to the dark place where it leads.

~Erica Jong

Courage is found in action. It has to be learned—and earned.

~Doug Hall

Clear thinking requires courage rather than intelligence.

~Thomas Szasz

It is courage, courage, courage, that raises the blood of life to crimson splendor. Live bravely and present a brave front to adversity.

~Horace

Any coward can fight a battle when he's sure of winning; but give me the man who has the pluck to fight when he's sure of losing.

~George Eliot

Whatever enlarges hope will also exalt courage.

~Samuel Johnson

Be scared. You can't help that. But don't be afraid. Ain't nothing in the woods going to hurt you if you don't corner it, or it don't smell that you are afraid. A bear or a deer has got to be scared of a coward the same as a brave man has got to be.

~William Faulkner

All things are possible for the one who believes.

~Mark 9:23 English Standard Version

Courage and perseverance have a magical talisman, before which difficulties disappear and obstacles vanish into air.

~John Quincy Adams

Sometimes we all have to do things we don't want to do. Even if they seem strange and scary at first.

~Audrey Penn

You gain strength, courage and confidence by every experience in which you really stop to look fear in the face . . . You must do the thing you think you cannot do.
~Eleanor Roosevelt

To do anything in this world worth doing, we must not stand back shivering and thinking of the cold and danger, but jump in, and scramble through as well as we can.
~Sydney Smith

Coward

To see what is right and not to do it is want of courage, or of principle.
~Confucius

Any coward can fight a battle when he's sure of winning; but give me the man who has the pluck to fight when he's sure of losing.
~George Eliot

To sin by silence, when they should protest, makes cowards of men.
~Ella Wheeler Wilcox

Creativity

Whatever creativity is, it is in part a solution to a problem.
~Brian Aldiss

Creativity is not the finding of a thing, but the making something out of it after it is found.
~James Russell Lowell

In an industrial society which confuses work and productivity, the necessity of producing has always been an enemy of the desire to create.
~Raoul Vaneigem

We must use time creatively—and forever realize that the time is always hope to do right.
~Martin Luther King Jr.

It is through creating, not possessing, that life is revealed.
~Vida D. Scudder

[Happiness] lies in the joy of achievement, in the thrill of creative effort.
~Franklin D. Roosevelt

To create you must quiet your mind. You need a quiet mind so that ideas will have a chance of connecting.
~Eric Maisel

To live a creative life, we must lose our fear of being wrong.
~Joseph Chilton Pearce

It is the supreme art of the teacher to awaken joy in creative expression and knowledge.
~Albert Einstein

Creativity is not the finding of a thing, but the making something out of it after it is found.
~James Russell Lowell

In order to create there must be a dynamic force, and what force is more potent than love?
~Igor Stravinsky

I lived in solitude in the country and noticed how the monotony of a quiet life stimulates the creative mind.
~Albert Einstein

One of the major factors which differentiates creative people from lesser creative people is that creative people pay attention to their small ideas.
~Roger von Tech

Bringing out your own unique brand of creativity into your life and the world can be the most significant thing you'll ever do.
~Lorna Catford

Crisis

Great crises produce great men and great deeds of courage.
~John F. Kennedy

When written in Chinese, the word "crisis" is composed of two characters. One represents danger and the other represents opportunity.

~John F. Kennedy

Criticism

If a man is often the subject of conversation, he soon becomes the subject of criticism.

~Immanuel Kant

Pay no attention to what the critics say. A statue has ever been erected in honor of a critic.

~Jean Sibelius

Cruelty

My doctrine is this, that if we see cruelty or wrong that we have the power to stop, and do nothing, we make ourselves sharers in the guilt.

~Anna Sewell

A critic is someone who never actually goes to the battle, yet who afterwards comes out shooting the wounded.

~Tyne Daly

Cry

I have wept to see thee weep.

~Mary Robinson

If the world's a vale of tears, Smile, till rainbows span it.

~Lucy Larcom

A good laugh is good for the spirits it's true, but a good cry is good for the soul.

~Bette Midler

Curiosity

Curiosity is one of the most permanent and certain characteristics of a vigorous intellect.

~Samuel Johnson

Life was meant to be lived, and curiosity must be kept alive. One must never, for whatever reason, turn his back on life.

~Eleanor Roosevelt

Curiosity is the wick in the candle of learning.

~William A. Ward

We just keep moving forward . . . because we're curious and curiosity keeps leading us down new paths.

~Walt Disney

The cure for boredom is curiosity. There is no cure for curiosity.

~Dorothy Parker

Custom

What custom hath endeared; we part with sadly, tho we prize it not.

~Joanna Baillie

Dance

Work like you don't need the money. Dance like no one is watching. And love like you've never been hurt.

~Mark Twain

On with the dance, let the joy be unconfined, is my motto; whether there's any dance to dance or any joy to unconfined.

~Mark Twain

We're fools whether we dance or not, so we might as well dance.
~Japanese Proverb

Danger

Avoiding danger is no safer in the long run than outright exposure. The fearful are caught as often as the bold.
~Helen Keller

Dare

All serious daring starts from within.
~Eudora Welty

Those who dare to fail miserably can achieve greatly.
~John F. Kennedy

It is not because things are difficult that we do not dare, it is because we do not dare that they are difficult.
~Lucius Annaeus Seneca

To dare is to lose one's footing momentarily. Not to dare is to lose oneself.
~Søren Kierkegaard

Darkness

Darkness cannot drive out darkness; only light can do that. Hate cannot drive out hate; only love can do that.
~Martin Luther King, Jr

Deadline

I love deadlines. I like the whooshing sound they make as they fly by.
~Douglas Adams

Death

The man who has accomplished all that he thinks worthwhile has begun to die.

~E. T. Trigg

Live as you will have wished to have lived when you are dying.
~Christian F. Gellert

We are ever dying to one world and being born into another.
~Henry David Thoreau

Be ashamed to die until you have won some victory for humanity.
~Horace Mann

There is no cure for birth and death save to enjoy the interval.
~George Santayana

Only those are fit to live who do not fear to die; and none are fit to die who have shrunk from the joy of life and the duty of life. Both life and death are parts of the same Great Adventure.
~Theodore Roosevelt

Decisions

No trumpets sound when the important decisions of our life are made. Destiny is made known silently.

~Agnes de Mille

I have to be wrong a certain number of times in order to be right a certain number of times. However, in order to be either, I must first make a decision.

~Frank N. Giampietro

The more decisions that you are forced to make alone, the more you are aware of your freedom to choose.
~Thornton Wilder

When your values are clear to you, making decisions becomes easier.
~Roy Disney

Again and again, the impossible problem is solved when we see that the problem is only a tough decision waiting to be made.
~Robert H. Schuller

I feel that one . . . must scan every life choice with rational thinking, but then base the decision on whether one's heart will be in it.
~Jean Shinoda Bolen

Somewhere deep down we know that in the final analysis we do decide things and that even our decisions to let someone else decide are really our decisions, however pusillanimous.
~Harvey G. Cox

The first step towards getting somewhere is to decide that you are not going to stay where you are.
~J. P. Morgan

Any fool can criticize, complain, and condemn—and most fools do. But it takes character and self-control to be understanding and forgiving.
~Dale Carnegie

I base most of my fashion taste on what doesn't itch.
~Gilda Radner

Deeds

The smallest good deed is better than the grandest good intention.
~Duguet

Words are nothing but words; power lies in deeds. Be a person of action.
~Mali Oriot Mamadu Konyate

Things you do for other people are usually some of the best things you do.
~Gabriela Ortiz

I have always thought the actions of men the best interpreters of their thoughts.
~John Locke

Defeat

Defeat is not the worst of failure. Not to have tried is the true failure.

~George E. Woodberry

Being defeated is often a temporary condition. Giving up is what makes it permanent.

~Marilyn vos Savant

A man is not finished when he is defeated. He is finished when he quits.

~Richard M. Nixon

I never thought of losing, but now that it's happened, the only thing is to do it right. That's my obligation to all the people who believe in me. We all have to take defeats in life.

~Muhammad Ali

Man is not made for defeat. A man can be destroyed, but not defeated.

~Earnest Hemingway

Never confuse a single defeat with a final defeat.

~F. Scott Fitzgerald

The most common way people give up their power is by thinking they don't have any.

~Alice Walker

Defeat is not the worst of failure. Not to have tried is the true failure.

~George Edward Woodberry

Departure

There is a time for departure even when there's no certain place to go.

~Tennessee Williams

Deserve

We accept the love we think we deserve.

~Stephen Chbosky

Whatever you want in life, other people are going to want it too. Believe in yourself enough to accept the idea that you have an equal right to it.

~Diane Sawyer

Desire

The starting point of all achievement is desire.

~Napoleon Hill

In my experience, there is only one motivation, and that is desire. No reasons or principles contain it or stand against it.

~Jane Smiley

Whatever you want in life, other people are going to want it too. Believe in yourself enough to accept the idea that you have an equal right to it.

~Diane Sawyer

He that can have patience can have what he will.

~Benjamin Franklin

There are only two tragedies in life: not getting what you want — and the getting it.

~Oscar Wilde

Longing performs all things.

~Mary Renault

I count him braver who overcomes his desires than him who overcomes his enemies.

~Aristotle

See the things you want as already yours. Think of them as yours, as belonging to you, as already in your possession.

~Robert Collier

The eyes of other people are the eyes that ruin us. If all but myself were blind, I should want neither fine clothes, fine houses, nor fine furniture.

~Benjamin Franklin

An object in possession seldom retains the same charm that it had in pursuit.

~Pliny the Elder

Destiny

No trumpets sound when the important decisions of our life are made. Destiny is made known silently.

~Agnes de Mille

Control your own destiny or someone else will.

~Jack Welch

By your thoughts you are daily, even hourly, building your life; you are carving your destiny.

~Ruth Barrick Golden

There is a mysterious cycle in human events. To some generations much is given. Of other generations much is expected. This generation of Americans has a rendezvous with destiny.

~Franklin D. Roosevelt

I am not afraid. . . . I was born to do this.

~Joan of Arc

Ideals are like stars; you will not succeed in touching them with your hands. . . . you choose them as your guides, and following them, you will reach your destiny.

~Carl Schurz

We are destined to evolve beyond the nature of duality.

~Gary Zukav

Destroyed

But man is not made for defeat. A man can be destroyed but not defeated.

~Ernest Hemingway

Determination

Failure will never overtake me if my determination to succeed is strong enough.

~Og Mandino

When people keep telling you that you can't do a thing, you kind of like to try it.

~Margaret Chase Smith

I came, I saw, I conquered.

~Julius Caesar

The best way out is always through.

~Robert Frost

By prevailing over all obstacles and distractions, one may unfailingly arrive at his chosen goal or destination.

~Christopher Columbus

It is energy—the central element of which is will—that produces the miracles of enthusiasm in all ages. Everywhere it is the mainspring of what is called force of character, and the sustaining power of all great action.

~Samuel Smiles

I will act now. Success will not wait. If I delay, success will become wed to another and lost to me forever. This is the time. This is the place. I am the person.

~Og Mandino

Most folks are as happy as they make up their minds to be.

~Abraham Lincoln

Put your heart, mind, and soul into even your smallest acts. This is the secret of success.

~Swami Sivananda

The first thing I do in the morning is to make my bed and while I am making up my bed I am making up my mind as to what kind of day I am going to have.

~Robert Frost

Know the true value of time; snatch, seize, and enjoy every moment of it. No idleness, no laziness, no procrastination: never put off till tomorrow what you can do today.

~Philip Stanhope

Difference

In order to be irreplaceable one must always be different.

~Coco Chanel

It's easy to make a buck. It's a lot tougher to make a difference.

~Tom Brokaw

So, let us not be blind to our differences—but let us also direct attention to our common interests and to the means by which those differences can be resolved.

~John F. Kennedy

Each child has . . . an equal opportunity, not to become equal, but to become different—to realize whatever unique potential of body, mind and spirit he or she possesses.

~John Fischer

Difficulties

Out of difficulties, grow miracles.

~Jean de La Bruyère

Have patience. All things are difficult before they become easy.

~Saadi

All things are difficult before they are easy.

~Thomas Fuller

Difficulty shows what men are.

~Epictetus

It is not because things are difficult that we do not dare, it is because we do not dare that they are difficult.

~Lucius Annaeus Seneca

Difficulties are meant to rouse, not discourage. The human spirit is to grow strong by conflict.

~William Ellery Channing

Real life isn't always going to be perfect or go our way, but the recurring acknowledgement of what is working in our lives can help us not only to survive but surmount our difficulties.

~Sara Ban Breathnach

Out of difficulties, grow miracles.

~Jean de La Bruyère

It is our attitude at the beginning of a difficult task which, more than anything else, will affect its successful outcome.

~William James

Many things which cannot be overcome when they are together, yield themselves up when taken little by little.

~Plutarch

Dignity

The ideal man bears the accidents of life with dignity and grace, making the best of circumstances.

~Aristotle

The most luxurious possession, the richest treasure anybody has, is his personal dignity.

~Jackie Robinson

Diligence

Care and diligence bring luck.

~Thomas Fuller

Direction

If you don't know where you are going, you might wind up someplace else.

~Yogi Berra

It isn't where you come from; it's where you're going that counts.
~Ella Fitzgerald

If you don't know where you are going, any road will get you there.

~Lewis Carroll

Disappointment

We must accept finite disappointment, but we must never lose infinite hope.

~Martin Luther King Jr.

The setting of a great hope is like the setting of the sun. The brightness of our life is gone.

~Henry Wadsworth Longfellow

Discernment

Anybody can become angry — that is easy, but to be angry with the right person and to the right degree and at the right time and for the right purpose, and in the right way — that is not within everybody's power and is not easy.

~Aristotle

Discipline

You never will be the person you can be if pressure, tension and discipline are taken out of your life.

~James G. Bilkey

Silence is the element in which great things fashion themselves together.

~Thomas Carlyle

Old minds are like old horses; you must exercise them if you wish to keep them in working order.

~John Adams

Discontentment

The grass is greener somewhere else. Our thoughts persuade, and we comply. And when we get to someplace else, we find the grass is often dry.

~Dolores Dahl

Discovery

Discovery consists of seeing what everybody has seen and thinking what nobody has thought.
~Albert von Szent-Györgyi

They are ill discoverers that think there is no land when they can see nothing but sea.
~Francis Bacon

A discovery is said to be an accident meeting a prepared mind.
~Albert Szent-Györgyi

One of the advantages of being disorderly is that one is constantly making exciting discoveries.
~A. A. Milne

The greatest obstacle to discovery is not ignorance—it is the illusion of knowledge.
~Daniel J. Boorstin

The seeds of great discoveries are constantly floating around, but they only take root in minds well prepared to receive them.
~Joseph Henry

The whole secret of the study of nature lies in learning how to use one's eyes.
~George Sand

Never be afraid to ask a question, especially of yourself. Discovery is the mission of life.
~Brian Kates

Diversity

Diversity: the art of thinking independently together.
~Malcolm Forbes

Doubt

A mind troubled by doubt cannot focus on the course to victory.
~Arthur Golden

Doubt, of whatever kind, can be ended by action alone.
~Thomas Carlyle

Never doubt that you can change history. You already have.
~Marge Piercy

It's not what you are that holds us back, it's what you think you are not.
~Denis Waitley

The only limit to our realization of tomorrow will be our doubts of today. Let us move forward with strong and active faith.
~Franklin D. Roosevelt

When in doubt, mumble; when in trouble, delegate; when in charge, ponder.
~James H. Boren

Dread

I have a new philosophy. I'm only going to dread one day at a time.
~Charles Schulz

Dream

It has never been my object to record my dreams, just the determination to realize them.
~Man Ray

If you can dream it, you can do it.
~Walt Disney

You are never too old to set another goal or to dream a new dream.
~Les Brown

Happy are those who dream dreams and are ready to pay the price to make them come true.
~Tupac Shakur

In forming a bridge between body and mind, dreams may be used as a springboard from which man can leap to new realms of experience lying outside his normal state of consciousness and enlarge his vision.
~Ann Faraday

The best way to make your dreams come true is to wake up.
~Paul Valéry

A No. 2 pencil and a dream can take you anywhere.
~Joyce A. Myers

Hold fast to dreams, for if dreams die, life is a broken-winged bird that cannot fly.
~Langston Hughes

Dream passionate dreams. Design their reality.
~Candis Fancher

Every great dream begins with a dreamer. Always remember, you have within you the strength, the patience, and the passion to reach for the stars to change the world.
~Harriet Tubman

To make a great dream come true, you must first have a great dream.
~Hans Selye

Nothing much happens without a dream. For something really great to happen, it takes a really great dream.
~Robert Greenleaf

Dream have as much influence as actions.
~Stéphane Mallarmé

If a little dreaming is dangerous, the cure for it is not to dream less but to dream more, to dream all the time.
~Marcel Proust

A goal is a dream with its feet on the ground.
~Frank Vizarre

Dreams can still come true; you need a great deal of energy and determination, and a little bit of luck.
~Stefano Gabbana

Who looks outside, dreams; who looks inside, awakes.
~Carl Jung

Let me remember lessons learned, and profit from the past, and may I build a bridge of dreams, that shall forever last.
~Grace E. Easley

There will always be dreams grander or humbler than your own, but there will never be a dream exactly like your own . . . for you are unique and more wondrous than you know!
~Linda Staten

If you can imagine it, you can achieve it; if you can dream it, you can become it.
~William Arthur Ward

What would you attempt to do if you knew you would not fail?
~Robert H. Schuller

If your dream is big enough, the facts don't count.
~Don Ward

Reach for your dreams and they will reach for you.
~Hana Rosa Zadra

Keep true to the dreams of thy youth.
~Johann Friedrich Von Schiller

Dreams come a size too big so that we can grow into them.
~Josie Bissett

The only thing that can stop you from fulfilling your dreams is you.
~Tom Bradley

Dreamers are mocked as impractical. The truth is they are the most practical, as their innovations lead to progress and a better way of life for all of us.
~Robin S. Sharma

Hope is not a dream, but a way of making dreams become a reality.
~Leon Jozef Cardinal Suenens

When we stop dreaming, we stop living.
~Lorrie Morgan

Dreaming and seeing precede doing.
~Margaret Sangster

My dreams have become puny with the reality my life has become.
~Imelda Marcos

Reach high, for stars lie hidden in your soul. Dream deep, for every dream precedes the goal.
~Pamela Vaull Starr

The armored cars of dreams, contrived to let us do so many a dangerous thing.
~Elizabeth Bishop

Dreams come true. Without possibility, nature would not incite us to have them.
~John Updike

Duty

There is no duty we so much underrate as the duty of being happy.
~Robert Louis Stevenson

Life is not so important as the duties of life.
~John Randolph

Do not pray for tasks equal to your powers. Pray for powers equal to your tasks.
~Phillips Brooks

I slept and dreamt that life was joy. I awoke and saw that life was service. I acted and behold, service was joy.
~Rabindranath Tagore

Our greatest duty and our main responsibility is to help others. But please, if you can't help them, would you please not hurt them.
~Dalai Lama

There is nothing in the universe that I fear, but that I shall not know all my duty, or shall fail to do it.
~Mary Lyon

Duty, then, is the sublimest word in our language. Do your duty in all things. . . . You cannot do more, you should never wish to do less.

~Robert E. Lee

Earth

To see the earth as it truly is, small and blue and beautiful in that eternal silence where it floats, is to see ourselves as riders on the Earth together, brothers on that bright loveliness in the eternal cold.

~Archibald MacLeish

For those who have seen the Earth from space . . . the experience most certainly changes your perspective. The things that we share in our world are far more valuable than those which divide us.

~Donald E. Williams

Easter

Loveliest of trees, the cherry now is hung with bloom along the bough, and stands about the woodland ride wearing white for Eastertide.

~A. E. Housman

Education

The arts must be considered an essential element of education . . . . They are tools for living life reflectively, joyfully and with the ability to shape the future.

~Shirley Trusty Corey

Education is not the filling of a pail, but the lighting of a fire.
~William Butler Yeats

What sculpture is to a block of marble, education is to the soul.
~Joseph Addison

The very spring and root of honesty and virtue lie in good education.

~Plutarch

The great want of our race is perfect educators to train new-born minds, who are infallible teachers of what is right and true.
~Catherine E. Beecher

Education must, then, be not only a transmission of culture but also a provider of alternative views of the world and a strengthener of the will to explore them.
~Jerome S. Bruner

Education's purpose is to replace an empty mind with an open one.
~Malcolm Forbes

I prefer the company of peasants because they have not been educated sufficiently to reason incorrectly.
~Michel de Montaigne

You see, real ongoing, lifelong education doesn't answer questions; it provokes them.
~Luci Swindoll

What is really important in education is . . . that the mind is matured, that energy is aroused.
~Søren Kierkegaard

Education is a progressive discovery of our own ignorance.
~Will Durant

If you would thoroughly know anything, teach it to others.
~Tryon Edwards

Effort

Effort is only effort when it begins to hurt.
~José Ortega y Gasset

Luck is what you have left over after you give 100 percent.
~Langston Coleman

Put your heart, mind, and soul into even your smallest acts. This is the secret of success.
~Swami Sivananda

We have to do the best we can. This is our sacred human responsibility.

~Albert Einstein

Nobody who ever gave his best regretted it.

~George Halas

It isn't success after all, is it, if it isn't an expression of your deepest energies?

~Marilyn French

Ego

Avoid having your ego so close to your position that when your position fails, your ego goes with it.

~Colin Powell

Elegance

Elegance is inferior to virtue.

~Mary Wollstonecraft

Email

E-mail is a unique communication vehicle for a lot of reasons. However e-mail is not a substitute for direction interaction.

~Bill Gates

Emergencies

Watch out for emergencies. They are your big chance.

~Fritz Reiner

Emergencies have always been necessary to progress. It was darkness which produced the lamp . . . . Fog that produced the compass . . . . Hunger that drove us to exploration. And it took a depression to teach us the real value of a job.

~Victor Hugo

Emotions

Each of us makes his own weather, determines the color of the skies in the emotional universe which he inhabits.
~Fulton J. Sheen

Your intellect may be confused, but your emotions will never lie to you.
~Roger Ebert

The kinds of people who can go on to greater emotional maturity are those who really like themselves, even if the world seems to turn against them.
~Theodore Irwin

I've learned what is reality, and what is make-believe, and that it isn't smart to wear one's heart upon one's sleeve.
~Grace E. Easley

The acceptance of the truth that joy and sorrow, laughter and tears are not confined to any particular time, place or people, but are universally distributed, should make us more tolerant of and more interested in the lives of others.
~William M. Peck

Anyone who is happy all the time is nuts.
~Leo Rosten

Empathy

True kindness presupposes the faculty of imagining as one's own the suffering and joys of others.
~André Gide

I have wept to see thee weep.
~Mary Robinson

Those who have suffered understand suffering and therefore extend their hand.
~Patti Smith

Do not believe that he who seeks to comfort you lives untroubled among the simple and quiet words that sometimes do you good. His life has much difficulty . . . Were it otherwise he would never have been able to find those words.

~Rainer Marie Rilke

Empowerment

Empowerment is all about letting go so that others can get going.
~Kenneth Blanchard

Encouragement

Encouragement after censure is as the sun after a shower.
~Johann Wolfgang von Goethe

There are high spots in all of our lives and most of them come about through encouragement from someone else . . . Encouragement is oxygen to the soul.

~George Madison Adams

Correction does much, but encouragement does more.
~Johann Wolfgang von Goethe

Try to be a rainbow in someone's cloud.

~Maya Angelou

Run with your head the first two thirds of a race and with your heart the final one third.

~Jack Daniels

We can't all be heroes because somebody has to sit on the curb and applaud when they go by.

~Will Rogers

If you can dream it, you can do it.

~Walt Disney

Life only demands from you the strength you possess.
~Dag Hammarskjöld

Pursue your passion and live your dream.
~Katherine Logan

Celebrate what you want to see more of.
~Tom Peters

All of us, in the glow of feeling we have pleased, want to do more to please.
~William James

Smile, for everyone lacks self-confidence and more than any other one thing a smile reassures them.
~André Maurois

Even if you fall on your face, you're still moving forward.
~Victor Kiam

Endurance

Endurance is not just the ability to bear a hard thing, but to turn it into glory.
~William Barclay

The blues of mental and physical wear and tear are not as devastating as the yellows of the quitter.
~James J. Walker

The best way out is always through.
~Robert Frost

The men who learn endurance, are they who call the whole world, brother.
~Charles Dickens

Enemies

Time is my greatest enemy.
~Evita Perón

Always forgive your enemies; nothing annoys them so much.
~Oscar Wilde

Energy

Within each of us is a hidden store of energy. Energy we can release to compete in the marathon of life.

~Roger Dawson

Thoughts are energy, and you can make your world or break your world by your thinking.

~Susan L. Taylor

Energy and persistence conquer all things.

~Benjamin Franklin

Most people never run far enough on their first wind to find out they've got a second. Give your dreams all you've got and you'll be amazed at the energy that comes out of you.

~William James

Life engenders life. Energy creates energy. It is by spending oneself that one becomes rich.

~Sarah Bernhardt

Enjoyment

The best way to pay for a lovely moment is to enjoy it.

~Richard Bach

The luxury of doing good surpasses every other personal enjoyment.

~John Gay

It is not how much we have, but how much we enjoy, that makes happiness.

~Charles H. Spurgeon

My advice to you is not to inquire why or whither, but just enjoy your ice cream while it's on your plate.

~Thornton Wilder

On with the dance, let the joy be unconfined, is my motto; whether there's any dance to dance or any joy to unconfined.

~Mark Twain

There is a strange reluctance on the part of most people to admit that they enjoy life.
~William Lyon Phelps

Enthusiasm

When enthusiasm is driven by confidence, any goal can be attained.
~Robert E. Regent

The real secret of success is enthusiasm.
~Walter P. Chrysler

Every production of genius must be the production of enthusiasm.
~Benjamin Disraeli

Enthusiasm reflects confidence, spreads good spirit, raises morale, arouses loyalty, and laughs at adversity . . . it is beyond price.
~Admiral James Stockdale

Vigor is contagious, and whatever makes us either think or feel strongly adds to our power and enlarges our field of action.
~Ralph Waldo Emerson

If you give your child only one gift, let it be enthusiasm.
~Bruce Barton

Envious

Do not overrate what you have received, nor envy others. He who envies others does not obtain peace of mind.
~Buddha

Let age, not envy, draw wrinkles on thy cheeks.
~Thomas Browne

Equality

Even on the most exalted throne in the world we are only sitting on our own bottom.
~Michel Eyquem de Montaigne

Evil

The lesser evil is also evil.

~Naomi Mitchison

A good End cannot sanctify evil Means; nor must we ever do Evil, that Good may come of it.

~William Penn

Evolution

We are destined to evolve beyond the nature of duality.

~Gary Zukav

While animals survive by adjusting themselves to their background, man survives by adjusting his background to himself.

~Ayn Rand

Examine

Re-examine all that you have been told . . . dismiss that which insults your own soul.

~Walt Whitman

Example

If you can't be a good example, then you'll just have to be a horrible warning.

~Catherine Aird

I talk and talk and talk, and I haven't taught people in 50 years what my father taught by example in one week.

~Mario Cuomo

The first great gift we can bestow on others is a good example.

~Thomas Morell

Excellence

Excellence is not a skill, it's an attitude.

~Ralph Marston

Excellence is achieved by the mastery of fundamentals.
~Vince Lombardi

*The quality of a person's life is in direct proportion to their com-
mitment to excellence, regardless of their chosen field of endeavor.*
~Vince Lombardi

*It's your life, your one and only life—so take excellence very per-
sonally.*

~Scott Johnson

Excellence in any pursuit is the late, ripe fruit of toil.
~W. M. L. Jay

*I am careful not to confuse excellence with perfection. Excellence,
I can reach for; perfection is God's business.*

~Michael J. Fox

Exceptions

*The young man knows the rules but the old man knows the excep-
tions.*

~Oliver Wendell Holmes

Excuse

Never ruin an apology with an excuse.

~Benjamin Franklin

Existence

*It is so easy to waste our lives: our days, our hours, our minutes .
. . It is so easy to exist instead of live.*

~Anna Quindlen

*Man is a fountain of immense meaning, not merely a drop in the
ocean of being.*

~Abraham Joshua Heschel

I have an existential map; it has 'you are here' written all over it.
~Steven Wright

Expectation

This is the precept by which I have lived: Prepare for the worst; expect the best; and take what comes.

~Hannah Arendt

The quality of our expectations determines the quality of our actions.

~André Godin

A pint can't hold a quart — if it holds a pint it is doing all that can be expected of it.

~Margaret Deland

All of us failed to match our dreams of perfection. So I rate us on the basis of our splendid failure to do the impossible.

~William Faulkner

Unhappiness is best defined as the difference between our talents and our expectations.

~Edward de Bono

Act like you expect to get into the end zone.

~Christopher Morley

High expectations are the key to everything.

~Sam Walton

Believe me, there is no such thing as expecting too much.

~Susan Cheever

It's expectation that differentiates us from the dead.

~Sheila Ballantyne

No one rises to low expectations.

~Les Brown

I do my thing, and you do your thing. I am not in this world to live up to your expectations.

~Frederick S. Perls

Expect the best.

~Joe Batten

Don't spend time beating on a wall, hoping to transform it into a door.

~Coco Chanel

Life's under no obligation to give us what we expect. We take what we get and are thankful it's no worse than it is.

~Margaret Mitchell

Experience

One thorn of experience is worth a whole wilderness of warning.

~James Russell Lowell

Experience is a great teacher.

~John Legend

Be brave. Take risks. Nothing can substitute experience.

~Paulo Coelho

If history repeats itself, and the unexpected always happens, how incapable must man be of learning from experience.

~George Bernard Shaw

The purpose of life is to live it, to taste experience to the utmost, to reach out eagerly and without fear for newer and richer experience.

~Eleanor Roosevelt

The past is finished. There is nothing to be gained by going over it. Whatever it gave us in the experiences it brought us was something we had to know.

~Rebecca Beard

In forming a bridge between body and mind, dreams may be used as a springboard from which man can leap to new realms of experience lying outside his normal state of consciousness and enlarge his vision.

~Ann Faraday

Never, for the sake of peace and quiet, deny your own experience and convictions.

~Dag Hammarskjöld

All experience is an arch, to build upon.

~Henry Brooks Adams

Dedicate some of your life to others. Your dedication will not be a sacrifice. It will be an exhilarating experience because it is intense effort applied toward a meaningful end.

~Thomas Dooley

We can experience nothing but the present moment, live in no other second of time, and to understand this is as close as we can get to eternal life.

~P. D. James

I think your whole life shows in your face and you should be proud of that.

~Lauren Bacall

Experience keeps a dear school, but fools will learn in no other.

~Benjamin Franklin

Oh for a life of sensations rather than of thoughts.

~John Keats

The story of any one man's real experience finds its startling parallel in that of every one of us.

~James Russell Lowell

Experience is how life catches up with us and teaches us to love and forgive each other.

~Judy Collins

No, you never get any fun out of the things you haven't done.

~Ogden Nash

The next best thing to winning is losing! At least you've been in the race.

~Nellie Hershey Tullis

Experience is a hard teacher because she gives the test first, the lesson afterward.

~Vernon Sanders Law

Explore

The greatest explorer on this earth never takes voyages as long as those of the man who descends to the depth of his heart.

~Julien Green

The self-explorer, whether he wants to or not, becomes the explorer of everything else.

~Elias Canetti

Education must, then, be not only a transmission of culture but also a provider of alternative views of the world and a strengthener of the will to explore them.

~Jerome S. Bruner

Exposure

Avoiding danger is no safer in the long run than outright exposure. The fearful are caught as often as the bold.

~Helen Keller

Extraordinary

The difference between ordinary and extraordinary is that little extra.

~Jimmy Johnson

Facts

Get your facts first, and then you can distort them as much as you please.

~Mark Twain

I'm not afraid of facts, I welcome facts but a congeries of facts is not equivalent to an idea. This is the essential fallacy of the so-called "scientific" mind. People who mistake facts for ideas are incomplete thinkers; they are gossips.

~Cynthia Ozick

I am not one of those who in expressing opinions confine themselves to facts.

~Mark Twain

Failure

Even if you fall on your face, you're still moving forward.
~Victor Kiam

Defeat is not the worst of failure. Not to have tried is the true failure.
~George E. Woodberry

You may be disappointed if you fail, but you are doomed if you don't try.
~Beverly Sills

By failing to prepare, you are preparing to fail.
~Benjamin Franklin

Success is not final, failure is not fatal: it is the courage to continue that counts.
~Winston Churchill

A man's life is interesting primarily when he has failed—I well know. For it's a sign that he tried to surpass himself.
~Georges Clemenceau

My great concern is not whether you have failed, but whether you are content with your failure.
~Abraham Lincoln

The greatest mistake you can make in life is to be continually fearing you will make one.
~Elbert Hubbard

Think twice before you speak, because your words and influence will plant the seed of either success or failure in the mind of another.
~Napoleon Hill

Act as if it were impossible to fail.
~Dorothea Brande

It is the individual who is not interested in his fellow men who has the greatest difficulties in life and provides the greatest injury to others. It is from among such individuals that all human failures spring.

~Alfred Adler

It's fine to celebrate success but it is more important to heed the lessons of failure.

~Bill Gates

Success is never final. Failure is never fatal. It's courage that counts.

~Winston Churchill

What great thing would you attempt if you knew you could not fail?

~Robert H. Schuller

Many of life's failures are people who did not realize how close they were to success when they gave up.

~Thomas Edison

Ever tried. Ever failed. No matter. Try again. Fail again. Fail better.

~Samuel Beckett

Take chances, make mistakes. That's how you grow. Pain nourishes your courage. You have to fail in order to practice being brave.

~Mary Tyler Moore

Failure will never overtake me if my determination to succeed is strong enough.

~Og Mandino

If you fell down yesterday, stand up today.

~H. G. Wells

Success makes us intolerant of failure and failure makes us intolerant of success.

~William Feather

There is no failure except in no longer trying.

~Elbert Hubbard

Be of good cheer. Do not think of today's failures, but of the success that may come tomorrow.

~Helen Keller

It is wise to keep in mind that neither success nor failure is ever final.

~Roger Babson

I have not failed. I've just found 10,000 ways that won't work.

~Thomas A. Edison

Those who dare to fail miserably can achieve greatly.

~John F. Kennedy

Ninety percent of all those who fail are not actually defeated. They simply quit.

~Paul J. Meyer

Failure is the foundation of success: success is the lurking place of failure.

~Lao Tzu

It is possible to fail in many ways . . . while to succeed is possible only in one way.

~Aristotle

We fail far more often by timidity than by over-daring.

~David Grayson

Failure is a detour, not a dead-end street.

~Zig Ziglar

If you don't accept failure as a possibility, you don't set high goals, you don't branch out, you don't try—you don't take the risk.

~Rosalynn Carter

I don't believe in failure. It is not failure if you enjoyed the process.

~Oprah Winfrey

Faith

Be faithful to that which exists nowhere but in yourself.

~André Gide

It wasn't raining when Noah built the ark.
~Howard Ruff

Faith is a knowledge within the heart, beyond the reach of proof.
~Khalil Gibran

It is necessary to the happiness of man that he be mentally faithful to himself. Infidelity does not consist in believing or disbelieving; it consists in professing to believe what one does not believe.
~Thomas Paine

If we really want to be full and generous in spirit, we have no choice by to trust at some level.
~Rita Dove

The mason asks but a narrow shelf to spring his brick from; man requires only an infinitely narrower one to spring his arch of faith from.
~Henry David Thoreau

He who has faith has . . . an inward reservoir of courage, hope, confidence, calmness, and assuring trust that all will come out well—even though to the world it may appear to come out most badly.
~B. C. Forbes

Tell a man that there are 500 billion stars in the universe and he will believe you. Tell him a fence has just been painted and he has to touch it to find out that it has been.
~Herb Cohen

Fall

Even if you fall on your face, you're still moving forward.
~Victor Kiam

Fame

A celebrity is a person who is known for his well-knownness.
~Daniel J. Boorstin

Never suffer youth to be an excuse for inadequacy, nor age and fame to be an excuse for indolence.

~Benjamin Hayden

It's marvelous to be popular, but foolish to think it will last.

~Dusty Springfield

Family

As a family, we had a code, which was to do the right thing, do it the best we could, never complain and never take advantage.

~Margaret Truman

Having family responsibilities and concerns just has to make you a more understanding person.

~Sandra Day O'Connor

Home is the place where, when you have to go there, they have to take you in.

~Robert Frost

The act of nutrition is not a purely physiological event . . . . The family meal is a formality that cultivates in us . . . a capacity for sharing, generosity, thoughtfulness, a talent for civilized conversation.

~Francine Du Plessix Gray

Perhaps the greatest social service that can be rendered by anybody to the country and to mankind is to bring up a family.

~George Bernard Shaw

The maelstrom of fatherhood is a chance to show grace under real pressure, to be cool despite the chaos of your son's room. That's something that's worth a fellow's time.

~Hugh O'Neill

The most important work you will ever do will be within the wall of your own homes.

~Harold B. Lee

A man should never neglect his family for business.

~Walt Disney

If you have only one smile in you, give it to the people you love. Don't be surly at home, then go out in the street and start grinning good morning at total stranger.

~Maya Angelou

Fate

Fate is not an eagle, it creeps like a rat.

~Elizabeth Bowen

Fate gives us the hand, and we play the cards.

~Arthur Schopenhauer

I do not know beneath what sky nor on what seas shall be thy fate: I only know it shall be high, I only know it shall be great.

~Richard Hovey

Fatherhood

A father is a man who expects his son to be as good a man as he meant to be.

~Frank A. Clark

My father gave me the greatest gift anyone could give another person, he believed in me.

~Jim Valvano

Favor

A favor well bestowed is almost as great an honor to him who confers it as to him who receives it.

~Richard Steele

Fear

The greatest mistake you can make in life is to be continually fearing you will make one.

~Elbert Hubbard

I have come to realize that all my trouble with living has come from fear and smallness within me.

~Angela L. Wozniak

I have learned over the years that when one's mind is made up, this diminishes fear; knowing what must be done does away with fear.
~Rosa Parks

I'm not afraid of storms, for I'm learning how to sail my ship.
~Louisa May Alcott

Don't let the fear of the time it will take to accomplish something stand in the way of your doing it.
~Earl Nightingale

Courage is resistance to fear, mastery of fear—not absence of fear.
~Mark Twain

I learned that courage was not the absence of fear, but the triumph over it. The brave man is not he who does not feel afraid, but he who conquers that fear.
~Nelson Mandela

Nothing in life is to be feared, it is only to be understood. Now is the time to understand more, so that we may fear less.
~Marie Curie

Don't be afraid to take a big step. You can't cross a chasm in two small jumps.
~David Lloyd George

Avoiding danger is no safer in the long run than outright exposure. The fearful are caught as often as the bold.
~Helen Keller

To live a creative life, we must lose our fear of being wrong.
~Joseph Chilton Pearce

Don't be afraid to give up the good for the great.
~John D. Rockefeller

Fear is actually related to love, as are all passions. Fear is the emotion that rises in us when there is a danger facing something or someone we love. . . . The catalogue of fears is the catalogue of loves. Love is an attraction for an object; fear is flight from it.
~Fulton J. Sheen

I believe that anyone can conquer fear by doing the things he fears to do, provided he keeps doing them until he gets a record of successful experience behind him.

~Eleanor Roosevelt

To do anything in this world worth doing, we must not stand back shivering and thinking of the cold and danger, but jump in, and scramble through as well as we can.

~Sydney Smith

Do the thing you fear, and the death of fear is certain.

~Ralph Waldo Emerson

You gain strength, courage and confidence by every experience in which you really stop to look fear in the face . . . You must do the thing you think you cannot do.

~Eleanor Roosevelt

If you listen to your fears, you will die never knowing what a great person you might have been.

~Robert H. Schuller

Feelings

In order to feel anything, you need strength.

~Anna Maria Ortese

Teach my unskilled mind to sing the feelings of my heart.

~Anna Young Smith

Hope is the feeling you have that the feeling you have isn't permanent.

~Jean Kerr

You cannot make yourself feel something you do not feel, but you can make yourself do right in spite of your feelings.

~Pearl S. Buck

The more often [a man] feels without acting, the less he will ever be able to act, and, in the long run, the less he will be able to feel.

~C. S. Lewis

Half of our mistakes in life arise from feeling where we ought to think, and thinking where we ought to feel.

~John Churton Collins

Teach my unskilled mind to sing the feelings of my heart.
~Anna Young Smith

Sentiment is the poetry of imagination.
~Alphonse de Lamartine

Finances

A big part of financial freedom is having your heart and mind free from worry about the what-ifs of life.
~Suze Orman

Our incomes are like our shoes; if too small, they gall and pinch us; but if too large, they cause us to stumble and to trip.
~John Locke

As sure as the spring will follow the winter, prosperity and economic growth will follow recession.
~Bo Bennett

Let him who would enjoy a good fortune waste none of his present.
~Roger Babson

Finger-Pointing

It is almost impossible to throw dirt on someone without getting a little on yourself.
~Abigail Van Buren

Finishing

The whole point of getting things done is knowing what to leave undone.
~Oswald Chambers

Focus

Only he who keeps his eye fixed on the far horizon will find his right road.
~Dag Hammarskjöld

Live life to the fullest, and focus on the positive.
~Matt Cameron

The secret of concentration is the secret of self-discovery. You reach inside yourself to discover your personal resources, and what it takes to match them to the challenge.

~Arnold Palmer

As concentration and attention increase, the mind becomes clear and balanced.

~Jack Kornfield

Food

A good cook is like a sorceress who dispenses happiness.

~Elsa Shiaparelli

All great change in America begins at the dinner table.

~Ronald Reagan

Foolishness

A fool is someone whose pencil wears out before its eraser does.

~Marilyn vos Savant

If fifty million people say a foolish thing, it is still a foolish thing.

~Anatole France

We're fools whether we dance or not, so we might as well dance.

~Japanese Proverb

The point of living, and of being an optimist, is to be foolish enough to believe the best is yet to come.

~Peter Ustinov

Each day, and the living of it, has to be a conscious creation in which discipline and order are relieved with some play and pure foolishness.

~May Sarton

The fool doth think he is wise, but the wise man knows himself to be a fool.

~William Shakespeare

A fool bolts pleasure, then complains of moral indigestion.

~Minna Antrim

Those who wish to appear wise among fools, among the wise seem foolish.

~Quintilian

Forget

May I forget what ought to be forgotten; and recall, unfailing, all that ought to be recalled, each kindly thing, forgetting what might sting.

~Mary Caroline Davies

People will forget what you said. People will forget what you did, but people will never forget how you made them feel.

~Maya Angelou

I like second chances. I've given people second chances. You have fall-outs with friends, and forgiveness is a great thing to have. It's not easy to forgive. I definitely don't forget, but I do forgive.

~Odette Annable

Not the power to remember, but its very opposite, the power to forget, is a necessary condition for our existence.

~Sholem Asch

Life's best balm—forgetfulness.

~Felicia Dorothea Humans

Forgiveness

Never does the human soul appear so strong and noble as when it forgoes revenge, and dares to forgive an injury.

~Edwin Hubbell Chapin

I like second chances. I've given people second chances. You have fall-outs with friends, and forgiveness is a great thing to have. It's not easy to forgive. I definitely don't forget, but I do forgive.

~Odette Annable

Love is an act of endless forgiveness, a tender look which becomes a habit.

~Peter Ustinov

In the sphere of forgiveness, too many hatchets are buried alive.
~Lem Hubbard

Always forgive your enemies; nothing annoys them so much.
~Oscar Wilde

When a deep injury is done us, we never recover until we forgive.
~Alan Paton

Forgive yourself for your faults and your mistakes and move on.
~Les Brown

Forgiveness is a virtue of the brave.
~Indira Gandhi

Forgiveness says you are given another chance to make a new beginning.
~Desmond Tutu

Life has taught me to forgive much, but to seek forgiveness still more.
~Otto von Bismarck

Anger makes you smaller, while forgiveness forces you to grow beyond what you were.
~Chérie Carter-Scott

Forgiveness is the economy of the heart . . . forgiveness saves the expense of anger, the cost of hatred, the waste of spirits.
~Hannah More

An eye for an eye only ends up making the whole world blind.
~Mohandas Gandhi

Every man should keep a fair-sized cemetery in which to bury the faults of his friends.
~Henry Ward Beecher

Fortitude

Character contributes to beauty. It fortifies a woman as her youth fades. A mode of conduct, a standard of courage, discipline, fortitude, and integrity can do a great deal to make a woman beautiful.
~Jacqueline Bisset

As strong as my legs are, it is my mind that has made me a champion.

~Michael Johnson

What this power is I cannot say; all I know is that it exists and it becomes available only when a man is in that state of mind in which he knows exactly what he wants and is fully determined not to quit until he finds it.

~Alexander Graham Bell

Fortune

Fortune favors the prepared mind.

~Louis Pasteur

The day of fortune is like a harvest day. We must be busy when the corn is ripe.

~Johann Wolfgang von Goethe

The shortest and the best way to make your fortune is to let people see clearly that it is in their interests to promote yours.

~Jean de La Bruyère

Let fortune do her worst, whatever she makes us lose, so long as she never makes us lose our honesty and our independence.

~Alexander Pope

To make a fortune some assistance from fate is essential. Ability alone is insufficient.

~Ihara Saikaku

Foundation

Do you wish to be great? Then begin by being . . . . The higher your structure is to be, the deeper must be its foundation.

~St. Augustine

If you have built castles in the air, your work need not be lost. That is where they should be. Now put foundations under them.

~Henry David Thoreau

Free Will

I am no bird; and no net ensnares me; I am a free human being with an independent will.

~Charlotte Brontë

Freedom

In order to live free and happily you must sacrifice boredom. It is not always an easy sacrifice.

~Richard Bach

There is a certain enthusiasm in liberty, that makes human nature rise above itself, in acts of bravery and heroism.

~Alexander Hamilton

But the freedom that they fought for, and the country grand they wrought for, Is their monument to-day, and for aye.

~Thomas Dunn English

The deadliest foe of democracy is not autocracy but liberty frenzied.

~Otto Hermann Kahn

Among a people generally corrupt, liberty cannot long exist.

~Edmund Burke

Freedom lies in being bold.

~Robert Frost

True freedom lies in the realization and calm acceptance of the fact that there may very well be no perfect answer.

~Allen Reid McGinnis

Freedom is an internal achievement rather than an external adjustment.

~Powell Clayton

Freedom means the opportunity to be what we never thought we would be.

~Daniel J. Boorstin

Give me your tired, your poor, your huddled masses yearning to breathe free.

~Emma Lazarus

Everything can be taken from a man but one thing: the last of the human freedoms — to choose one's attitude in any given set of circumstances, to choose one's own way.

~Viktor E. Frankl

But what is Freedom? Rightly understood, A universal license to be good.

~Hartley Coleridge

Whoever will be free must make himself free. Freedom is no fairy gift to fall into a man's lap. What is freedom? To have the will to be responsible for one's self.

~Max Stirner

We are all. Free. To do. Whatever. We want. To do.

~Richard Bach

Responsibility is the price of freedom.

~Elbert Hubbard

The basic test of freedom is perhaps less in what we are free to do than in what we are free not to do.

~Eric Hoffer

The Flag and the Constitution stand for democracy and not tyranny; for freedom, not subjection.

~Franklin D. Roosevelt

We are as great as our belief in human liberty — no greater. And our belief in human liberty is only ours when it is larger than ourselves.

~Archibald MacLeish

Freedom is never dear at any price. It is the breath of life. What would a man not pay for living?

~Mohandas Gandhi

Friendship

To the soul, there is hardly anything more healing than friendship.
~Thomas Moore

A single rose can be my garden . . . a single friend, my world.
~Leo Buscaglia

Friends show their love in times of trouble, not in happiness.
~Euripides

A real friend is one who walks in when the rest of the world walks out.
~Walter Winchell

Getting people to like you is merely the other side of liking them.
~Norman Vincent Peale

He removes the greatest ornament of friendship who takes away from it respect.
~Marcus Tullius Cicero

Associate yourself with men of good quality, if you esteem your own reputation; for 'tis better to be alone than in bad company.
~George Washington

Shared laughter creates a bond of friendship. When people laugh together, they cease to be young and old, teacher and pupils, worker and boss. They become a single group of human beings.
~W. Lee Grant

The happiness we give to others makes us happier too, we find, just as friendship returns to the friendly, and kindness comes back to the kind.
~Keith Bennett

The only way to have a friend is to be one.
~Ralph Waldo Emerson

Be true to your work, your word, and your friend.
~John Boyle O'Reilly

If a friend is in trouble, don't annoy him by asking if there is anything you can do. Think up something appropriate and do it.
~Edgar Watson Howe

The good man is the friend of all living things.
~Mohandas Gandhi

There is nothing on this earth more to be prized than true friendship.
~Thomas Aquinas

There is nothing better than a friend, unless it is a friend with chocolate.

~Linda Grayson

And the song, from beginning to end, I found in the heart of a friend.

~Henry Wadsworth Longfellow

The friend who holds your hand and says the wrong thing is made of dearer stuff than the one who stays away.

~Barbara Kingsolver

It is said that love is blind. Friendship, on the other hand, is clairvoyant.

~Philippe Soupault

Boldness be my friend.

~William Shakespeare

One of the most beautiful qualities of true friendship is to understand and to be understood.

~Lucius Annaeus Seneca

Of all possessions a friend is the most precious.

~Herodotus

A friend is what the heart needs all the time.

~Henry Van Dyke

Remember that the most valuable antiques are dear old friends.

~H. Jackson Brown Jr.

No better relation than a prudent and faithful friend.

~Benjamin Franklin

Friends come and go, but with a precious few you should hold on . . . because the older you get, the more you need the people who knew you when you were young.

~Baz Luhrmann

From quiet homes and first beginning, out to the undiscovered ends, there's nothing worth the wear of winning, but laughter and the love of friends.

~Hilaire Belloc

Each friend represents a world in us, a world possibly not born until they arrive, and it is only by this meeting that a new world is born.

~Anaïs Nin

Friendship is the gift of the gods, and the most precious boon to man.

~Benjamin Disraeli

Sometimes being a friend means mastering the art of timing. There is a time for silence. A time to let go and allow people to hurl themselves into their own destiny. And a time to prepare to pick up the pieces when it's all over.

~Gloria Naylor

What a delight it is to make friends with someone you have despised!

~Colette

But every road is tough to me that has no friend to cheer it.

~Elizabeth Shane

That is just the way in this world; an enemy can partly ruin a man, but it takes a good-natured injudicious friend to complete the thing and make it perfect.

~Mark Twain

The ornament of a house is the friends who frequent it.

~Ralph Waldo Emerson

No distance of place or lapse of time can lessen the friendship of those who are thoroughly persuaded of each other's worth.

~Robert Southey

Be courteous to all, but intimate with few, and let those few be well-tried before you given them your confidence.

~George Washington

Animals are such agreeable friends—they ask no questions; they pass no criticisms.

~George Eliot

A true friend is forever a friend.

~George Macdonald

Laughter is the shortest distance between two people.

~Victor Borge

Never explain—your friends do not need it and your enemies will not believe you anyway.

~Elbert Hubbard

You must therefore love me, myself, and not my circumstances, if we are to be real friends.

~Marcus Tullius Cicero

A true friend never gets in your way unless you happen to be going down.

~Arnold H. Glasgow

It is one of the blessings of old friends that you can afford to be stupid with them.

~Ralph Waldo Emerson

Fulfillment

Only those who have learned the power of sincere and selfless contribution experience life's deepest joy: true fulfillment.

~Tony Robbins

Fun

If you obey all the rules, you miss all the fun.

~Katharine Hepburn

A little nonsense now and then is relished by the wisest men.

~Roald Dahl

When you have confidence, you can have a lot of fun. And when you have fun, you can do amazing things.

~Joe Namath

Future

Where the old tracks are lost, new country is revealed with its wonders.

~Rabindranath Tagore

The time is now, the place is here. Stay in the present. You can do nothing to change the past, and the future will never come exactly as you plan or hope for.

~Dan Millman

I feel that you are justified in looking into the future with true assurance, because you have a mode of living in which we find the joy of life and the joy of work harmoniously combined.

~Albert Einstein

Real generosity toward the future lies in giving all to the present.

~Albert Camus

I have learned to live each day as it comes, and not to borrow trouble by dreading tomorrow. It is the dark menace of the future that makes cowards of us.

~Dorothy Dix

As for the future, your task is not to foresee it, but to enable it.

~Antoine de Saint-Exupéry

I fear there will be no future for those who do not change.

~Louis L'Amour

The future belongs to people who see possibilities before they become obvious.

~John Sculley

Isn't it amazing the way the future succeeds in creating an appropriate past?

~John Leonard

The future is uncertain . . . but this uncertainty is at the very heart of human creativity.

~Ilya Prigogine

The future is much like the present, only longer.

~Don Quisenberry

Your future takes precedence over your past. Focus on your future, rather than on the past.

~Gary Ryan Blair

Happy is the soul that has something to look backward to with pride, and something to look forward to with hope.
~Oliver G. Wilson

The only limit to our realization of tomorrow will be our doubts of today. Let us move forward with strong and active faith.
~Franklin D. Roosevelt

We cannot always build the future for our youth, but we can always build our youth for the future.
~Franklin D. Roosevelt

Remember that our sons and grandsons are going to do things that would stagger us.
~Daniel H. Burnham

The future is sending back good wishes and waiting with open arms.
~Kobi Yamada

We always underestimate the future.
~Charles F. Kettering

A society grows great when old men plant trees whose shade they know they shall never sit in.
~Greek Proverb

To believe in something not yet proved and to underwrite it with our lives: it is the only way we can leave the future open.
~Lillian Smith

Real generosity toward the future lies in giving all to the present.
~Albert Camus

The future never just happened. It was created.
~Mae Jemison

Your future depends on many things, but mostly on you.
~Frank Tyger

Enough, if something from our hands have power, to live and act and serve the future hour.
~William Wordsworth

The future cannot be predicted, but futures can be invented.
~Dennis Gabor

Sometimes, I think the things we see are shadows of the things to be; that what we plan we build.
~Phoebe Cary

When we are planning for posterity, we ought to remember that virtue is not hereditary.
~Thomas Paine

Gain

To gain that which is worth having, it may be necessary to lose everything else.
~Bernadette Devlin

In this life we get only those things for which we hunt, for which we strive, and for which we are willing to sacrifice.
~George Matthew Adams

The grab for a quick killing is the mark of the worst kind of leadership, for it places immediate profit above the long-term interest of the organization and can lead ultimately only to disaster.
~Crawford H. Greenewalt

Gardening

Where would the gardener be if there were no more weeds?
~Chuang Tzu

To plant a garden is to believe in tomorrow.
~Audrey Hepburn

If you have a garden and a library, you have everything you need.
~Marcus Tullius Cicero

Generosity

Real generosity toward the future lies in giving all to the present.
~Albert Camus

*What I spent, is gone; what I kept, I lost; but what I gave away will
be mine forever.*

~Ethel Percy Andrus

Money is like muck, not good except it be spread.

~Francis Bacon

*I have found that there is a tremendous joy in giving. It is a very
important part of the joy of living.*

~William Black

Be a "go-giver" as well as a "go-getter."

~Leonard Hudson

Genius

Genius is the ability to put into effect what is on your mind.

~F. Scott Fitzgerald

Every production of genius must be the production of enthusiasm.

~Benjamin Disraeli

Patience is a necessary ingredient of genius.

~Benjamin Disraeli

Genius is nothing but a greater aptitude for patience.

~Benjamin Franklin

Sticking to it is the genius.

~Thomas Edison

Talent does what it can: genius does what it must.

~Edward G. Bulwer-Lytton

Gentleness

There is nothing stronger in this world than gentleness.

~Han Suyin

*Only the weak are cruel. Gentleness can only be expected from the
strong.*

~Leo Buscaglia

Force is all-conquering, but its victories are short lived.
~Abraham Lincoln

Gifts

Love the giver more than the gift.

~Brigham Young

If you set goals and go after them with all the determination you can muster, your gifts will take you places that will amaze you.
~Les Brown

The only gift is giving to the poor; all else is exchange.
~Thiruvalluvar

The first great gift we can bestow on others is a good example.
~Thomas Morell

Giving

Be a "go-giver" as well as a "go-getter."

~Leonard Hudson

Giving is the secret of a healthy life. Not necessarily money, but whatever a person has to give of encouragement, sympathy, and understanding.

~John D. Rockefeller

Love the giver more than the gift.

~Brigham Young

Remember that the happiest people are not those getting more, but those giving more.

~H. Jackson Brown Jr.

Real generosity toward the future lies in giving all to the present.
~Albert Camus

The heart that gives, gathers.

~Marianne Moore

You can give without loving, but you cannot love without giving.
~Amy Carmichael

I have found that there is a tremendous joy in giving. It is a very important part of the joy of living.

~William Black

What you give to humanity you get back. Bread cast upon the waters is much more wholesome and nourishing than pie in the sky.

~Melvin Jones

A harbor, even if it is a little harbor, is a good thing . . . it takes something from the world, and has something to give in return.

~Sarah Orne Jewett

Since you get more joy out of giving joy to others, you should put a good deal of thought into the happiness that you are able to give.

~Eleanor Roosevelt

Promise a lot and give even more.

~Anthony J. D'Angelo

A hug is like a boomerang—you get it back right away.

~Bil Keane

The more you love, the more you'll find that life is good and friends are kind. For only what we give away enriches us from day to day.

~Helen Steiner Rice

I've learned to be more tolerant, With others and myself, And that one cannot truly give . . . Until one gives himself.

~Grace E. Easley

Nothing that you have not given away will ever be really yours.

~C. S. Lewis

If instead of a gem, or even a flower, we should cast the gift of a loving thought into the heart of a friend, that would be giving as the angels give.

~George MacDonald

Goals

A successful individual typically sets his next goal somewhat but not too much above his last achievement. In this way he steadily raises his level of aspiration.

~Kurt Lewin

You are never too old to set another goal or to dream a new dream.
~Les Brown

If you can dream it, you can do it.
~Walt Disney

I can't change the direction of the wind, but I can adjust my sails to always reach my destination.
~Jimmy Dean

Most people fail in life not because they aim too high and miss, but because they aim too low and hit.
~Les Brown

By prevailing over all obstacles and distractions, one may unfailingly arrive at his chosen goal or destination.
~Christopher Columbus

When I was young, my ambition was to be one of the people who made a difference in this world.
~Jim Henson

When enthusiasm is driven by confidence, any goal can be attained.
~Robert E. Regent

If you don't know where you are going, you might wind up someplace else.
~Yogi Berra

Far away there in the sunshine are my highest aspirations. I may not reach them, but I can look up and see their beauty, believe in them, and try to follow where they lead.
~Louisa May Alcott

What we find is that if you have a goal that is very, very far out, and you approach it in little steps, you start to get there faster. Your mind opens up to the possibilities.
~Mae Jemison

Often the search proves more profitable than the goal.
~E. L. Konigsburg

I have resolved that from this day on, I will do all the business I can honestly, have all the fun I can reasonably, do all the good I can willingly, and save my digestion by thinking pleasantly.
~Robert Louis Stevenson

Each person has an ideal, a hope, a dream which represents the soul. We must give to it the warmth of love, the light of understanding and the essence of encouragement.
~Cathy Dorr Dam

If you set goals and go after them with all the determination you can muster, your gifts will take you places that will amaze you.
~Les Brown

A goal is a dream with its feet on the ground.
~Frank Vizarre

People with clear, written goals, accomplish more in a shorter period of time than people without them could ever imagine.
~Brian Tracy

Obstacles are those frightful things you see when you take your eyes off your goal.
~Henry Ford

Arriving at one goal is the starting point to another.
~John Dewey

Care enough for a result, and you will almost certainly attain it.
~William James

Set your goals to a paper and you're halfway there!
~Don Ward

When enthusiasm is driven by confidence, any goal can be attained.
~Robert E. Regent

Always plan with the end result in mind . . . Be clear. Be specific.
~Stephanie Goddard Davidson

Concentrate on finding your goal, then concentrate on reaching it.
~Michael Friedsam

Go for the moon. If you don't get it, you'll still be heading for a star.

~Willis Reed

In the absence of clearly-defined goals, we become strangely loyal to performing daily trivia until ultimately we become enslaved by it.

~Robert Heinlein

Goodness

Virtue is bold, and goodness never fearful.

~William Shakespeare

Patience and goodness will ever in the end conciliate the goodwill of others.

~Josephine

Doing good to others is not a duty. It is a joy, for it increases your own health and happiness.

~Zoroaster

Do all the good you can . . . to all the people you can, as long as ever you can.

~John Wesley

When you fall, pick something up.

~Oswald Theodore Avery

The majority of people perform well in a crisis and when the spotlight is on them; it's on the Sunday afternoons of this life, when the nobody is looking, that the spirit falters.

~Alan Bennett

The good man is the friend of all living things.

~Mohandas Gandhi

Find the good. It's all around you. Find it, showcase it, and you'll start believing in it.

~Jesse Owens

Power is the ability to do good things for others.

~Brooke Astor

Goodness does not consist in greatness, but greatness in goodness.
~Athenaeus

Don't let the good things of life rob you of the best things.
~Maltbie D. Babcock

What is beautiful is good, and who is good will soon also be beautiful.

~Sappho

What is alive, and open, and active, is good.

~D. H. Lawrence

We ought to do good to others as simply and naturally as a horse runs, or a bee makes honey, or a vine bears grapes season after season without thinking of the grapes it has borne.
~Marcus Aurelius

Don't be afraid to give up the good for the great.
~John D. Rockefeller

The good is the greatest rival of the best.
~Nellie L. McClung

Although the world is full of suffering, it is full also of the overcoming of it. My optimism, then, does not rest of the absence of evil, but on a glad belief in the preponderance of good and a willing effort always to cooperate with the good, that it may prevail.
~Helen Keller

A good head and a good heart are always a formidable combination.
~Nelson Mandela

There will always be a conflict between good and good enough.
~Henry Martyn Leland

Be so good they can't ignore you.

~Jerry Dunn

Oh, how easy it must be to be good when one has the power of doing good!
~Susan Edmonstone Ferrier

Goodness is easier to recognize than to define.
~W. H. Auden

We don't remain good if we don't always strive to become better.
~Gottfried Keller

The luxury of doing good surpasses every other personal enjoyment.
~John Gay

Gossip

I'm not afraid of facts, I welcome facts but a congeries of facts is not equivalent to an idea. This is the essential fallacy of the so-called "scientific" mind. People who mistake facts for ideas are incomplete thinkers; they are gossips.
~Cynthia Ozick

Government

The care of human life and happiness, and not their destruction, is the first and only legitimate object of good government.
~Thomas Jefferson

No man is good enough to govern another man without that other man's consent.
~Abraham Lincoln

Grace

The ideal man bears the accidents of life with dignity and grace, making the best of circumstances.
~Aristotle

You can't live a perfect day without doing something for someone who will never be able to repay you.
~John Wooden

Gratitude

Let's feel the magic of those two little, big words, "thank you."
~Ardath Rodale

Gratitude is born in hearts that take time to count up past mercies.
~Charles E. Jefferson

In relation to others, gratitude is good manners; in relation to ourselves, it is a habit of the heart and a spiritual discipline.
~Daphne Rose Kingma

Feeling gratitude and not expressing it is like wrapping a present and not giving it.
~William Arthur Ward

Gratitude is the sign of noble souls.
~Aesop

Gratitude makes sense of our past, brings peace for today, and creates a vision for tomorrow.
~Melody Beattie

As we express our gratitude, we must never forget that the highest appreciation is not to utter words, but to live by them.
~John F. Kennedy

There shall be eternal summer in the grateful heart.
~Celia Thaxter

Many a man curses the rain that falls upon his head, and knows not that it brings abundance to drive away hunger.
~Saint Basil

Your diamonds are not in far distant mountains or in yonder seas; they are in your own backyard, if you but dig for them.
~Russell H. Conwell

The hardest arithmetic to master is that which enables us to count our blessings.
~Eric Hoffer

In a full heart there is room for everything, and in an empty heart there is room for nothing.
~Antonio Porchia

Sincerity is the highest compliment you can pay.
~Ralph Waldo Emerson

I'm thankful for every moment.

~Al Green

Gratitude makes sense of our past, brings peace for today, and creates a vision for tomorrow.

~Melody Beattie

Say alleluia always, no matter the time of day, no matter the season of life.

~St. Benedict of Nursia

Gratitude is the fairest blossom which springs from the soul.

~Henry Ward Beecher

Greatness

It takes a great man to make a good listener.

~Calvin Coolidge

Do you wish to be great? Then begin by being . . . . The higher your structure is to be, the deeper must be its foundation.

~St. Augustine

The qualities which the great have to give, they give perpetually. Their gifts are taken into the pattern of life, and they appear thereafter in the fabric of the lives of nations, renewing themselves as the leaves of the trees are renewed by the seasons.

~Robert Trout

Great crises produce great men and great deeds of courage.

~John F. Kennedy

The human tendency to regard little things as important has produced very many great things.

~G. C. Lichtenberg

Goodness does not consist in greatness, but greatness in goodness.

~Athenaeus

Great men are rarely isolated mountain peaks; they are the summits of ranges.

~Thomas Wentworth Higginson

We cannot do great deeds unless we're willing to do the small things that make up the sum of greatness.

~Theodore Roosevelt

Hide not your talents. They for use were made. What's a sundial in the shade?

~Benjamin Franklin

An individual has not started living until he can rise above the narrow confines of his individualistic concerns to the broader concerns of all humanity.

~Martin Luther King Jr.

The greatest object in the universe, says the philosopher, is a good man struggling with adversity; yet there is still a greater, which is the good man who comes to relieve it.

~Oliver Goldsmith

The world knows nothing of its greatest men.

~Henry Taylor

A retentive memory may be a good thing, but the ability to forget is the true token of greatness.

~Elbert Hubbard

Great things are only possible with outrageous requests.

~Thea Alexander

Love and desire are the spirit's wings to great deeds.

~Johann Wolfgang von Goethe

It is the nature of all greatness not to be exact.

~Edmund Burke

Growth

The most powerful agent of growth and transformation is something much more basic than any technique: a change of heart.

~John Welwood

Take chances, make mistakes. That's how you grow. Pain nourishes your courage. You have to fail in order to practice being brave.

~Mary Tyler Moore

There are countless ways of achieving greatness, but any road to achieving one's maximum potential must be built on a bedrock of respect for the individual, a commitment to excellence, and a rejection of mediocrity.
~Buck Rodgers

A leaf that is destined to grow large is full of grooves and wrinkles at the start. Now if one has no patience and wants it smooth off-hand like a willow leaf, there is trouble ahead.
~Johann Wolfgang von Goethe

The proverb warns that "You should not bite the hand that feeds you." But maybe you should, if it prevents you from feeding yourself.
~Thomas Szasz

Few things can help an individual more than to place responsibility on him, and to let him know that you trust him.
~Booker T. Washington

Difficulties are meant to rouse, not discourage. The human spirit is to grow strong by conflict.
~William Ellery Channing

Only as high as I reach can I grow. Only as far as I seek can I go. Only as deep as I look can I see. Only as much as I dream can I be.
~Karen Ravn

Don't bother just to be better than your contemporaries or predecessors. Try to be better than yourself.
~William Faulkner

Anger makes you smaller, while forgiveness forces you to grow beyond what you were.
~Chérie Carter-Scott

You gain strength, courage and confidence by every experience in which you really stop to look fear in the face . . . You must do the thing you think you cannot do.
~Eleanor Roosevelt

As human beings, our greatness lies not so much in being able to remake the world . . . as in being able to remake ourselves.
~Mohandas K. Gandhi

If everything were perfect in this life, we would never learn any-
thing new. We would not be able to elevate our spirits through the
events that happen to us.

~Lynn V. Andrews

We are like eggs at present. And you cannot go on indefinitely
being just an ordinary, decent egg. We must be hatched or go bad.

~C. S. Lewis

A man's life is interesting primarily when he has failed—I well
know. For it's a sign that he tried to surpass himself.

~Georges Clemenceau

One's belief that one is sincere is not so dangerous as one's convic-
tion that one is right. We all feel we are right; but we felt the same
twenty years ago and today we know we weren't always right.

~Igor Stravinsky

Always be a work in progress.

~Emily Lillian

Dreams come a size too big so that we can grow into them.

~Josie Bissett

Change means movement. Movement means friction. Friction
means heat—and heat is required for growth.

~Dan Zadra

It's not trespassing when you cross your own boundaries.

~Johnnie Walker

The greatest thing is, at any moment, to be willing to give up who
we are in order to become all that we can become.

~Max De Pree

There are no such things as limits to growth, because there are
no limits to the human capacity for intelligence, imagination and
wonder.

~Ronald Reagan

Growth is never by mere chance; it is the result of forces working
together.

~James Cash Penney

Good, better, best. Never let it rest. 'Til your good is better and your better is best.

~St. Jerome

Growth, in some curious way, I suspect, depends on being always in motion just a little bit, one way or another.

~Norman Mailer

What great thing would you attempt if you knew you could not fail?

~Robert H. Schuller

I am not concerned that you have fallen — I am concerned that you arise.

~Abraham Lincoln

Security is mostly a superstition. It does not exist in nature. . . . Life is either a daring adventure, or nothing.

~Helen Keller

No matter how much pressure you feel at work, if you could find ways to relax for at least five minutes every hour, you'd be more productive.

~Joyce Brothers

If we learn to open our hearts, anyone, including the people who drive us crazy, can be our teacher.

~Pema Chodron

Make the most of yourself, for that is all there is of you.
~Ralph Waldo Emerson

The shell must break before the bird can fly.
~Alfred, Lord Tennyson

The appetite grows by what it feeds on.

~Ida B. Wells

To be tested is good. The challenged life may be the best therapist.
~Gail Sheehy

None of us suddenly becomes something overnight. The preparations have been in the making for a lifetime.

~Gail Godwin

To be thrown upon one's resources is to be cast into the very lap of fortune, for our faculties then undergo a development and display an energy of which they were previously unsusceptible.
~Benjamin Franklin

A man should never be ashamed to own he has been in the wrong . . . in other words, that he is wiser today than he was yesterday.
~Alexander Pope

Like an ability or a muscle, hearing your inner wisdom is strengthened by doing it.
~Robbie Gass

The degree to which I can create relationships, which facilitate the growth of others as separate persons, is a measure of the growth I have achieved in myself.
~Carl Rogers

Renewal is the principle—and the process—that empowers us to move on an upward spiral of growth and change, of continuous improvement.
~Stephen R. Covey

A mind that is stretched by a new experience can never go back to its old dimensions.
~Oliver Wendell Holmes Jr.

Nothing is a waste of time if you use the experience wisely.
~Auguste Rodin

Habits

Chaos often breeds life, when order breeds habit.
~Henry Brooks Adams

Our self-image and our habits tend to go together. Change one and you will automatically change the other.
~Maxwell Maltz

The habits of any culture fit the people who learn to use them like well-worn gloves.
~Ruth Benedict

Habit is a cable; we weave a thread of it every day, and at last we cannot break it.

~Horace Mann

Habit is overcome by habit.

~Thomas à Kempis

Curious things, habits. People themselves never knew they had them.

~Agatha Christie

Where the habits are simple, and the mind truly elevated, then is society in the best state.

~Mary Martha Sherwood

For the ordinary business of life an ounce of habit is worth a pound of intellect.

~Thomas B. Reed

To control our passions we must govern our habits, and keep watch over ourselves in the small details of everyday life.

~Sir John Lubbock

Bad habits are easier to abandon today than tomorrow.

~Yiddish Proverb

Good habits, which bring our lower passions and appetites under automatic control, leave our natures free to explore the larger experiences of life.

~Ralph W. Sockman

Any fool can criticize, complain, and condemn—and most fools do. But it takes character and self-control to be understanding and forgiving.

~Dale Carnegie

Habits are the shorthand of behavior.

~Julie Henderson

It is well to be up before daybreak, for such habits contribute to health, wealth, and wisdom.

~Aristotle

Halloween

I love the spirit of Halloween and the energy that comes with it.
~Katharine McPhee

Some people are born for Halloween, and some are just counting the days until Christmas.
~Stephen Graham Jones

Happiness

Happiness, like a refreshing stream, flows from heart to heart in endless circulation.
~Henry Grove

I must accept life unconditionally. Most people ask for happiness on condition. Happiness can only be felt if you don't set any condition.
~Artur Rubinstein

True happiness is to enjoy the present, without anxious dependence upon the future.
~Lucius Annaeus Seneca

Happy are those who dream dreams and are ready to pay the price to make them come true.
~Tupac Shakur

Happiness depends upon ourselves.
~Aristotle

Happiness resides not in possessions, and not in gold, happiness dwells in the soul.
~Democritus

The happiness of a man in this life does not consist in the absence but on the mastery of his passions.
~Alfred, Lord Tennyson

The most important thing is to enjoy your life—to be happy—it's all that matters.
~Audrey Hepburn

A smile is happiness you'll find right under your nose.
~Tom Wilson

You will never be happy if you continue to search for what happiness consists of. You will never live if you are looking for the meaning of life.
~Albert Camus

In order to live free and happily you must sacrifice boredom. It is not always an easy sacrifice.
~Richard Bach

So long as we can lose any happiness, we possess some.
~Booth Tarkington

It is not how much we have, but how much we enjoy, that makes happiness.
~Charles H. Spurgeon

Happiness is essentially a state of going somewhere, wholeheartedly, one-directionally, without regret or reservation.
~William H. Sheldon

Learn to value yourself, which means: fight for your happiness.
~Ayn Rand

Doing good to others is not a duty. It is a joy, for it increases your own health and happiness.
~Zoroaster

There is no duty we so much underrate as the duty of being happy.
~Robert Louis Stevenson

The summit of happiness is reached when a person is ready to be what he is.
~Erasmus

I am more and more convinced that our happiness or unhappiness depends more on the way we meet the events of life than on the nature of those events themselves.
~Wilhelm von Humboldt

Sir, there is nothing too little for so little creature as man. It is by studying little things that we attain the great art of having as little misery and as much happiness as possible.
~Samuel Johnson

Knowledge is happiness, because to have knowledge—broad, deep knowledge—is to know true ends from false, and lofty things from low.
~Helen Keller

The happiness we give to others makes us happier too, we find, just as friendship returns to the friendly, and kindness comes back to the kind.
~Keith Bennett

Happy people plan actions, they don't plan results.
~Denis Waitley

For every minute you are angry you lose sixty seconds of happiness.
~Ralph Waldo Emerson

Our brightest blazes of gladness are commonly kindled by unexpected sparks.
~Samuel Johnson

People don't notice whether it's winter or summer when they're happy.
~Anton Chekhov

Very little is needed to make a happy life; it is all within yourself, in your way of thinking.
~Marcus Aurelius

Happiness is not a goal . . . it is a by-product.
~Eleanor Roosevelt

[Happiness] lies in the joy of achievement, in the thrill of creative effort.
~Franklin D. Roosevelt

One must never look for happiness: one meets it by the way.
~Isabelle Eberhardt

Independence is happiness.

~Susan B. Anthony

Remember that the happiest people are not those getting more, but those giving more.

~H. Jackson Brown Jr.

Happiness, I have discovered, is nearly always a rebound from hard work.

~David Grayson

They must often change who would remain constant in happiness or wisdom.

~Confucius

The trick is in what one emphasizes. We either make ourselves miserable, or we make ourselves happy. The amount of work is the same.

~Carlos Castaneda

Happiness, like a refreshing stream, flows from heart to heart in endless circulation.

~Henry Grove

Don't miss out on happiness by looking toward the ground—but keep looking skyward, that's where the rainbow's found.

~Catherine Janssen Irwin

Learn to be happy. And think of life as a terminal illness because if you do you will live it with joy and passion, as it ought to be lived.

~Anna Quindlen

No man is happy who does not think himself so.

~Marcus Aurelius

If your happiness depends on what somebody else does, I guess you do have a problem.

~Richard Bach

One swallow does not make a summer, neither does one fine day; similarly one day or brief time of happiness does not make a person entirely happy.

~Aristotle

In about the same degree as you are helpful, you will be happy.
~Karl Reiland

Derive happiness in oneself from a good day's work from illuminating the fog that surrounds us.
~Henri Matisse

If the things we believe are different than the things we do, there can be no true happiness.
~Dana Telford

The purpose of our lives is to be happy.
~Dalai Lama

Some cause happiness wherever they go; others whenever they go.
~Oscar Wilde

Real happiness is cheap enough, yet how dearly we pay for its counterfeit.
~Hosea Ballou

It is only possible to live happily ever after on a daily basis.
~Margaret Bonanno

If I had not had so much ambition and had not tried to do so many things, I probably would have been happier, but less useful.
~Thomas Edison

Character is the basis of happiness, and happiness the sanction of character.
~George Santayana

The world is so full of a number of things. I'm sure we should all be as happy as kings.
~Robert Louis Stevenson

Man needs, for his happiness, not only the enjoyment of this or that, but hope and enterprise and change.
~Bertrand Russell

I feel very happy to see the sun come up every day. I feel happy to be around . . . I like to take this day—any day—and go to town with it.
~James Dickey

Now and then it's good to pause in our pursuit of happiness and just be happy.

~Guillaume Apollinaire

To enjoy true happiness we must travel into a very far country, and even out of ourselves.

~Thomas Browne

It is necessary to the happiness of man that he be mentally faithful to himself. Infidelity does not consist in believing or disbelieving; it consists in professing to believe what one does not believe.

~Thomas Paine

All the world is searching for joy and happiness, but these cannot be purchased for any price in any market place, because they are virtues that come from within.

~Lucille R. Taylor

Unless we think of others and do something for them, we miss one of the greatest sources of happiness.

~Ray Lyman Wilbur

Happiness is the only sanction of life; where happiness fails, existence remains a mad and lamentable experiment.

~George Santayana

Those who are not looking for happiness are the most likely to find it, because those who are searching forget that the surest way to be happy is to seek happiness for others.

~Martin Luther King Jr.

Happiness is good health and a bad memory.

~Ingrid Bergman

Unhappiness is best defined as the difference between our talents and our expectations.

~Edward de Bono

Practice hope. As hopefulness becomes a habit, you can achieve a permanently happy spirit.

~Norman Vincent Peale

I think I began learning long ago that those who are happiest are those who do the most for others.

~Booker T. Washington

That is happiness; to be dissolved into something complete and great.

~Willa Cather

Health and good humor are to the human body like sunshine to vegetation.

~Jean B. Massillon

Mankind are always happier for having been happy; so that, if you make them happy now, you make them happy twenty years hence by the memory of it.

~Sydney Smith

The truth is, there's no better time to be happy than right now . . . Your life will always be filled with challenges.

~Richard Carlson

Then give to the world the best you have. And the best will come back to you.

~Madeline Bridges

The habit of being uniformly considerate toward others will bring increased happiness to you.

~Greenville Kleiser

If you ever find happiness by hunting for it, you will find it, as the old woman did her lost spectacles, safe on her nose all the time.

~Josh Billings

Gladness can scarcely be a solitary thing.

~Dora Greenwell

The greatest happiness is to transform one's feelings into actions.

~Germaine de Staël

Continuity of purpose is one of the most essential ingredients of happiness in the long run, and for most men this comes chiefly through their work.

~Bertrand Russell

Happiness depends, as Nature shows, Less on exterior things than most suppose.

~William Cowper

Resolve to keep happy, and your joy and you shall form an invincible host against difficulties.

~Helen Keller

If you observe a really happy man, you will find . . . that he is happy in the course of living life twenty-four crowded hours each day.

~W. Beran Wolfe

There are shortcuts to happiness, and dancing is one of them.

~Vicki Baum

Many persons have a wrong idea of what constitutes true happiness. It is not attained through self-gratification but through fidelity to a worthy purpose.

~Helen Keller

I live what most people call the good life. I was happy, but deep inside I always felt that, with the short amount of time we are given to live and love in this world, we spend too much time loving things instead of people.

~Mother Antonia

I am still determined to be cheerful and happy, in whatever situation I may be; for I have also learned from experience that the greater part of our happiness or misery depends upon our dispositions, and not upon our circumstances.

~Martha Washington

Happiness makes up in height for what it lacks in length.

~Robert Frost

Sometimes the most proactive thing we can do is to be happy, just to genuinely smile. Happiness, like unhappiness, is a proactive choice.

~Stephen R. Covey

Harmony

With an eye made quiet by the power. Of harmony, and the deep power of joy. We see into the heart of things.
~William Wordsworth

I am fascinated by what is beautiful, strong, healthy, what is living. I seek harmony.
~Leni Riefenstahl

Hatred

Darkness cannot drive out darkness; only light can do that. Hate cannot drive out hate; only love can do that.
~Martin Luther King Jr.

We must remember that any oppression, any injustice, any hatred, is a wedge designed to attack our civilization.
~Franklin D. Roosevelt

All your life, you will be faced with a choice. You can choose love or hate . . . I choose love.
~Johnny Cash

"To hate" is to be pained by the hated one's happiness, just as "to love" is to delight in the beloved's happiness.
~Gottfried Wilhelm Leibniz

Health

A healthy body is guest chamber for the soul: a sick body is a prison.
~Francis Bacon

The body is the soul's house. Shouldn't we therefore take care of our house so that it doesn't fall into ruin?
~Philo Judaeus

Health and good humor are to the human body like sunshine to vegetation.
~Jean B. Massillon

Laughter is by definition healthy.

~Doris Lessing

Doing good to others is not a duty. It is a joy, for it increases your own health and happiness.

~Zoroaster

It is healthier to see the good points of others than to analyze our own bad ones.

~Françoise Sagan

My gift is that I'm not beautiful. My career was never about looks. It's about health and being in good shape.

~Shirley Maclaine

Those who think they have not time for bodily exercise will sooner or later have to find time for illness.

~Edward Stanley

Physical fitness is not only one of the most important keys to a healthy body, it is the basis of dynamic and creative intellectual activity.

~John F. Kennedy

I still need more healthy rest in order to work at my best. My health is the main capital I have and I want to administer it intelligently.

~Ernest Hemingway

Cheerfulness, sir, is the principal ingredient in the composition of health.

~Arthur Murphy

Take care of your body. It's the only place you have to live.

~Jim Rohn

Hear

To listen is to know for a moment. To hear is to know forever.

~Dana Cowley

Every man hears only what they understand.

~Johann Wolfgang von Goethe

Heart

The royal road to a man's heart is to talk to him about the things he treasures most.

~Dale Carnegie

The most powerful agent of growth and transformation is something much more basic than any technique: a change of heart.

~John Welwood

I must have something to engross my thoughts, some object in life which will fill this vacuum and prevent this sad wearing away of the heart.

~Elizabeth Blackwell

The heart that gives, gathers.

~Marianne Moore

The human heart is vast enough to contain all the world.

~Joseph Conrad

The greatest explorer on this earth never takes voyages as long as those of the man who descends to the depth of his heart.

~Julien Green

Don't be reckless with other people's hearts. Don't put up with people who are reckless with yours.

~Jimi Hendrix

I turn my head to sky rains falling, wash the wounds of numbness from my soul. Turn my heart in tides of fierce renewal, where love and rage run whole.

~Carolyn McDade

If your heart did not break now and then . . . how would you know it is there?

~Bette Bao Lord

The heart is a free and a fetterless thing. A wave of the ocean, a bird on the wing.

~Julia Pardoe

The only thing that makes one place more attractive to me than another is the quantity of heart I find in it.

~Jane Welsh Carlyle

Heaven and Hell

[Go to] heaven for the climate, hell for company.

~Mark Twain

Helpful

It is one of the most beautiful compensations of this life that no man can sincerely try to help another without helping himself.
~Ralph Waldo Emerson

Our prime purpose in this life is to help others. And if you can't help them, at least don't hurt them.

~Dalai Lama

If a friend is in trouble, don't annoy him by asking if there is any- thing you can do. Think up something appropriate and do it.
~Edgar Watson Howe

Lay hold of something that will help you, and then use it to help somebody else.

~Booker T. Washington

The greatest object in the universe, says the philosopher, is a good man struggling with adversity; yet there is still a greater, which is the good man who comes to relieve it.
~Oliver Goldsmith

Our greatest duty and our main responsibility is to help others. But please, if you can't help them, would you please not hurt them.
~Dalai Lama

There is no more noble occupation in the world than to assist an- other human being—to help someone succeed.
~Alan Loy McGinnis

In about the same degree as you are helpful, you will be happy.
~Karl Reiland

We can't help everyone, but everyone can help someone.
~Ronald Reagan

Very few burdens are heavy if everyone lifts.

~Sy Wise

Heroism

There is a certain enthusiasm in liberty, that makes human nature rise above itself, in acts of bravery and heroism.

~Alexander Hamilton

A hero is someone who has given his or her life to something bigger than oneself.

~Joseph Campbell

The new hero is the innovator.

~Alvin Toffler

I think a hero is an ordinary individual who finds the strength to persevere and endure in spite of overwhelming obstacles.

~Christopher Reeve

It takes a hero to be one of those men who goes into battle.

~Norman Schwarzkopf

Hard times don't create heroes. It is during the hard times when the 'hero' within us is revealed.

~Bob Riley

Life, misfortunes, isolation, abandonment, poverty, are battlefields that have their heroes; obscure heroes, sometimes greater than illustrious heroes.

~Victor Hugo

What makes Superman a hero is not that he has power, but that he has the wisdom and the maturity to use the power wisely.

~Christopher Reeve

I am not concerned that you have fallen—I am concerned that you arise.

~Abraham Lincoln

True heroism is remarkably sober, very undramatic. It is not the urge to surpass all others at whatever cost, but the urge to serve others at whatever cost.

~Arthur Ashe

Hindsight

By the time a man realizes that maybe his father was right, he usually has a son who thinks he's wrong.
~Charles Wadsworth

History

If history repeats itself, and the unexpected always happens, how incapable must man be of learning from experience.
~George Bernard Shaw

Never doubt that you can change history. You already have.
~Marge Piercy

There is no life that does not contribute to history.
~Dorothy West

To be ignorant of what occurred before you were born is to remain always a child.
~Marcus Tullius Cicero

The principle office of history I take to be this: to prevent virtuous actions from being forgotten, and that evil words and deeds should fear an infamous reputation with posterity.
~Tacitus

Home

It takes a heap o' living' in a house t' make it a home.
~Edgar A. Guest

The strength of a nation derives from the integrity of the home.
~Confucius

Home is where the heart is.
~Pliny the Elder

Eden is that old-fashioned house we dwell in every day without suspecting our abode, until we drive away.
~Emily Dickinson

As far as I'm concerned, I wouldn't want to go to any other country. It's good enough here.

~Orviel Kruse

All the places to love are here . . . no matter where you may live.
~Patricia MacLachlan

Honesty

No man can produce great things who is not thoroughly sincere in dealing with himself.

~James Russell Lowell

Be true to your work, your word, and your friend.
~John Boyle O'Reilly

No legacy is so rich as honesty.

~William Shakespeare

If we live truly, we shall see truly.

~Ralph Waldo Emerson

Being extremely honest with oneself is a good exercise.
~Sigmund Freud

The very spring and root of honesty and virtue lie in good education.

~Plutarch

When in doubt tell the truth.

~Mark Twain

Our lives improve only when we take chances—and the first and most difficult risk we can take is to be honest with ourselves.
~Walter Anderson

I hope I shall always possess firmness and virtue enough to maintain what I consider the most enviable of all titles, the character of an honest man.

~George Washington

Honesty has a beautiful and refreshing simplicity about it. No ulterior motives. No hidden meanings. An absence of hypocrisy, duplicity, political games, and verbal superficiality. As honesty and real integrity characterize our lives, there will be no need to manipulate others.

~Charles Swindoll

I have found that being honest is the best technique I can use. Right up front, tell people what you're trying to accomplish and what you're willing to sacrifice to accomplish it.

~Lee Iacocca

Keep true. Never be ashamed of doing right. Decide on what you think is right and stick to it.

~George Eliot

Prefer loss to the wealth of dishonest gain; the former vexes you for a time; the latter will bring you lasting remorse.

~Chilo

Honor

The greatest way to live with honor in this world is to be what we pretend to be.

~Socrates

Who sows virtue reaps honor.

~Leonardo da Vinci

No person was ever honored for what he received. Honor has been the reward for what he gave.

~Calvin Coolidge

Honor has not to be won; it must only not be lost.

~Arthur Schopenhauer

Reputation is what other people know about you. Honor is what you know about yourself.

~Lois McMaster Bujold

Hope

Hope is being able to see that there is light despite all of the darkness.

~Desmond Tutu

When there is hope in the future, there is power in the present.

~Zig Ziglar

Don't give up. Don't lose hope. Don't sell out.

~Christopher Reeve

Human pain does not let go of its grip at one point in time. Rather, it works its way out of our consciousness over time. There is a season of sadness. A season of anger. A season of tranquility. A season of hope.

~Robert Veninga

To live without hope is to cease to live.

~Fyodor Dostoyevsky

No matter how dark the moment, love and hope are always possible.

~George Chakiris

Make no little plans. They have no magic to stir men's blood . . . Make big plans, aim high in hope and work.

~Daniel H. Burnham

Hope smiles from the threshold of the year to come, whispering, "It will be happier."

~Alfred, Lord Tennyson

A day of unselfish purpose is always a day of confident hope.

~Woodrow Wilson

Hope is the feeling you have that the feeling you have isn't permanent.

~Jean Kerr

We must accept finite disappointment, but we must never lose infinite hope.

~Martin Luther King Jr.

Where there is no vision, there is no hope.
~George Washington Carver

Hope is . . . furnished with light and heat.
~Jeremy Collier

Man needs, for his happiness, not only the enjoyment of this or that, but hope and enterprise and change.
~Bertrand Russell

Everything that is done in the world is done by hope. No husbandman would sow one grain of corn, if he hoped not it would grow up and become seed.
~Martin Luther

There is a light in this world, a healing spirit more powerful than any darkness we may encounter.
~Mother Teresa

You must not lose faith in humanity. Humanity is an ocean; if a few drops of the ocean are dirty, the ocean does not become dirty.
~Mohandas K. Gandhi

Whatever enlarges hope will also exalt courage.
~Samuel Johnson

Expect to have hope rekindled. Expect your prayers to be answered in wondrous ways. The dry seasons in life do not last. The spring rains will come again.
~Sarah Ban Breathnach

Hope begins in the dark, the stubborn hope that if you just show up and try to do the right thing, the dawn will come. You wait and watch and work: you don't give up.
~Anne Lamott

When we become aware that we do not have to escape our pains, but that we can mobilize them into a common search for life, those very pains are transformed from expressions of despair into signs of hope.
~Henri J. M. Nouwen

Fairy tales are more than true: not because they tell us that dragons exist, but because they tell us that dragons can be beaten.

~G. K. Chesterton

Practice hope. As hopefulness becomes a habit, you can achieve a permanently happy spirit.

~Norman Vincent Peale

True hope dwells on the possible, even when life seems to be a plot written by someone who wants to see how much adversity we can overcome. True hope responds to the real world, to real life; it is an active effort.

~Walter Anderson

Those who are animated by hope can perform what would seem impossibilities to those who are under the depressing influence of fear.

~Maria Edgeworth

There is no medicine like hope, no incentive so great, and no tonic so powerful as expectation of something better tomorrow.

~Orison Marden

Hope is the only bee that makes honey without flowers.

~Robert Green Ingersoll

Each time someone stands up for an ideal, or acts to improve the lot of others, or strikes out against injustice, he sends forth a tiny ripple of hope.

~Robert F. Kennedy

Every year on your birthday, you get a chance to start new.

~Sammy Hagar

The world is not respectable; it is mortal, tormented, confused, deluded forever; but it is shot through with beauty, with love, with glints of courage and laughter; and in these, the spirit blooms timidly, and struggles to the light amid the thorns.

~George Santayana

Hope is like the sun, which, as we journey towards it, casts the shadow of our burden behind us.

~Samuel Smiles

Hospitality

Christmas is a season for kindling the fire of hospitality in the hall, the genial flame of charity in the heart.

~Washington Irving

Hostility

A loving person lives in a loving world. A hostile person lives in a hostile world: everyone you meet is your mirror.

~Ken Keyes Jr.

Humanity

You must not lose faith in humanity. Humanity is an ocean; if a few drops of the ocean are dirty, the ocean does not become dirty.

~Mohandas K. Gandhi

The most perfect expression of human behavior is a string quartet.

~Jeffrey Tate

The bow cannot always stand bent, nor can human frailty subsist without some lawful recreation.

~Miguel de Cervantes

By learning to discover the value our ordinariness, we nurture a friendliness toward ourselves and the world that is the essence of a healthy soul.

~Thomas Moore

A man shares his days with hunger, thirst, and cold, with the good times and the bad, and the first part of being a man is to understand that.

~Louis L'Amour

Be ashamed to die until you have won some victory for humanity.

~Horace Mann

Man is an imagining being.

~Gaston Bachelard

One might well say that mankind is divisible into two great classes: hosts and guests.

~Sir Max Beerbohm

We are all one.

~A. H. Almaas

I am no bird; and no net ensnares me; I am a free human being with an independent will.

~Charlotte Brontë

The man who is forever disturbed about the condition of humanity either has no problems of his own or has refused to face them.

~Henry Miller

I we can find ways to awaken the full power of awareness, we could enter a new phase of human evolution and revitalize ourselves and our world.

~Tarthang Tulku

Man is, at one and the same time, a solitary being and a social being.

~Albert Einstein

We are luminous beings. We are perceivers. We are an awareness.

~Carlos Castaneda

I sometimes think we expect too much of Christmas Day. We try to crowd into it the long arrears of kindliness and humanity of the whole year. As for me, I like to take Christmas a little at a time, all through the year.

~David Grayson

As human beings, our greatness lies not so much in being able to remake the world . . . as in being able to remake ourselves.

~Mohandas K. Gandhi

We have to do the best we can. This is our sacred human responsibility.

~Albert Einstein

The world knows nothing of its greatest men.

~Henry Taylor

I can think of no more stirring symbol of man's humanity to man than a fire engine.

~Kurt Vonnegut

Humans are amphibians—half spirit and half animal. As spirits they belong to the eternal world, but as animals they inhabit time.

~C. S. Lewis

The great renewal of the world will perhaps consist in this, that man and woman . . . shall no longer seek each other as opposites, but as . . . neighbors, and will unite as human beings.

~Rainer Maria Rilke

We are all one.

~A. H. Almaas

No man is an island entire of itself; every man is . . . a part of the main. . . . any man's death diminishes me, because I am involved in mankind, and therefore never send to know for whom the bell tolls; it tolls for thee.

~John Donne

Our most basic common link is that we all inhabit this planet. We all breathe the same air. We all cherish our children's future. And we all are mortal.

~John F. Kennedy

What we have done for ourselves alone dies with us; what we have done for others and the world remains and is immortal.

~Albert Pike

The true value of a human being is determined primarily by the measure and the sense in which he has attained to liberation from the self.

~Albert Einstein

Dedicate some of your life to others. Your dedication will not be a sacrifice. It will be an exhilarating experience because it is intense effort applied toward a meaningful end.

~Thomas Dooley

There is no more noble occupation in the world than to assist another human being—to help someone succeed.

~Alan Loy McGinnis

It is the individual who is not interested in his fellow men who has the greatest difficulties in life and provides the greatest injury to others. It is from among such individuals that all human failures spring.

~Alfred Adler

The greatest achievement of the human spirit is to live up to one's opportunities and make the most of one's resources.

~Luc de Clapiers

Humility

Life is a long lesson in humility.

~James M. Barrie

Humility is not thinking less of yourself, it's thinking of yourself less.

~C. S. Lewis

The true way to be humble is not to stoop until you are smaller than yourself, but to stand at your real height against some higher nature that will show you what the real smallness of your greatness is.

~Phillips Brooks

Drop the idea that you are Atlas carrying the world on your shoulders. The world would go on even without you. Don't take yourself so seriously.

~Norman Vincent Peale

Never be haughty to the humble; never be humble to the haughty.
~Jefferson Davis

No matter what accomplishments you achieve, somebody helped you.

~Althea Gibson

Tremendous humility comes from others having faith in you.
~Dag Hammarskjöld

Be silent as to services you have rendered, but speak of favours you have received.

~Lucius Annaeus Seneca

Silence is the element in which great things fashion themselves together.

~Thomas Carlyle

What we must decide is perhaps how we are valuable rather than how valuable we are.

~Edgar Z. Friedenberg

It is far more impressive when others discover your good qualities without your help.

~Judith Martin

When we were children, we used to think that when we were grown-up, we would no longer be vulnerable. But to grow up is to accept vulnerability . . . To be alive is to be vulnerable.

~Madeleine L'Engle

It is in the character of very few men to honor without envy a friend who has prospered.

~Aeschylus

There is nobody so irritating as somebody with less intelligence and more sense than we have.

~Don Herold

Humor

A sense of humor is a major defense against minor troubles.

~Mignon McLaughlin

The importance of laughter and humor in the workplace can't be emphasized enough.

~Mike Vance and Diane Deacon

Humor can alter any situation and help us cope at the very instant we are laughing.

~Allen Klein

Health and good humor are to the human body like sunshine to vegetation.

~Jean B. Massillon

There is certainly no defense against adverse fortune which is, on the whole, so effectual as an habitual sense of humor.
~Thomas W. Higginson

Humor is the instinct for taking pain playfully.
~Max Eastman

A good laugh is good for the spirits it's true, but a good cry is good for the soul.
~Bette Midler

It is characteristic of all deep human problems that they are not to be approached without some humor and some bewilderment.
~Freeman Dyson

Humor is the instinct for taking pain playfully.
~Max Eastman

You may not be able to change a situation, but with humor you can change your attitude about it.
~Allen Klein

Like a welcome summer rain, humor may suddenly cleanse and cool the earth, the air and you.
~Langston Hughes

A little perspective, like a little humor, goes a long way.
~Allen Klein

The ability to laugh at life is right at the top, with love and communication, in the hierarchy of our needs.
~Sara Davidson

I asked my caddie for a sand wedge and he came back ten minutes later with a ham on rye.
~Chi Chi Rodriguez

You can tell how smart people are by what they laugh at.
~Tina Fey

We owe a lot to Thomas Edison—if it wasn't for him, we'd be watching television by candlelight.
~Milton Berle

If you could choose one characteristic that would get you through life, choose a sense of humor.

~Jennifer Jones

A sense of humor can help you overlook the unattractive, tolerate the unpleasant, cope with the unexpected, and smile through the unbearable.

~Moshe Waldoks

A well-developed sense of humor is the pole that adds balance to your steps as you walk the tightrope of life.

~William Arthur Ward

Humor is the great thing, the saving thing. The minute it crops up, all our irritations and resentments slip away and a sunny spirit takes their place.

~Mark Twain

The brain is a wonderful organ; it starts working the moment you get up in the morning and does not stop until you get into the office.

~Robert Frost

Analyzing humor is like dissecting a frog. Few people are interested and the frog dies of it.

~E. B. White

Get your facts first, and then you can distort them as much as you please.

~Mark Twain

Common sense and a sense of humor are the same thing, moving at different speeds. A sense of humor is just common sense, dancing.

~Clive James

I like nonsense, it wakes up the brain cells. Fantasy is a necessary ingredient in living, it's a way of looking at life through the wrong end of a telescope. Which is what I do, and that enables you to laugh at life's realities.

~Theodor Seuss Geisel (Dr. Seuss)

Hurry

Wisely and slow; they stumble that run fast.

~William Shakespeare

Don't hurry. Don't worry.

~Walter Hagan

Hypocrisy

Don't say things. What you are stands over you the while, and thunders so that I cannot hear what you say to the contrary.

~Ralph Waldo Emerson

The trouble is that not enough people have come together with the firm determination to live the things which they say they believe.

~Eleanor Roosevelt

If the things we believe are different than the things we do, there can be no true happiness.

~Dana Telford

Ideals

Ideals are like stars; you will not succeed in touching them with your hands. . . . you choose them as your guides, and following them, you will reach your destiny.

~Carl Schurz

The ideal man bears the accidents of life with dignity and grace, making the best of circumstances.

~Aristotle

Hearts are the strongest when they beat in response to noble ideals.

~Ralph Bunche

Ideology has very little to do with "consciousness"—it is profoundly unconscious.

~Louis Althusser

Ideas

Nothing is more dangerous than an idea, when you only have one idea.

~Emile Chartier Alain

I have never yet seen any plan which has not been mended by the observations of those who were much inferior in understanding to the person who took the lead in the business.

~Edmund Burke

I'm not afraid of facts, I welcome facts but a congeries of facts is not equivalent to an idea. This is the essential fallacy of the so-called "scientific" mind. People who mistake facts for ideas are incomplete thinkers; they are gossips.

~Cynthia Ozick

If I have a thousand ideas and only one turns out to be good, I am satisfied.

~Alfred Nobel

Getting an idea should be like sitting on a pin; it should make you jump up and do something.

~E. L. Simpson

One clear idea is too precious a treasure to lose.

~Caroline Gilman

Play with your ideas; thinking should be fun.

~Harold R. McAlindon

No matter what people tell you, words and ideas can change the world.

~Robin Williams

Great ideas need landing gear as well as wings.

~C. D. Jackson

To create you must quiet your mind. You need a quiet mind so that ideas will have a chance of connecting.

~Eric Maisel

Just one great idea can completely revolutionize your life.
~Earl Nightingale

If you have an apple and I have an apple and we exchange these apples then you and I will still each have one apple. But if you have an idea and I have an idea and we exchange these ideas, then each of us will have two ideas.
~George Bernard Shaw

Ideas bring people together, but ideals hold them together.
~Dan Zadra

Form the habit of saying 'Yes' to your good ideas. Then write down all the reasons why they will work. There will always be plenty of people around to tell you why they won't work.
~Gil Atkinson

Ideas come from everywhere.
~Alfred Hitchcock

People will accept your idea much more readily if you tell them Benjamin Franklin said it first.
~David H. Comins

If you don't execute your ideas, they die.
~Roger von Oech

To stay ahead, you must have your next idea waiting in the wings.
~Rosabeth Moss Kanter

Don't let ideas die of neglect.
~Harold R. McAlindon

An idea in a cage is like a silver dollar buried in the ground. Both are safe, but neither produces anything.
~Myron S. Allen

If you wish to win a man over to your ideas, first convince him that you are his true friend.
~Abraham Lincoln

The vitality of thought is in adventure. Ideas won't keep. Something must be done about them.
~Alfred North Whitehead

All the forces in the world . . . is so powerful as an idea whose time has come.

~Victor Hugo

Identity

The privilege of a lifetime is being who you are.

~Joseph Campbell

The more you like yourself, the less you are like anyone else, which makes you unique.

~Walt Disney

Every story I create, creates me. I write to create myself.

~Octavia E. Butler

In great matters men show themselves as they wish to be seen; in small matters, as they are.

~Gamaliel Bradford

Look within. Within is the fountain of good, and it will ever bubble up, if thou wilt ever dig.

~Marcus Aurelius

It is very important to know who you are. To make decisions. To show who you are.

~Malala Yousafzai

I'm Irish on St. Patrick's Day. I'm Italian on Columbus Day. I'm a New Yorker every day.

~Tamara Tunie

The ablest man I ever met is the man you think you are.

~Franklin D. Roosevelt

No one can make you feel inferior without your consent.

~Eleanor Roosevelt

When you are content to be simply yourself and don't compare or compete, everybody will respect you.

~Lao Tzu

Never be bullied into silence. Never allow yourself to be made a victim. Accept no one's definition of your life, but define yourself.
~Harvey Fierstein

Public opinion is a weak tyrant compared with our own private opinion. What a man thinks of himself, that it is which determines, or rather indicates, his fate.
~Henry David Thoreau

I've learned to take time for myself and to treat myself with a great deal of love and respect because I like me . . . I think I'm kind of cool.
~Whoopi Goldberg

The world is a great mirror. It reflects back to you what you are.
~Thomas Dreier

Guided by my heritage of a love of beauty and a respect for strength—in search of my mother's garden, I found my own.
~Alice Walker

To be yourself in a world that is constantly trying to make you something else is the greatest accomplishment.
~Ralph Waldo Emerson

The ideal man bears the accidents of life with dignity and grace, making the best of circumstances.
~Aristotle

You are a child of the universe, no less than the trees and the stars; you have a right to be here.
~Max Ehrmann

What lies ahead of you and what lies behind you is nothing compared to what lies within you.
~Mohandas Gandhi

Knowing yourself is the beginning of all wisdom.
~Aristotle

Finding ourselves takes time. It is hard work and it is worth doing.
~Anne Wilson Schaef

I have to live with myself, and so I want to be fit for myself to know.
~Edgar A. Guest

You never find yourself until you face the truth.
~Pearl Bailey

You have got to discover you, what you do, and trust it.
~Barbra Streisand

We see things as we are, not as they are.
~Jennifer Stone

There is nothing deep down inside us except what we have put there ourselves.
~Richard Rorty

Self-knowledge is best learned, not by contemplation, but by action. Strive to do your duty and you will soon discover of what stuff you are made.
~Johann Wolfgang von Goethe

Men are created different; they lose their social freedom and their individual autonomy in seeking to become like each other.
~David Riesman

Always be a first-rate version of yourself, instead of a second-rate version of somebody else.
~Judy Garland

One must not always think so much about what one should do, but rather what one should be. Our works do not ennoble us; but we must ennoble our works.
~Meister Eckhart

What you think of yourself is much more important than what others think of you.
~Lucius Annaeus Seneca

We don't know who we are until we see what we can do.
~Martha Grimes

If you are what you do, then when you don't . . . you aren't.
~Wayne Dyer

After all, it's what we've done that makes us what we are.
~Jim Croce

An identity would seem to be arrived at by the way in which the person faces and uses his experience.
~James Baldwin

Idleness

Work is not always required . . . there is such a thing as sacred idleness, the cultivation of which is now fearfully neglected.
~George MacDonald

You must learn to be still in the midst of activity and be vibrantly alive in repose.
~Indira Gandhi

Ignorance

There are two things which cannot be attacked in front: ignorance and narrow-mindedness. They can only be shaken by the simple development of the contrary qualities.
~John Emerich Edward Dalberg-Acton

We allow our ignorance to prevail upon us and make us think we can survive alone, alone in patches, alone in groups, alone in races, even alone in genders.
~Maya Angelou

I know absolutely nothing. That is why each new day, each new moment, is truly an adventure.
~Ross Fields

Everyone is ignorant, only on different subjects.
~Will Rogers

There is nothing more frightening than ignorance in action.
~Johann Wolfgang von Goethe

Imagination

This world is but a canvas to our imagination.
~Henry David Thoreau

I doubt that the imagination can be suppressed. If you truly eradicated it in a child, he would grow up to be an eggplant.
~Ursula K. Le Guin

I believe in the imagination. What I cannot see is infinitely more important than what I can see.
~Duane Michals

Man is an imagining being.
~Gaston Bachelard

The true sign of intelligence is not knowledge but imagination.
~Albert Einstein

Imagination is the eye of the soul.
~Joseph Joubert

The man who has no imagination has no wings.
~Muhammad Ali

Imagination is more important than knowledge. Knowledge is limited. Imagination encircles the world.
~Albert Einstein

A rock pile ceases to be a rock pile the moment a single man contemplates it, bearing within him the image of a cathedral.
~Antoine de Saint-Exupéry

Give me matter, and I will construct a world out of it!
~Immanuel Kant

The soul without imagination is what an observatory would be without a telescope.
~Henry Ward Beecher

Inspiration and imagination go hand in hand.
~Suzanna Hatch

What creates despair is the imagination, which . . . insists on predicting millions of moments, thousands of days, and so drains you that you cannot live the moment at hand.
~Andre Dubus

If one advances confidently in the direction of his dreams, and endeavors to live the life which he has imagined, he will meet with a success unexpected in common hours.

~Henry David Thoreau

Immorality

The only immorality is not to do what one has to do when one has to do it.

~Jean Anouilh

Old age has deformities enough of its own. It should never add to them the deformity of vice.

~Eleanor Roosevelt

Impatience

There art two cardinal sins from which all others spring: Impatience and Laziness.

~Franz Kafka

Patience is the art of concealing your impatience.

~Guy Kawasaki

Importance

The human tendency to regard little things as important has produced very many great things.

~G. C. Lichtenberg

Impossible

Start by doing what's necessary; then do what's possible; and suddenly you are doing the impossible.

~Francis of Assisi

Aerodynamically, the bumble bee shouldn't be able to fly, but the bumble bee doesn't know it, so it goes on flying anyway.

~Mary Kay Ash

It is difficult to say what is impossible, for the dream of yesterday is the hope of today and the reality of tomorrow.
~Robert H. Goddard

You must do the thing you think you cannot do.
~Eleanor Roosevelt

Improvement

Never leave well enough alone.
~Raymond Loewy

If you can't make it better, you can laugh at it.
~Erma Bombeck

Practice without improvement is meaningless.
~Chuck Knox

The place to improve the world is first in one's own heart and head and hands, and then work outward from there.
~Robert M. Pirsig

Each of us must work for his own improvement, and at the same time share a general responsibility for all humanity.
~Marie Curie

There's only one corner of the universe you can be certain of improving, and that's your own self.
~Aldous Huxley

Independence

Independence is happiness.
~Susan B. Anthony

To be truly and really independent is to support ourselves by our own exertions.
~Jane Porter

If you expect someone else to guide you, you'll be lost.
~James Earl Jones

The proverb warns that "You should not bite the hand that feeds you." But maybe you should, if it prevents you from feeding yourself.

~Thomas Szasz

Influence

Who shall set a limit to the influence of a human being?
~Ralph Waldo Emerson

As one lamp lights another, nor grows less, so nobleness enkindleth nobleness.

~James Russell Lowell

Pull the string, and it will follow wherever you wish. Push it, and it will go nowhere at all.

~Dwight D. Eisenhower

No man can become rich without himself enriching others.
~Andrew Carnegie

Everyone can do something that makes a difference.
~Todd R. Wagner

There are those whose lives affect all others around them. Quietly touching one heart, who in turn, touches another. Reaching out to ends further than they would ever know.

~William Bradfield

Quality begins on the inside . . . then works its way out.
~Bob Moawad

Vote early and vote often.

~Al Capone

You must be the change you wish to see in the world.
~Mohandas Gandhi

The more light you allow within you, the brighter the world you live in will be.

~Shakti Gawain

Happiness, like a refreshing stream, flows from heart to heart in endless circulation.

~Henry Grove

Ingenuity

Just because something doesn't do what you planned it to do doesn't mean it's useless.

~Thomas Edison

It still holds true that man is most uniquely human when he turns obstacles into opportunities.

~Eric Hoffer

Never tell people how to do things. Tell them what to do, and they will surprise you with their ingenuity.

~George S. Patton

Make it new.

~Ezra Pound

Injury

Singular indeed that the people should be writhing under oppression and injury, and yet not one among them to be found, to raise the voice of complaint.

~Abraham Lincoln

Injustice

We must remember that any oppression, any injustice, any hatred, is a wedge designed to attack our civilization.

~Franklin D. Roosevelt

Injustice anywhere is a threat to justice everywhere.

~Martin Luther King Jr.

Innovation

The new hero is the innovator.

~Alvin Toffler

Innovation distinguishes between a leader and a follower.

~Steve Jobs

Yesterday's answer usually has nothing to do with today's problem.

~Bill Gates

Inspiration

Inspiration never arrived when you were searching for it.

~Lisa Alther

We should be taught not to wait for inspiration to start a thing. Action always generates inspiration. Inspiration seldom generates action.

~Frank Tibolt

If you can imagine it, you can achieve it; if you can dream it, you can become it.

~William Arthur Ward

Hearts are the strongest when they beat in response to noble ideals.

~Ralph Bunche

If your actions inspire others to dream more, learn more, do more, and become more, you are a leader.

~John Quincy Adams

This, then, is the test we must set for ourselves; not to march alone but to march in such a way that others will wish to join us.

~Hubert Humphrey

Inspiration and imagination go hand in hand.

~Suzanna Hatch

Education is not the filling of a pail, but the lighting of a fire.

~William Butler Yeats

A man is fortunate if he encounters living examples of vice, as well as of virtue, to inspire him.

~Brendan Behan

Use what talents you possess; the woods would be very silent if no birds sang there except those that sang best.

~Henry Van Dyke

Every great dream begins with a dreamer. Always remember, you have within you the strength, the patience, and the passion to reach for the stars to change the world.

~Harriet Tubman

You are educated. Your certification is in your degree. You may think of it as the ticket to the good life. Let me ask you to think of an alternative. Think of it as your ticket to change the world.

~Tom Brokaw

Let us make future generations remember us as proud ancestors just as, today, we remember our forefathers.

~Roh Moo-hyun

Instinct

It is only by following your deepest instinct that you can lead a rich life, and if you let your fear of consequence prevent you from following your deepest instinct, then your life will be safe, expedient and thin.

~Katharine Butler Hathaway

Trust your own instinct. Your mistakes might as well be your own, instead of someone else's.

~Billy Wilder

Good instincts usually tell you what to do long before your head has figured it out.

~Michael Burke

Integrity

Integrity is never painless.

~M. Scott Peck

Character contributes to beauty. It fortifies a woman as her youth fades. A mode of conduct, a standard of courage, discipline, fortitude, and integrity can do a great deal to make a woman beautiful.

~Jacqueline Bisset

A man should be upright, not be kept upright.
~Marcus Aurelius

Be true to your work, your word, and your friend.
~John Boyle O'Reilly

If we live truly, we shall see truly.
~Ralph Waldo Emerson

The strength of a nation derives from the integrity of the home.
~Confucius

Honest hearts produce honest actions.
~Brigham Young

Remember this—that there is a proper dignity and proportion to be observed in the performance of every act of life.
~Marcus Aurelius

The truth of the matter is that you always know the right thing to do. The hard part is doing it.
~Norman Schwarzkopf

Be true to your work and your word.
~Ben Morrow

A life lived with integrity—even if it lacks the trappings of fame and fortune is a shining star in whose light others may follow in the years to come.
~Denis Waitley

The most important persuasion tool you have in your entire arsenal is integrity.
~Zig Ziglar

If the things we believe are different than the things we do, there can be no true happiness.
~Dana Telford

Intelligence

Every true genius is bound to be naive.
~Friedrich von Schiller

For the ordinary business of life an ounce of habit is worth a pound of intellect.

~Thomas B. Reed

A man of genius makes no mistakes. His errors are volitional and are the portals of discovery.

~James Joyce

It takes people a long time to learn the difference between talent and genius, especially ambitious young men and women.

~Louisa May Alcott

The exact measure of the progress of civilization is the degree in which the intelligence of the common mind has prevailed over wealth and brute force.

~George Bancroft

You're braver than you believe, stronger than you seem, and smarter than you think.

~A. A. Milne

Intelligence is quickness to apprehend as distinct from ability, which is capacity to act wisely on the thing apprehended.

~Alfred North Whitehead

Talent wins games, but teamwork and intelligence win championships.

~Michael Jordan

The true sign of intelligence is not knowledge but imagination.

~Albert Einstein

Intelligence is the ability to adapt to change.

~Stephen Hawking

Clear thinking requires courage rather than intelligence.

~Thomas Szasz

An intellectual is a man who takes more words than necessary to tell more than he knows.

~Dwight D. Eisenhower

Time has a way of demonstrating the most stubborn are the most intelligent.

~Yevgeny Yevtushenko

Physical fitness is not only one of the most important keys to a healthy body, it is the basis of dynamic and creative intellectual activity.

~John F. Kennedy

Intentions

The smallest good deed is better than the grandest good intention.

~Duguet

Intolerance

No loss by flood and lightning, no destruction of cities and temples by hostile forces of nature, has deprived man of so many noble lives and impulses as those which his intolerance has destroyed.

~Helen Keller

Success makes us intolerant of failure and failure makes us intolerant of success.

~William Feather

Isolation

It's like magic. When you live by yourself, all your annoying habits are gone!

~Merrill Markoe

Associate yourself with men of good quality, if you esteem your own reputation; for 'tis better to be alone than in bad company.

~George Washington

Journey

It's all about the journey, not the outcome.

~Carl Lewis

Joy

Only those who have learned the power of sincere and selfless contribution experience life's deepest joy: true fulfillment.

~Tony Robbins

On with the dance, let the joy be unconfined, is my motto; whether there's any dance to dance or any joy to unconfined.

~Mark Twain

Accept the pain, cherish the joys, resolve the regrets; then can come the best of benedictions — "If I had my life to live over, I'd do it all the same."

~Joan McIntosh

For present joys are more to flesh and blood, than a dull prospect of a distant good.

~John Dryden

Joy is prayer; joy is strength; joy is love; joy is a net of love by which you can catch souls.

~Mother Teresa

Joy is not in things, it is in us.

~Richard Wagner

Learn to be happy. And think of life as a terminal illness because if you do you will live it with joy and passion, as it ought to be lived.

~Anna Quindlen

With an eye made quiet by the power. Of harmony, and the deep power of joy. We see into the heart of things.

~William Wordsworth

I have found that there is a tremendous joy in giving. It is a very important part of the joy of living.

~William Black

All the world is searching for joy and happiness, but these cannot be purchased for any price in any market place, because they are virtues that come from within.

~Lucille R. Taylor

Since you get more joy out of giving joy to others, you should put a good deal of thought into the happiness that you are able to give.

~Eleanor Roosevelt

I slept and dreamt that life was joy. I awoke and saw that life was service. I acted and behold, service was joy.

~Rabindranath Tagore

Joy is the will which labors, which overcomes obstacles, which knows triumph.

~William Butler Yeats

One of the sanest, surest, and most generous joys of life comes from being happy over the good fortune or others.

~Archibald Rutledge

Joys are our wings, sorrows our spurs.

~Jean Paul Richter

An eye can threaten like a loaded and leveled gun, or can insult like hissing or kicking; or, in its altered mood, by beams of kindness, it can make the heart dance with joy.

~Ralph Waldo Emerson

Judgment

As a man advances in life, he gets what is better than admiration — judgment, to estimate things at their true value.

~Samuel Johnson

We judge ourselves by what we feel capable of doing, while others judge us by what we have already done.

~Henry Wadsworth Longfellow

If you must speak ill of another, do not speak it, write it in the sand near the water's edge.

~Napoleon Hill

Everyone is a genius. But if you judge a fish by its ability to climb a tree, it will live its whole life believing it is stupid.

~Albert Einstein

Justice

Extremism in the defense of liberty is no vice. Moderation in the pursuit of justice is no virtue.

~Barry Goldwater

Kindness

Be kind; everyone you meet is fighting a hard battle.
~John Watson

Let me be a little kinder, Let me be a little blinder, To the faults of those around me, Let me praise a little more.
~Edgar A. Guest

Perhaps you will forget tomorrow the kind words you say today, but the recipient may cherish them over a lifetime.
~Dale Carnegie

A warm smile is the universal language of kindness.
~William Arthur Ward

May I forget what ought to be forgotten; and recall, unfailing, all that ought to be recalled, each kindly thing, forgetting what might sting.
~Mary Caroline Davies

The happiness we give to others makes us happier too, we find, just as friendship returns to the friendly, and kindness comes back to the kind.
~Keith Bennett

Kindness in words creates confidence. Kindness in thinking creates profoundness. Kindness in giving creates love.
~Lao Tzu

True kindness presupposes the faculty of imagining as one's own the suffering and joys of others.
~André Gide

Recompense injury with justice, and recompense kindness with kindness.
~Confucius

A little word in kindness spoken, a motion, or a tear, has often healed the heart that's broken and made a friend sincere.
~John Greenleaf Whittier

I sometimes think we expect too much of Christmas Day. We try to crowd into it the long arrears of kindliness and humanity of the whole year. As for me, I like to take Christmas a little at a time, all through the year.

~David Grayson

The habit of being uniformly considerate toward others will bring increased happiness to you.

~Greenville Kleiser

Wherever there is a human being, there is an opportunity for a kindness.

~Lucius Annaeus Seneca

Kind words are the music of the world. They have a power which seems to be beyond natural causes, as if they were some angel's song which had lost its way and come on earth.

~Frederick William Faber

What wisdom can you find that is greater than kindness.

~Jean Jacques Rousseau

Never lose a chance of saying a kind word.

~William Makepeace Thackeray

Kindness is an inner desire that makes us want to do good things even if we do not get anything in return. It is the joy of our life to do them. When we do good things from this inner desire, there is kindness in everything we think, say, want and do.

~Emanuel Swedenborg

It is futile to judge a kind deed by its motives. Kindness can become its own motive. We are made kind by being kind.

~Eric Hoffer

Good temper, like a sunny day, sheds a brightness over everything; it is the sweetener of toil and the soother of disquietude.

~Washington Irving

So, be swift to love and make haste to be kind.

~Henri-Frédéric Amiel

Kindness is the sunshine in which virtue grows.

~Robert G. Ingersoll

Too often we underestimate the power of a touch, a smile, a kind word, a listening ear, an honest compliment, or the smallest act of caring, all of which have the potential to turn a life around.

~Leo Buscaglia

An eye can threaten like a loaded and leveled gun, or can insult like hissing or kicking; or, in its altered mood, by beams of kindness, it can make the heart dance with joy.

~Ralph Waldo Emerson

You must give time to your fellow men—even if it's a little thing, do something for others—something for which you get no pay but the privilege of doing it.

~Albert Schweitzer

Kind words can be short and easy to speak, but their echoes are truly endless.

~Mother Teresa

What you would not have done to yourselves, never do unto others.

~Alexander Severus

Be generous with kindly words, especially about those who are absent.

~Johann Wolfgang von Goethe

Decency is like gold, the same in all countries.

~Li Hung Chang

Knowledge

As knowledge increases, wonder deepens.

~Charles Morgan

Never mistake knowledge for wisdom. One helps you make a living; the other helps you make a life.

~Eleanor Roosevelt

Knowledge comes, but wisdom lingers.

~Alfred, Lord Tennyson

Nothing is too small to know, and nothing is too big to attempt.

~William Van Horne

Knowledge is happiness, because to have knowledge—broad, deep knowledge—is to know true ends from false, and lofty things from low.

~Helen Keller

We know next to nothing about virtually everything. It is not necessary to know the origin of the universe; it is necessary to want to know. Civilization depends not on any particular knowledge, but on the disposition to crave knowledge.

~George F. Will

You know more than you think you know.

~Oscar Wilde

The larger the island of knowledge, the longer the shoreline of wonder.

~Ralph W. Sockman

The true sign of intelligence is not knowledge but imagination.

~Albert Einstein

Imagination is more important than knowledge. Knowledge is limited. Imagination encircles the world.

~Albert Einstein

The old believe everything; the middle-aged suspect everything; the young know everything.

~Oscar Wilde

Knowledge will give you power, but character respect.

~Bruce Lee

Knowledge must come through action.

~Sophocles

Love is ever the beginning of knowledge, as fire is of light.

~Thomas Carlyle

The utmost extent of man's knowledge, is to know that he knows nothing.

~Joseph Addison

The next best thing to being clever is being able to quote someone who is.

~Mary Pettibone Poole

Any fool can criticize, complain, and condemn—and most fools do. But it takes character and self-control to be understanding and forgiving.

~Dale Carnegie

The best-informed man is not necessarily the wisest.

~Dietrich Bonhoeffer

I was brought up to believe that the only thing worth doing was to add to the sum of accurate information in the world.

~Margaret Mead

Where there is much desire to learn, there of necessity will be much arguing, much writing, many opinions; for opinions in good men is but knowledge in the making.

~John Milton

A superstition is a premature explanation that overstays its time.

~George Iles

Labor Day

If all the cars in the United States were placed end to end, it would probably be Labor Day Weekend.

~Doug Larson

Language

Language most shews a man: Speak, that I may see thee.

~Ben Jonson

Language is memory and metaphor.

~Storm Jameson

Laughter

Laughter is by definition healthy.

~Doris Lessing

The importance of laughter and humor in the workplace can't be emphasized enough.

~Mike Vance and Diane Deacon

Humor can alter any situation and help us cope at the very instant we are laughing.

~Allen Klein

A good laugh is good for the spirits it's true, but a good cry is good for the soul.

~Bette Midler

Laughter is an instant vacation.

~Milton Berle

Anyone who takes himself too seriously always runs the risk of looking ridiculous; anyone who can consistently laugh at himself does not.

~Václav Havel

Shared laughter creates a bond of friendship. When people laugh together, they cease to be young and old, teacher and pupils, worker and boss. They become a single group of human beings.

~W. Lee Grant

Laughter is the shortest distance between two people.

~Victor Borge

If you can't make it better, you can laugh at it.

~Erma Bombeck

The most wasted of all days is one without laughter.

~E. E. Cummings

Hearty laughter is a good way to jog internally without having to go outdoors.

~Norman Cousins

I had rather be the cause of her laughter, than of her tears.

~Caroline Lamb

Always laugh when you can. It is cheap medicine.

~Lord Byron

A day without laughter is a day wasted.
~Charlie Chaplin

For what do we live, but to make sport for our neighbors and laugh at them in our turn?
~Jane Austen

From quiet homes and first beginning, out to the undiscovered ends, there's nothing worth the wear of winning, but laughter and the love of friends.
~Hilaire Belloc

A good laugh is sunshine in a house.
~William Makepeace Thackeray

The only honest art form is laughter, comedy. You can't fake it . . . try to fake three laughs in an hour—ha ha ha ha ha—they'll take you away, man. You can't.
~Lenny Bruce

Laughter is the tonic, the relief, the surcease for pain.
~Charlie Chaplin

If we may believe our logicians, man is distinguished from all other creatures by the faculty of laughter. He has a heart capable of mirth, and naturally disposed to it.
~Joseph Addison

Laughter is inner jogging.
~Norman Cousins

Laziness

Laziness may appear attractive, but work gives satisfaction.
~Anne Frank

A man who dares to waste one hour of time has not discovered the values of life.
~Charles Darwin

Leadership

A leader is a dealer in hope.

~Napoleon Bonaparte

The leader who exercises power with honor will work from the inside out, starting with himself.

~Blaine Lee

Outstanding leaders go out of the way to boost the self-esteem of their personnel. If people believe in themselves, it's amazing what they can accomplish.

~Sam Walton

A person always doing his or her best becomes a natural leader, just by example.

~Joe DiMaggio

Making personal leadership (influence) a choice is like having the freedom to play the piano. It is a freedom that has to be earned—only then can leadership become a choice.

~Stephen R. Covey

Management is doing things right; leadership is doing the right things.

~Peter Drucker

Leadership and learning are indispensable to each other.

~John F. Kennedy

A leader has to be one of two things: he either has to be a brilliant visionary himself, a truly creative strategist, in which case he can do what he likes and get away with it; or else he has to be a true empowerer who can bring out the best in others.

~Henry Mintzberg

The grab for a quick killing is the mark of the worst kind of leadership, for it places immediate profit above the long-term interest of the organization and can lead ultimately only to disaster.

~Crawford H. Greenewalt

Of all the things I've done, the most vital is coordinating the talents of those who work for us and pointing them toward a certain goal.

~Walt Disney

A good objective of leadership is to help those who are doing poorly to do well and to help those who are doing well do even better.
~Jim Rohn

The final test of a leader is that he leaves behind him in other men the conviction and the will to carry on.
~Walter Lippmann

The leader who exercises power with honor will work from the inside out, starting with himself.
~Blaine Lee

Few things can help an individual more than to place responsibility on him, and to let him know that you trust him.
~Booker T. Washington

A leader is one who ventures and takes the risks of going out ahead to show the way and whom others follow, voluntarily, because they are persuaded that the leader's path is the right one—for them, probably better than they could devise for themselves.
~Robert K. Greenleaf

Leaders walk their talk. In true leaders, there is no gap between the theories they espouse and the life they practice.
~Warren G. Bennis

If your actions inspire others to dream more, learn more, do more, and become more, you are a leader.
~John Quincy Adams

Management is efficiency in climbing the ladder of success; leadership determines whether the ladder is leaning against the right wall.
~Stephen Covey

Empowerment is all about letting go so that others can get going.
~Kenneth Blanchard

The leader . . . is rarely the brightest person in the group. Rather, they have extraordinary taste, which makes them more curators than creators. They are appreciators of talent and nurturers of talent and they have the ability to recognize valuable ideas.
~Warren G. Bennis

Pull the string, and it will follow wherever you wish. Push it, and it will go nowhere at all.

~Dwight D. Eisenhower

The crazier the times are, the more important it is for leaders to develop and to trust their intuition.

~Tom Peters

Leadership consists of nothing but taking responsibility for everything that goes wrong and giving your subordinates credit for everything that goes well.

~Dwight D. Eisenhower

Let him who would move and convince others, be first moved and convinced himself.

~Thomas Carlyle

One of the true tests of leadership is the ability to recognize a problem before it becomes an emergency.

~Arnold H. Glasow

He that would make his own liberty secure must guard even his enemy from oppression; for if he violates this duty, he establishes a precedent that will reach to himself.

~Thomas Paine

Nothing so conclusively proves a man's ability to lead others as what he does from day to day to lead himself.

~Thomas J. Watson Sr.

I am certainly not one of those who need to be prodded. In fact, if anything, I am the prod.

~Winston Churchill

Learning

Bad times have a scientific value. These are occasions a good learner would not miss.

~Ralph Waldo Emerson

If history repeats itself, and the unexpected always happens, how incapable must man be of learning from experience.

~George Bernard Shaw

In a time of drastic change it is the learners who inherit the future. The learned usually find themselves equipped to live in a world that no longer exists.

~Eric Hoffer

Sir, there is nothing too little for so little creature as man. It is by studying little things that we attain the great art of having as little misery and as much happiness as possible.

~Samuel Johnson

It is better to know some of the questions than all of the answers.

~James Thurber

We know next to nothing about virtually everything. It is not necessary to know the origin of the universe; it is necessary to want to know. Civilization depends not on any particular knowledge, but on the disposition to crave knowledge.

~George F. Will

Learning is not attained by chance, it must be sought for with ardor and attended to with diligence.

~Abigail Adams

It's amazing how much you can learn if your intentions are truly earnest.

~Chuck Berry

Curiosity is the wick in the candle of learning.

~William A. Ward

I know absolutely nothing. That is why each new day, each new moment, is truly an adventure.

~Ross Fields

There's more learning than is taught in books.

~Lady Isabella Augusta Gregory

Every day learn something new.

~Holly Solomon

Sit down before fact as a little child, be prepared to give up every preconceived notion . . . or you shall learn nothing.

~Thomas Henry Huxley

I have learned throughout my life as a composer chiefly through my mistakes and pursuits of false assumptions, not by my exposure to founts of wisdom and knowledge.

~Igor Stravinsky

Who is wise? He that learns from everyone. Who is powerful? He that governs his passions. Who is rich? He that is content.

~Benjamin Franklin

Learn to see in another's calamity the ills which you should avoid.

~Publilius Syrus

In the pursuit of learning, every day something is acquired.

~Lao Tzu

We cannot teach people anything; we can only help them discover it within themselves.

~Galileo Galilei

Do not seek to follow in the footsteps of the wise; seek what they sought.

~Matsuo Basho

Leadership and learning are indispensable to each other.

~John F. Kennedy

Try to learn something about everything and everything about something.

~Thomas Huxley

I hear and I forget. I see and I remember. I do and I understand.

~Confucius

Live as if you were to die tomorrow. Learn as if you were to live forever.

~Mohandas K. Gandhi

All men should strive to learn before they die, what they are running from, to, and why.

~James Thurber

Let me remember lessons learned, and profit from the past, and may I build a bridge of dreams, that shall forever last.

~Grace E. Easley

Who are the learned? Those who practice what they know.
~Elijah Muhammad

Someone has said that all living is just learning the meaning of words. That does not mean the long ten syllable words we have to look up in the dictionary. The really great words to master are short ones—work, love, hope, joy, pain, home, child, life, death.
~Halford E. Luccock

Live as if you were to die tomorrow. Learn as if you were to live forever.
~Mohandas K. Gandhi

Experience keeps a dear school, but fools will learn in no other.
~Benjamin Franklin

What we actually learn, from any given set of circumstances, determines whether we become increasingly powerless or more powerful.
~Blaine Lee

Just because something doesn't do what you planned it to do doesn't mean it's useless.
~Thomas Edison

We read to train the mind, to fill the mind, to rest the mind, to recreate the mind, or to escape the mind.
~Holbrook Jackson

Now here is the best of my days, but I don't really know it, yes.
~Peter Breinholt

A house without books is like a room without windows.
~Horace Mann

The more you learn what to do with yourself, and the more you do for others, the more you will learn to enjoy the abundant life.
~William Boetcker

They know enough who know how to learn.
~Henry Brooks Adams

We differ, blind and seeing, one from another, not in our senses, but in the use we make of them, in the imagination and courage with which we seek wisdom beyond the senses.

~Helen Keller

Keep learning about the world. Use your mind to the hilt. Life passes quickly and, towards the end, gathers speed like a freight train running downhill. The more you know, the more you enrich yourself and others.

~Susan Trott

Anyone who stops learning is old, whether at twenty or eighty. Anyone who keeps learning stays young. The greatest thing in life is to keep your mind young.

~Henry Ford

Legacy

No legacy is so rich as honesty.

~William Shakespeare

Let us make future generations remember us as proud ancestors just as, today, we remember our forefathers.

~Roh Moo-hyun

Do not seek to follow in the footsteps of the wise; seek what they sought.

~Matsuo Basho

You ask me how I want to be remembered, what I want on my tombstone? "Si se puede—It can be done."

~Dolores Huerta

We are remembered for what we do when it counts.

~Don Ward

Liberty

Among a people generally corrupt, liberty cannot long exist.
~Edmund Burke

The shallow consider liberty a release from all law, from every constraint. The wise man sees in it, on the contrary, the potent Law of Laws.

~Walt Whitman

Liberty, when it begins to take root, is a plant of rapid growth.

~George Washington

Where liberty dwells, there is my country.

~Benjamin Franklin

Extremism in the defense of liberty is no vice. Moderation in the pursuit of justice is no virtue.

~Barry Goldwater

The deadliest foe of democracy is not autocracy but liberty frenzied.

~Otto Hermann Kahn

Liberty, too, must be limited in order to be possessed.

~Edmund Burke

He that would make his own liberty secure must guard even his enemy from oppression; for if he violates this duty, he establishes a precedent that will reach to himself.

~Thomas Paine

Light

A candle loses nothing by lighting another candle.

~James Keller

The more light you allow within you, the brighter the world you live in will be.

~Shakti Gawain

You can't have light without a dark to stick in it.

~Arlo Guthrie

Darkness cannot drive out darkness; only light can do that. Hate cannot drive out hate; only love can do that.

~Martin Luther King Jr.

There is light in the world, a healing spirit more powerful than any darkness may encounter.

~Mother Theresa

Limitations

Argue for your limitations, and sure enough, they're yours.

~Richard Bach

If you accept your limitations, you go beyond them.

~Brendan Behan

Listening

It takes a great man to make a good listener.

~Calvin Coolidge

One advantage of talking to yourself is that you know at least somebody's listening.

~Franklin P. Jones

To listen is to know for a moment. To hear is to know forever.

~Dana Cowley

Nature has given us two ears but only one mouth.

~Benjamin Disraeli

The more and more you listen, the more and more you will hear. The more you hear, the more and more deeply you will understand.

~Khyentse Rinpohe

One of the most sincere forms of respect is actually listening to what another has to say.

~Bryant H. McGill

We have two ears and one mouth so that we can listen twice as much as we speak.

~Epictetus

One of the best ways to persuade others is with your ears—by listening to them.

~Dean Rusk

It seems rather incongruous that in a society of super-sophisticated communication, we often suffer from a shortage of listeners.
~Erma Bombeck

There are two types of people who will tell you that you cannot make a difference in this world: those who are afraid to try and those who are afraid you will succeed.
~Ray Goforth

Listeners who pretend interest don't fool us for long — even though they sometimes fool themselves. . . . Real listeners don't charm, flatter, provoke or interrupt. . . . They suspend the self and listen.
~Michael P. Nichols

As soon as you're open and listening and willing to dialogue, people are remarkably receptive and changes speed up rapidly.
~Mort Topfer

Know how to listen, and you will profit even from those who talk badly.
~Plutarch

Living

Life is not lost by dying; life is lost minute by minute, day by dragging day, in all the thousand small uncaring ways.
~Stephen Vincent Benét

Life is made up, not of great sacrifices or duties, but of little things.
~Sir Humphry Davy

Life only demands from you the strength you possess.
~Dag Hammarskjöld

I must accept life unconditionally. Most people ask for happiness on condition. Happiness can only be felt if you don't set any condition.
~Artur Rubinstein

Live as if you were to die tomorrow. Learn as if you were to live forever.
~Mohandas K. Gandhi

Be ashamed to die until you have won some victory for humanity.
~Horace Mann

When I hear somebody sigh that "Life is hard," I am always tempt-ed to ask, "Compared to what?"

~Sydney J. Harris

I think your whole life shows in your face and you should be proud of that.

~Lauren Bacall

The measure of a man's life is the well spending of it, and not the length.

~Plutarch

Life is a great big canvas, and you should throw all the paint you can on it.

~Danny Kaye

I slept and dreamt that life was joy. I awoke and saw that life was service. I acted and behold, service was joy.

~Rabindranath Tagore

Life's most persistent and urgent question is, "What are you doing for others?"

~Martin Luther King Jr.

If you miss love, you miss life.

~Leo Buscaglia

Life lived for tomorrow will always be just a day away from being realized.

~Leo Buscaglia

The little things? The little moments? They aren't little.
~Jon Kabat-Zinn

Maybe you are here on earth to learn that life is what you make it, and it's to be enjoyed.

~Dick Sutphen

Each day is a little life: every waking and rising a little birth, every fresh morning a little youth, every going to rest and sleep a little death.

~Arthur Schopenhauer

Do you qualify to be alive or is the limit of your senses so as only to survive . . . ?

~Ray Stevens

If you want to live on the edge of life, you need to be flexible.

~Kim Novak

The secret of life is to know when enough is enough.

~Vincent Ryan

If you can spend a perfectly useless afternoon in a perfectly useless manner, you have learned how to live.

~Lin Yutang

I don't want to get to the end of my life and find that I just lived the length of it. I want to have lived the width of it as well.

~Diane Ackerman

My grandfather always said that living is like licking honey off a thorn.

~Louise Adamic

Only those are fit to live who do not fear to die; and none are fit to die who have shrunk from the joy of life and the duty of life. Both life and death are parts of the same Great Adventure.

~Theodore Roosevelt

If you are to be, you must begin by assuming responsibility. You alone are responsible for every moment of your life, for every one of your acts.

~Antoine de Saint-Exupéry

How far you go in life depends on your being tender with the young, compassionate with the aged, sympathetic with the striving, and tolerant of the weak and the strong. Because someday in life you will have been all of these.

~George Washington Carver

Don't let the good things of life rob you of the best things.
~Maltbie D. Babcock

One way to get the most out of life is to look upon it as an adventure.
~William Feather

Life can only be understood backwards; but it must be lived forwards.
~Søren Kierkegaard

People find life entirely too time-consuming.
~Stanisław Jerzy Lec

The man who has accomplished all that he thinks worthwhile has begun to die.
~E. T. Trigg

Every moment and every event of every man's life on earth plants something in his soul.
~Thomas Merton

There are only two ways to approach life—as a victim or as a gallant fighter—and you must decide if you want to act or react.
~Merle Shain

The most important thing is to enjoy your life—to be happy—it's all that matters.
~Audrey Hepburn

Life is really simple, but we insist on making it complicated.
~Confucius

Life is a book and you are its author. You determine its plot and pace and you—only you—turn its pages.
~Beth Mende Conny

Within each of us is a hidden store of energy. Energy we can release to compete in the marathon of life.
~Roger Dawson

Incident piled on incident no more makes life than brick piled on brick makes a house.

~Edith Ronald Mirrielees

Life is 10% what happens to you and 90% how you react to it.
~Charles R. Swindoll

Life imitates art far more than art imitates life.
~Oscar Wilde

The more sand that has escaped from the hourglass of our life, the clearer we should see through it.
~Jean-Paul Sartre

It is only by following your deepest instinct that you can lead a rich life, and if you let your fear of consequence prevent you from following your deepest instinct, then your life will be safe, expedient and thin.
~Katharine Butler Hathaway

I have found that if you love life, life will love you back.
~Arthur Rubinstein

Do not take life too seriously. You will never get out of it alive.
~Elbert Hubbard

Searching is half the fun: life is much more manageable when thought of as a scavenger hunt as opposed to a surprise party.
~Jimmy Buffet

Life is not a problem to be solved, but a reality to be experienced.
~Søren Kierkegaard

Life is a long lesson in humility.
~James M. Barrie

Life is a paradise for those who love many things with a passion.
~Leo Buscaglia

You are responsible for your life. You can't keep blaming somebody else for your dysfunction. Life is really about moving on.
~Oprah Winfrey

Is not this the true romantic feeling; not to desire to escape life, but to prevent life from escaping you.
~Thomas Wolfe

I look upon every day to be lost, in which I do not make a new acquaintance.

~Samuel Johnson

Life isn't fair, it's just fairer than death, that's all.

~William Goldman

The greatest of all miracles is to be alive.

~Thich Nhat Hanh

You will never be happy if you continue to search for what happiness consists of. You will never live if you are looking for the meaning of life.

~Albert Camus

Life would be tragic if it weren't funny.

~Stephen Hawking

Believe that life is worth living, and your belief will help create the fact.

~William James

For the ordinary business of life an ounce of habit is worth a pound of intellect.

~Thomas B. Reed

In this life we get only those things for which we hunt, for which we strive, and for which we are willing to sacrifice.

~George Matthew Adams

The purpose of life is to live it, to taste experience to the utmost, to reach out eagerly and without fear for newer and richer experience.

~Eleanor Roosevelt

Man is born a predestined idealist, for he is born to act. To act is to affirm the worth of an end, and to persist in affirming the worth of an end is to make an ideal.

~Oliver Wendell Holmes Sr.

I have come to realize that all my trouble with living has come from fear and smallness within me.

~Angela L. Wozniak

Man is born to live, not to prepare for life.

~Boris Pasternak

Could we change our attitude, we should not only see life differently, but life itself would come to be different. Life would undergo a change of appearance because we ourselves had undergone a change of attitude.

~Katherine Mansfield

Beyond happiness or unhappiness, though it is both things, love is intensity; it does not give us eternity but life, that second in which the doors of time and space open just a crack: here is there and now is always.

~Octavio Paz

Accept the pain, cherish the joys, resolve the regrets; then can come the best of benedictions — "If I had my life to live over, I'd do it all the same."

~Joan McIntosh

Today, this hour, this minute is the day, the hour, the minute for each of us to sense the fact that life is good, with all of its trials and troubles, and perhaps more interesting because of them.

~Robert R. Updegraff

Life is not easy for any of us. But what of that? We must have perseverance and, above all, confidence in ourselves. We must believe that we are gifted for something, and that this thing must be attained.

~Marie Curie

Live as you will have wished to have lived when you are dying.

~Christian F. Gellert

Life isn't a matter of milestones, but of moments.

~Rose Kennedy

The first half of life consists of the capacity to enjoy without the chance; the last half consists of the chance without the capacity.

~Mark Twain

Life is what happens to you while you're busy making other plans.

~John Lennon

The best years of your life are the ones in which you decide your problems are your own. You don't blame them on your mother, the ecology, or the president. You realize that you control your own destiny.

~Albert Ellis

If you observe a really happy man, you will find . . . that he is happy in the course of living life twenty-four crowded hours each day.

~W. Beran Wolfe

I like living. I have sometimes been wildly, despairingly, acutely miserable, racked with sorrow, but through it all I still know quite certainly that just to be alive is a grand thing.

~Agatha Christie

I began to have an idea of my life, not as the slow shaping of achievement to fit my preconceived purposes, but as the gradual discovery and growth of a purpose which I did not know.

~Marion Milner

Love is a good thing.

~Sheryl Crow

Life is what happens to you while you're busy making other plans.

~John Lennon

Life is a song—sing it. Life is a game—play it. Life is a challenge—meet it. Life is a dream—realize it. Life is a sacrifice—offer it. Life is love—enjoy it.

~Sai Baba

In the end, it's not the years in your life that count. It's the life in your years.

~Abraham Lincoln

Your life does not get better by chance, it gets better by change.

~Jim Rohn

No life is so hard that you can't make it easier by the way you take it.

~Ellen Glasgow

Life shrinks or expands in proportion to one's courage.
~Anaïs Nin

Life stands before me like an eternal spring with new and brilliant clothes.
~Carl Friedrich Gauss

Life is not long, and too much of it must not pass in idle deliberation how it shall be spent.
~Samuel Johnson

Life is not a problem to be solved, but a reality to be experienced.
~Søren Kierkegaard

Life is about not knowing, having to change, taking the moment and making the best of it, without knowing what's going to happen next. Delicious ambiguity.
~Gilda Radner

My chief study all my life has been to lighten misfortunes and multiply pleasures, as far as human nature can.
~Mary Wortley Montagu

Dedicate some of your life to others. Your dedication will not be a sacrifice. It will be an exhilarating experience because it is intense effort applied toward a meaningful end.
~Thomas Dooley

To live without hope is to cease to live.
~Fyodor Dostoyevsky

It is the appreciation of beauty and truth, the striving for knowledge which makes life worth living.
~Morris Ralphael Cohen

Life is like a landscape. You live in the midst of it but can describe it only from the vantage point of distance.
~Charles Lindbergh

Life was meant to be lived, and curiosity must be kept alive. One must never, for whatever reason, turn his back on life.
~Eleanor Roosevelt

Life is either a great adventure or nothing.

~Helen Keller

Don't ever confuse the two, your life and your work . . . The second is only part of the first.

~Anna Quindlen

Let how you live your life stand for something, no matter how small and incidental it may seem.

~Jodie Foster

Everything has been figured out except how to live.

~Jean-Paul Sartre

When the days are too short, chances are you are living at your best.

~Earl Nightingale

There is no life that does not contribute to history.

~Dorothy West

Life is for most of us a continuous process of getting used to things we hadn't expected.

~Martha Lupton

The quality of a person's life is in direct proportion to their commitment to excellence, regardless of their chosen field of endeavor.

~Vince Lombardi

It is so easy to waste our lives: our days, our hours, our minutes . . . It is so easy to exist instead of live.

~Anna Quindlen

Learn to be happy. And think of life as a terminal illness because if you do you will live it with joy and passion, as it ought to be lived.

~Anna Quindlen

Life is nothing but a series of moments. Start living the moments and the years will take care of themselves.

~Gary W. Fenchuk

I slept and dreamt that life was joy. I awoke and saw that life was service. I acted and behold, service was joy.

~Rabindranath Tagore

Enjoy life—there are no re-runs.

~Shirl Lowery

Live in each season as it passes; breathe the air, drink the drink, taste the fruit, and resign yourself to the influences of each.

~Henry David Thoreau

Life is not complex. We are complex. Life is simple, and the simple thing is the right thing.

~Oscar Wilde

Life is a great and wondrous mystery, and the only thing we know that we have for sure is what is right here right now. Don't miss it.

~Leo Buscaglia

Live your life as though there is great joy to be experienced . . . an abundance of goodness in each person you come in contact with, and the knowledge that you have enough inner wisdom to answer the mysteries that challenge you.

~Meladee McCarty

Your living is determined not so much by what life brings to you as by the attitude you bring to life; not so much by what happens to you as by the way your mind looks at what happens.

~Kahlil Gibran

Life is like a ten-speed bike. Most of us have gears we never use.

~Charles Schulz

The art of living is more like wrestling than dancing.

~Marcus Aurelius

Is life worth living? Aye, with the best of us, heights of us, depths of us—life is the test of us!

~Corinne Roosevelt Robinson

All of us tend to put off living. We are all dreaming of some magical rose garden over the horizon—instead of enjoying the roses that are blooming outside our windows today.

~Dale Carnegie

There is no cure for birth and death save to enjoy the interval.

~George Santayana

There is more to life than simply increasing its speed.
~Mohandas Gandhi

Live life to the fullest, and focus on the positive.
~Matt Cameron

Life is a moderately good play with a badly written third act.
~Truman Capote

Life is a tragedy when seen in close-up, but a comedy in long-shot.
~Charlie Chaplin

Life is 10 percent what you make it, and 90 percent how you take it.
~Irving Berlin

When you arise in the morning, think of what a precious privilege it is to be alive—to breathe, to think, to enjoy, to love.
~Marcus Aurelius

Live as if you were to die tomorrow. Learn as if you were to live forever.
~Mohandas K. Gandhi

Get a life in which you are not alone. Find people you love, and who love you. And remember that love is not leisure, it is work.
~Anna Quindlen

I live what most people call the good life. I was happy, but deep inside I always felt that, with the short amount of time we are given to live and love in this world, we spend too much time loving things instead of people.
~Mother Antonia

It had been my repeated experience that when you say to life calmly and firmly . . . "I trust you; do what you must," life had an uncanny way of responding to your need.
~Olga Ilyin

Men, for the sake of getting a living, forget to live.
~Margaret Fuller

Life for every person should be a journey in jubilance.
~Charles Fillmore

*You [are] the only person alive who has sole custody of your life . .
. . Your entire life . . . . Not just the life of your mind, but the life of
your heart. Not just your bank account, but your soul.*
~Anna Quindlen

*This is the only chance you will ever have on earth with this excit-
ing adventure called life. So why not plan it, and try to live it as
richly, as happily as possible?*
~Dale Carnegie

*Get a life. A real life, not a manic pursuit of the next promotion,
the bigger paycheck, the larger house.*
~Anna Quindlen

Any man who does not accept the conditions of life sells his soul.
~Charles Baudelaire

*When you write down your life, every page should contain some-
thing no one has ever heard about.*
~Elias Canetti

*There is only one success . . . to be able to spend your life in your
own way, and not to give others absurd maddening claims upon it.*
~Christopher Morley

*Life is like a library owned by an author. In it are a few books
which he wrote himself, but most of them were written for him.*
~Harry Emerson Fosdick

*Someone has said that all living is just learning the meaning of
words. That does not mean the long ten syllable words we have
to look up in the dictionary. The really great words to master are
short ones—work, love, hope, joy, pain, home, child, life, death.*
~Halford E. Luccock

*I think that, as life is action and passion, it is required of a man
that he should share the passion and action of his time at peril of
being judged not to have lived.*
~Oliver Wendell Holmes

Life is a mission. Every other definition of life is false, and leads all who accept it astray. Religion, science, philosophy, though still at variance upon many points, all agree in this, that every existence is an aim.

~Giuseppe Mazzini

And this our life, exempt from public haunt, finds tongues in trees, books in the running brooks, sermons in stones, and good in everything.

~William Shakespeare

The proper function of man is to live, not to exist. I shall not waste my days in trying to prolong them. I shall use my time.

~Jack London

Do right. Do your best. Treat others as you want to be treated.

~Lou Holtz

Let us live while we live.

~Philip Doddridge

To be is to do.

~Kurt Vonnegut

You've gotta dance like there's nobody watching, love like you'll never be hurt, sing like there's nobody listening, and live like it's heaven on earth.

~William W. Purkey

Life's like a movie, write your own ending. Keep believing, keep pretending.

~Jim Henson

There are only two tragedies in life: not getting what you want—and the getting it.

~Oscar Wilde

I would rather have 30 minutes of "wonderful" than a lifetime of nothing special.

~Julia Roberts

Life is too short to short yourself on life.

~Terri Zadra

A change in bad habits leads to a change in life.
~Jenny Craig

Alertness and courage are life's shield.
~Filipino Proverb

You only live once—but if you do it right, once is enough.
~Mae West

"Is life worth living?" The question does not make any sense.
~Erich Fromm

I wouldn't miss life for anything!
~Anne Wilson Schaef

People talk about "finding" their lives. In reality, your life is not something you find—it's something you create.
~David Phillips

It's your life, your one and only life—so take excellence very personally.
~Scott Johnson

Once you say you're going to settle for second, that's what happens to you in life, I find.
~John F. Kennedy

Make each day your masterpiece.
~John Wooden

Life is in the here and now. Either we meet it, we live it—or we miss it.
~Vimala Thakar

Seek and you will find. Don't be willing to accept an ordinary life.
~Salle Merrill Redfield

That it will never come again is what makes life so sweet.
~Emily Dickinson

Life is ours to be spent, not to be saved.
~D. H. Lawrence

We are here, and it is now. What else is there?

~Kobi Yamada

Life is like an onion. You peel it off one layer at a time, and some-times you weep.

~Carl Sandburg

If you don't think every day is a good day, just try missing one.

~Cavett Robert

I want to convince you that you must learn to make every act count, since you are going to be here for only a short while.

~Don Juan

The aim of life is to live, and to live means to be aware, joyously, drunkenly, serenely, divinely aware.

~Henry Miller

Say yes to life, even though you know it may devour you.

~Stephen Larsen

I would like to learn, or remember, how to live.

~Annie Dillard

Life is a succession of moments. To live each one is to succeed.

~Corita Kent

Because of the routines we follow, we often forget that life is an ongoing adventure.

~Maya Angelou

Day after day, we discover our own lives. Because we never know what we will find, every discovery is an unexpected gift we give to ourselves.

~Barbara J. Esbensen

For the happiest life, days should be rigorously planned, nights left open to chance.

~Mignon McLaughlin

From father to son, so it goes on.

~Ashanti Proverb

I want to be able to say in the last four seconds of my life that I tried to do my best.

~Rubén Blades

Your time is limited, so don't waste it living someone else's life.

~Steve Jobs

Tomorrow's life is too late. Live today.

~Marcus Valerius Martialis

The tragedy of life is not so much what we suffer, but what we miss.

~Thomas Carlyle

Life is short and you've got to get the most out of it.

~Gwen Stefani

This life is worth living, we can say, since it is what we make it.

~William James

This is the urgency: Live! and have your blooming in the noise of the whirlwind.

~Gwendolyn Brooks

We cannot put off living until we are ready. The most salient characteristic of life is its coerciveness . . . "here and now" without any possible postponement. Life is fired at us point blank.

~José Ortega y Gasset

Whatever you want in life, other people are going to want it too. Believe in yourself enough to accept the idea that you have an equal right to it.

~Diane Sawyer

Life is pure adventure and the sooner we realize that, the quicker we will be able to treat life as art. . . . We need to remember that we are created creative and can invent new scenarios as frequently as they are needed.

~Maya Angelou

Life's under no obligation to give us what we expect. We take what we get and are thankful it's no worse than it is.

~Margaret Mitchell

Any idiot can face a crisis — it's day to day living that wears you out.

~Anton Chekhov

What would life be if we had no courage to attempt anything?
~Vincent van Gogh

Happiness comes more from loving than being loved; and often when our affection seems wounded it is only our vanity bleeding. To love, and to be hurt often, and to love again — this is the brave and happy life.

~J. E. Buckrose

Just when I discovered the meaning of life, they changed it.
~George Carlin

The ordinary acts we practice every day at home are of more importance to the soul than their simplicity might suggest.
~Thomas Moore

Life is constantly providing us with new funds, new resources, even when we are reduced to immobility. In life's ledger there is no such thing as frozen assets.

~Henry Miller

My message to the world is "Let's swing, sing, shout, make noise! Let's not mimic death before our time comes!"
~Mel Brooks

There are no little events in life, those we think of no consequence may be full of fate, and it is at our own risk if we neglect the acquaintances and opportunities that seem to be casually offered, and of small importance.

~Amelia E. Barr

One can survive everything, nowadays, except death, and live down anything except a good reputation.
~Oscar Wilde

What I love about noise is that it camouflages life.
~Germaine de Staël

In small proportions we just beauties see; And in short measures, life may perfect be.

~Ben Jonson

Live all you can; it's a mistake not to.

~Henry James

Life is absolutely super and wonderful.

~Edward Albee

In the time of your life, live!

~William Saroyan

There is a strange reluctance on the part of most people to admit that they enjoy life.

~William Lyon Phelps

Is not amusement the very soul of life?

~Frances Milton Trollope

Life itself is the proper binge.

~Julia Child

There are only two ways to live your life. One is as though nothing is a miracle. The other is as though everything is a miracle.

~Albert Einstein

Life takes on meaning when you become motivated, set goals and charge after them in an unstoppable manner.

~Les Brown

Live out of your imagination, not your history.

~Stephen Covey

Life engenders life. Energy creates energy. It is by spending oneself that one becomes rich.

~Sarah Bernhardt

Logic

Reason itself is fallible, and this fallibility must find a place in our logic.

~Nicola Abbagnano

Losing

If we win, nobody will care. If we lose, there will be nobody to care.
~Winston Churchill

Winning is a habit. Unfortunately so is losing.
~Vince Lombardi

Love

The greatest thing you'll ever learn is just to love and be loved in return.
~Eden Ahbez

Two persons love in one another the future good which they aid one another to unfold.
~Margaret Fuller

In a full heart there is room for everything, and in an empty heart there is room for nothing.
~Antonio Porchia

If you miss love, you miss life.
~Leo Buscaglia

The more you love, the more you'll find that life is good and friends are kind. For only what we give away enriches us from day to day.
~Helen Steiner Rice

We love the things we love for what they are.
~Robert Frost

It's times like these when my faith I feel And I know how I love you.
~Dave Matthews

Love is letting-be.
~John Macquarrie

I'll love you forever, I'll like you for always, As long as I'm living my baby you'll be.
~Robert Munsch

Perhaps the feelings that we experience when we are in love represent a normal state. Being in love shows a person who he should be.

~Anton Chekhov

So, be swift to love and make haste to be kind.

~Henri-Frédéric Amiel

Keep love in your heart. A life without it is like a sunless garden when the flowers are dead.

~Oscar Wilde

Fear is actually related to love, as are all passions. Fear is the emotion that rises in us when there is a danger facing something or someone we love. . . . The catalogue of fears is the catalogue of loves. Love is an attraction for an object; fear is flight from it.

~Fulton J. Sheen

Love is when you meet someone who tells you something new about yourself.

~Andre Breton

If I truly love one person I love all persons, I love the world, I love life.

~Erich Fromm

Darkness cannot drive out darkness; only light can do that. Hate cannot drive out hate; only love can do that.

~Martin Luther King Jr.

Love is a binding force, by which another is joined to me and cherished as myself.

~Thomas Aquinas

Love is composed of a single soul inhabiting two bodies.

~Aristotle

Work like you don't need the money. Dance like no one is watching. And love like you've never been hurt.

~Mark Twain

Love doesn't make the world go 'round. Love is what makes the ride worthwhile.

~Franklin P. Jones

Spread love everywhere you go. Let no one ever come to you without leaving happier.

~Mother Teresa

All problems boil down to limited choices, and the choice we often forget is love.

~Tom Daly

A life without love is of no account. Love is the water of life. Drink it down with heart and soul.

~Rumi

Being deeply loved by someone gives you strength, while loving someone deeply gives you courage.

~Lao Tzu

Being heard is so close to being loved that for the average person, they are almost indistinguishable.

~David W. Augsburger

Do not think that love in order to be genuine has to be extraordinary. What we need is to love without getting tired. Be faithful in small things because it is in them that your strength lies.

~Mother Teresa

Don't forget to love yourself.

~Søren Kierkegaard

Every heart sings a song, incomplete, until another heart whispers back. Those who wish to sing always find a song. At the touch of a lover, everyone becomes a poet.

~Plato

Every time you smile at someone, it is an action of love, a gift to that person, a beautiful thing.

~Mother Teresa

Everyone discusses my art and pretends to understand, as if it were necessary to understand, when it is simply necessary to love.

~Claude Monet

I have found the paradox, that if you love until it hurts, there can be no more hurt, only more love.

~Mother Teresa

I'm selfish, impatient and a little insecure. I make mistakes, I am out of control and at times hard to handle. But if you can't handle me at my worst, then you sure as hell don't deserve me at my best.
~Marilyn Monroe

It is better to be hated for what you are than to be loved for what you are not.

~André Gide

It's not how much we give but how much love we put into giving.
~Mother Teresa

Love all, trust a few, do wrong to none.

~William Shakespeare

Love is patient, love is kind. It does not envy, it does not boast, it is not proud. It is not rude, it is not self-seeking, it is not easily angered, it keeps no record of wrongs. Love does not delight in evil but rejoices with the truth. It always protects, always trusts, always hopes, always perseveres.
~1 Corinthians 13:1 New International Version

Love is an act of endless forgiveness, a tender look which becomes a habit.

~Peter Ustinov

Love never dies a natural death. It dies because we don't know how to replenish its source. It dies of blindness and errors and betrayals. It dies of illness and wounds; it dies of weariness, of withering, of tarnishing.

~Anaïs Nin

Love yourself first and everything else falls into line. You really have to love yourself to get anything done in this world.
~Lucille Ball

Love yourself instead of abusing yourself.
~Karolina Kurkova

Never love anyone who treats you like you're ordinary.
~Oscar Wilde

Nobody has ever measured, not even poets, how much the heart can hold.
~Zelda Fitzgerald

One is loved because one is loved. No reason is needed for loving.
~Paulo Coelho

Plant your own garden and decorate your own soul, instead of waiting for someone to bring you flowers.
~Veronica A. Shoffstall

The first duty of love is to listen.
~Paul Tillich

The giving of love is an education in itself.
~Eleanor Roosevelt

There are two basic motivating forces: fear and love. When we are afraid, we pull back from life. When we are in love, we open to all that life has to offer with passion, excitement, and acceptance. We need to learn to love ourselves first, in all our glory and our imperfections. If we cannot love ourselves, we cannot fully open to our ability to love others or our potential to create. Evolution and all hopes for a better world rest in the fearlessness and open-hearted vision of people who embrace life.
~John Lennon

There is nothing I would not do for those who are really my friends. I have no notion of loving people by halves, it is not my nature.
~Jane Austen

This is a good sign, having a broken heart. It means we have tried for something.
~Elizabeth Gilbert

Time is too slow for those who wait, too swift for those who fear, too long for those who grieve, too short for those who rejoice, but for those who love, time is eternity.
~Henry Van Dyke

'Tis better to have loved and lost than never to have loved at all.
~Alfred, Lord Tennyson

To love yourself right now, just as you are, is to give yourself heaven. Don't wait until you die. If you wait, you die now. If you love, you live now.

~Alan Cohen

To tell the truth is to become beautiful, to begin to love yourself, value yourself. And that's political, in its most profound way.

~June Jordan

We're all a little weird. And life is a little weird. And when we find someone whose weirdness is compatible with ours, we join up with them and fall into mutually satisfying weirdness—and call it love—true love.

~Robert Fulghum

What can you do to promote world peace? Go home and love your family.

~Mother Teresa

What is this precious love and laughter budding in our hearts? It is the glorious sound of a soul waking up!"

~Hafiz

When you do not require a person to show up as you imagine you need them to be, then you can drop expectation. Then you love them exactly as they are. Yet this can only happen when you love your self exactly as you are.

~N. D. Walsch

Where there is love there is life.

~Mohandas Gandhi

You know you're in love when you can't fall asleep because reality is finally better than your dreams.

~Theodor Seuss Geisel (Dr. Seuss)

You, yourself, as much as anybody in the entire universe, deserve your love and affection.

~Buddha

Your task is not to seek for love, but merely to seek and find all the barriers within yourself that you have built against it.

~Rumi

Behold thyself in glory. Love thyself as I love you. In this way you honour me. It is my duty to love myself deeply, totally, unconditionally. To see myself as something of great worth. To do less is to deny the task for which I was born. What of my faults and inadequacies? I resolve to love them as part of who I am. I am beautiful because of them. They are part of my uniqueness, like markings on a wild animal. They give me flavour. Make me real. I allow myself and others to make mistakes, miss opportunities and make foolish decisions. I recognise and accept my vulnerability and fragility. My quirks and idiosyncrasies—all part of who I am. I am beautiful and special because of my humanness—in fact, this is where my true beauty lies. As the day accepts the sun and the night accepts the moon, so I accept myself. And so I become complete and whole.

~John Kehoe

The heart is the thousand-stringed instrument that can only be tuned with love.

~Hafiz

What greater thing is there for two human souls than to feel that they are joined for life—to strengthen each other . . . to be one with each other in silent unspeakable memories.

~George Eliot

Man must evolve for all human conflict a method which rejects revenge, aggression and retaliation. The foundation of such a method is love.

~Martin Luther King Jr.

Person to person, moment to moment, as we love, we change the world.

~Samahria Lyte Kaufman

Beyond happiness or unhappiness, though it is both things, love is intensity; it does not give us eternity but life, that second in which the doors of time and space open just a crack: here is there and now is always.

~Octavio Paz

Love is, above all, the gift of oneself.

~Jean Anouilh

Love is the ability and willingness to allow those that you care for to be what they choose for themselves without any insistence that they satisfy you.

~Wayne Dyer

Love is being stupid together.

~Paul Valéry

There is no difficulty that enough love will not conquer: no disease that enough love will not heal: no door that enough love will not open.

~Emmet Fox

We may not have it all together, but together we have it all.

~Ruth Rogers

A loving person lives in a loving world. A hostile person lives in a hostile world: everyone you meet is your mirror.

~Ken Keyes Jr.

What love we've given, we'll have forever. What love we fail to give, will be lost for all eternity.

~Leo Buscaglia

We accept the love we think we deserve.

~Stephen Chbosky

Because of a great love, one is courageous.

~Lao Tzu

Love the giver more than the gift.

~Brigham Young

It's such an amazing thing to be loved for who you are.

~Debra Winger

Let us always meet each other with smile, for the smile is the beginning of love.

~Mother Teresa

For small creatures such as we the vastness is bearable only through love.

~Carl Sagan

If music be the food of love, play on.

~William Shakespeare

All your life, you will be faced with a choice. You can choose love or hate . . . I choose love.

~Johnny Cash

No matter how dark the moment, love and hope are always possible.

~George Chakiris

A loving heart is the truest wisdom.

~Charles Dickens

Whoso loves believes the impossible.

~Elizabeth Barrett Browning

Love for the joy of loving, and not for the offerings of someone else's heart.

~Marlene Dietrich

You can give without loving, but you cannot love without giving.

~Amy Carmichael

There is more pleasure in loving than in being beloved.

~Thomas Fuller

Love is a good thing.

~Sheryl Crow

True love cannot be found where it does not exist, nor can it be denied where it does.

~Torquato Tasso

Whoever loves much, does much.

~Thomas à Kempis

Get a life in which you are not alone. Find people you love, and who love you. And remember that love is not leisure, it is work.

~Anna Quindlen

In love, one and one are one.

~Jean-Paul Sartre

I live what most people call the good life. I was happy, but deep inside I always felt that, with the short amount of time we are given to live and love in this world, we spend too much time loving things instead of people.

~Mother Antonia

Human love serves to love those dear to us but to love one's enemies we need divine love.

~Leo Tolstoy

One moment of loving is good for the soul, it's something I know — not what I've been told.

~Mildred H. Bell

Familiar acts are beautiful through love.

~Percy Bysshe Shelly

Love is ever the beginning of knowledge, as fire is of light.

~Thomas Carlyle

Never forget that the most powerful force on earth is love.

~Nelson Rockefeller

"To hate" is to be pained by the hated one's happiness, just as "to love" is to delight in the beloved's happiness.

~Gottfried Wilhelm Leibniz

Love must be learned and learned again; there is no end to it.

~Katherine Anne Porter

It is said that love is blind. Friendship, on the other hand, is clairvoyant.

~Philippe Soupault

Romance is tempestuous. Love is calm.

~Mason Cooley

True love is like ghosts, which everyone talks about and few have seen.

~François de La Rochefoucauld

Where we love is home, home that our feet may leave, but not our hearts.

~Oliver Wendell Holmes

Choose thy love. Love thy choice.

~German Proverb

Loving is half of believing.

~Victor Hugo

The greatest gift you can give to others is the gift of unconditional love and acceptance.

~Brian Tracy

There is a land of the living and a land of the dead and the bridge is love, the only survival, the only meaning.

~Thornton Wilder

Man, while he loves, is never quite depraved.

~Charles Lamb

We need so little to feel loved; all we need to do is begin to notice the multitude of tiny gifts and small miracles that punctuate each day we are alive.

~Wayne Muller

Say little, and love much; give all; judge no man; aspire to all that is pure and good.

~White Eagle

Love that lasts involves a real and genuine concern for others as persons, for their values as they feel them, for their development and growth.

~Ana Liu

Like threads of silver seen through crystal beads Let love through good deeds show.

~Edwin Arnold

To love deeply is one direction makes us more loving in all others.
~Anne-Sophie Swetchine

If you have only one smile in you, give it to the people you love. Don't be surly at home, then go out in the street and start grinning good morning at total stranger.

~Maya Angelou

Love doesn't just sit there, like a stone, it has to be made, like bread; remade all the time, made new.
~Ursula K. Le Guin

Life began with waking up and loving my mother's face.
~George Eliot

If instead of a gem, or even a flower, we should cast the gift of a loving thought into the heart of a friend, that would be giving as the angels give.
~George MacDonald

Where love is concerned, too much is not even enough.
~Pierre Beaumarchais

Luck

Care and diligence bring luck.
~Thomas Fuller

Luck is what you have left over after you give 100 percent.
~Langston Coleman

The amount of good luck coming your way depends on your willingness to act.
~Barbara Sher

I am a great believer in luck, and I find the harder I work the more I have of it.
~Stephen Leacock

What helps luck is a habit of watching for opportunities, of having a patient but restless mind, of sacrificing one's ease or vanity, or uniting a love of detail to foresight, and of passing through hard times bravely and cheerfully.
~Victor Cherbuliez

Luck is the dividend of sweat. The more you sweat, the luckier you get.
~Ray Kroc

There is no one luckier than he who thinks himself so.
~German Proverb

I believe luck is preparation meeting opportunity.
~Oprah Winfrey

You've got to think lucky. If you fall into a mudhole, check your back pocket—you might have caught a fish.
~Darrell Royal

Majority

Whenever you find yourself on the side of the majority, it is time to pause and reflect.
~Mark Twain

Management

Management is doing things right; leadership is doing the right things.
~Peter Drucker

Management is efficiency in climbing the ladder of success; leadership determines whether the ladder is leaning against the right wall.
~Stephen Covey

By working faithfully eight hours a day, you may eventually get to be boss and work twelve hours a day.
~Robert Frost

The importance of laughter and humor in the workplace can't be emphasized enough.
~Mike Vance and Diane Deacon

One cannot manage too many affairs: like pumpkins in the water, one pops up while you try to hold down the other.
~Chinese Proverb

Competitive strategy is about being different. It means deliberately choosing a different set of activities to deliver a unique mix of value.
~Michael Porter

Manners

Good manners will open doors that the best education cannot.
~Clarence Thomas

The hardest job kids face today is learning good manners without seeing any.
~Fred Astaire

There is always a best way of doing everything, if it be to boil an egg. Manners are the happy ways of doing things.
~Ralph Waldo Emerson

Marriage

A good marriage is that in which each appoints the other guardian of his solitude.
~Rainer Maria Rilke

What greater thing is there for two human souls than to feel that they are joined for life—to strengthen each other . . . to be one with each other in silent unspeakable memories.
~George Eliot

There is no more lovely, friendly and charming relationship, communion, or company than a good marriage.
~Martin Luther

Women and men have to fight together to change society—and both will benefit . . . Partnership, not dependence, is the real romance in marriage.
~Muriel Fox

One advantage of marriage, it seems to me, is that when you fall out of love with him, or he falls out of love with you, it keeps you together until you maybe fall in love again.
~Judith Viorst

Though he had Eden to live in, Man cannot be happy alone.
~Josephine Pollard

Two persons love in one another the future good which they aid one another to unfold.

~Margaret Fuller

Married couples who love each other tell each other a thousand things without talking.

~Chinese Proverb

A successful marriage requires falling in love many times, always with the same person.

~Mignon McLaughlin

Memories

There is not any memory with less satisfaction than the memory of some temptation we resisted.

~James Branch Cabell

We do not remember days, we remember moments.

~Cesare Pavese

When I was younger, I could remember anything, whether it had happened or not.

~Mark Twain

God gave us memory so that we might have roses in December.

~James M. Barrie

In 20 years, you'll look back at photos of yourself and recall in a way you can't grasp now how much possibility lay before you and how fabulous you really looked.

~Mary Schmich

May memory restore again and again the smallest color of the smallest day.

~Delmore Schwartz

How we remember, what we remember, and why we remember form the most personal map of our individuality.

~Christina Baldwin

Sometimes you will never know the value of a moment until it becomes a memory.

~Theodor Seuss Geisel (Dr. Seuss)

Praising what is lost makes the remembrance dear.
~William Shakespeare

A retentive memory may be a good thing, but the ability to forget is the true token of greatness.
~Elbert Hubbard

Memory is a man's real possession . . . In nothing else is he rich . . . in nothing else is he poor.
~Alexander Smith

Men

Man has his will—but woman has her way.
~Oliver Wendell Holmes

There is very little difference between men and women in space.
~Helen Sharman

Charm is a woman's strength just as strength is a man's charm.
~Havelock Ellis

Mercy

I have always found that mercy bears richer fruits than strict justice.
~Abraham Lincoln

Gratitude is born in hearts that take time to count up past mercies.
~Charles E. Jefferson

Sweet mercy is nobility's true badge.
~William Shakespeare

Mercy among the virtues is like the moon among the stars—not so sparkling and vivid as many, but dispensing a calm radiance that hallows the whole.
~Edwin Hubbell Chapin

Mind

The trouble with having an open mind, of course, is that people will insist on coming along and trying to put things in it.
~Terry Pratchett

Rule your mind or it will rule you.
~Horace

Where the habits are simple, and the mind truly elevated, then is society in the best state.
~Mary Martha Sherwood

Teach my unskilled mind to sing the feelings of my heart.
~Anna Young Smith

When you rule your mind you rule your world. When you choose your thoughts you choose results.
~Imelda Shanklin

Beauty is no quality in things themselves: it exists merely in the mind which contemplates them.
~David Hume

A discovery is said to be an accident meeting a prepared mind.
~Albert Szent-Györgyi

What impresses men is not mind, but the result of mind.
~Walter Bagehot

Fortune favors the prepared mind.
~Louis Pasteur

Genius is the ability to put into effect what is on your mind.
~F. Scott Fitzgerald

To the dull mind all of nature is leaden. To the illumined mind the whole world burns and sparkles with light.
~Ralph Waldo Emerson

Minds are like parachutes. They only function when open.
~Thomas Dewar

To create you must quiet your mind. You need a quiet mind so that ideas will have a chance of connecting.

~Eric Maisel

The mind is not a storehouse to be filled but an instrument to be used.

~John Gardner

Little minds attain and are subdued by misfortunes; but great minds rise above them.

~Washington Irving

Peace of mind is that mental condition in which you have accepted the worst.

~Lin Yutang

You cannot have a positive life and a negative mind.

~Joyce Meyer

It is the mind that makes the body.

~Sojourner Truth

The mind is not a vessel to be filled but a fire to be kindled.

~Plutarch

The mind ought sometimes to be diverted that it may return to better thinking.

~Phaedrus

In the province of the mind, what one believes to be true either is true or becomes true.

~John Lilly

To create you must quiet your mind. You need a quiet mind so that ideas will have a chance of connecting.

~Eric Maisel

The mind doth shape itself to its own wants and can bear all things.
~Joanna Baillie

The true, strong, and sound mind is the mind that can embrace equally great things and small.

~Samuel Johnson

Every human mind is a great slumbering power until awakened by a keen desire and a definite resolution to do.

~Edgar F. Roberts

Keep learning about the world. Use your mind to the hilt. Life passes quickly and, towards the end, gathers speed like a freight train running downhill. The more you know, the more you enrich yourself and others.

~Susan Trott

Anyone who stops learning is old, whether at twenty or eighty. Anyone who keeps learning stays young. The greatest thing in life is to keep your mind young.

~Henry Ford

Our minds are like certain vehicles—when they have little to carry they make much noise about it, but when heavily loaded they run quietly.

~Elihu Burritt

Miracles

The most incredible thing about miracles is that they happen.

~G. K. Chesterton

Every day is a miracle.

~James Gould Cozzens

Every day holds the possibility of a miracle.

~Elizabeth David

We couldn't conceive of a miracle if none had ever happened.

~Libbie Fudim

Unselfish acts are the real miracles out of which all the reported miracles grow.

~Ralph Waldo Emerson

Out of difficulties, grow miracles.

~Jean de La Bruyère

The greatest of all miracles is to be alive.

~Thich Nhat Hanh

There are only two ways to live your life. One is as though nothing is a miracle. The other is as though everything is a miracle.
~Albert Einstein

Expectancy is the atmosphere for miracles.
~Edwin Louis Cole

Miserable

Be miserable. Or motivate yourself. Whatever has to be done, it's always your choice.
~Wayne Dyer

Sir, there is nothing too little for so little creature as man. It is by studying little things that we attain the great art of having as little misery and as much happiness as possible.
~Samuel Johnson

If you're not making mistakes, then you're not doing anything. I'm positive that a doer makes mistakes.
~John Wooden

The trick is in what one emphasizes. We either make ourselves miserable, or we make ourselves happy. The amount of work is the same.
~Carlos Castaneda

The only way to avoid being miserable is not to have enough leisure to wonder whether you are happy or not.
~George Bernard Shaw

It's the most unhappy people who most fear change.
~Mignon McLaughlin

Misfortunes

Little minds attain and are subdued by misfortunes; but great minds rise above them.
~Washington Irving

There is certainly no defense against adverse fortune which is, on the whole, so effectual as an habitual sense of humor.
~Thomas W. Higginson

Mistakes

The greatest mistake you can make in life is to be continually fearing you will make one.
~Elbert Hubbard

Success does not consist in never making mistakes but in never making the same one a second time.
~George Bernard Shaw

Take chances, make mistakes. That's how you grow. Pain nourishes your courage. You have to fail in order to practice being brave.
~Mary Tyler Moore

Trust your own instinct. Your mistakes might as well be your own, instead of someone else's.
~Billy Wilder

Mistakes are part of the dues one pays for a full life.
~Sophia Loren

A life spent making mistakes is not only more honorable but more useful than a life spent doing nothing.
~George Bernard Shaw

Nobody made a greater mistake than he who did nothing because he could do only a little.
~Edmund Burke

A person who has never made a mistake never tried anything new.
~Albert Einstein

Half of our mistakes in life arise from feeling where we ought to think, and thinking where we ought to feel.
~John Churton Collins

A man of genius makes no mistakes. His errors are volitional and are the portals of discovery.
~James Joyce

When you make a mistake, don't look back at it long. Take the reason of the thing into your mind and then look forward. Mistakes are lessons of wisdom. The past cannot be changed. The future is yet in your power.

~Hugh White

Modesty

Be modest, be respectful of others, try to understand.

~Lakhdar Brahimi

The great charm of all power is modesty.

~Louisa May Alcott

The superior man is modest in his speech, but exceeds in his actions.

~Confucius

Moments

Life isn't a matter of milestones, but of moments.

~Rose Kennedy

We do not remember days, we remember moments.

~Cesare Pavese

If we take care of the moments, the years will take care of themselves.

~Maria Edgeworth

Cherish all your happy moments: they make a fine cushion for old age.

~Christopher Morley

Money

A big part of financial freedom is having your heart and mind free from worry about the what-ifs of life.

~Suze Orman

Our incomes are like our shoes; if too small, they gall and pinch us; but if too large, they cause us to stumble and to trip.
~John Locke

It's easy to make a buck. It's a lot tougher to make a difference.
~Tom Brokaw

Money is like muck, not good except it be spread.
~Francis Bacon

It's good to have money and the things that money can buy, but it's good, too, to check up once in a while and make sure that you haven't lost the things that money can't buy.
~George Horace Lorimer

Money and time are the heaviest burdens of life, and . . . the un-happiest of all mortals are those who have more of either than they know how to use.
~Samuel Johnson

Money sometimes makes fools of important persons, but it may also make important persons of fools.
~Walter Winchell

Remember that time is money.
~Benjamin Franklin

Debt is like any other trap, easy enough to get into, but hard enough to get out of.
~Josh Billings

If you would be wealthy, think of saving as well as getting.
~Benjamin Franklin

Wisdom outweighs any wealth.
~Sophocles

He that is of opinion money will do everything may well be suspected of doing everything for money.
~Benjamin Franklin

Morality

The highest possible stage in moral culture is when we recognize that we ought to control our thoughts.

~Charles Darwin

The art of acting morally is behaving as if everything we do matters.

~Gloria Steinem

I have never believed there was one code of morality for a public [man] and another for a private man.

~Thomas Jefferson

There is only one morality . . . just as there is only one geometry.

~Voltaire

I know only that what is moral is what you feel good after and what is immoral is what you feel bad after.

~Ernest Hemmingway

Compassion is the basis of all morality.

~Arthur Schopenhauer

Motherhood

Mothers are the necessity of invention.

~Bill Watterson

All-Gracious! Grant, to those that bear a mother's charge, the strength and light to lead the steps that own their care in ways of Love, and Truth, and Right.

~William Cullen Bryant

The natural state of motherhood is unselfishness. When you become a mother, you are no longer the center of your own universe.

~Jessica Lange

We bear the world and we make it . . . . There was never a great man who had not a great mother — it is hardly an exaggeration.

~Oliver Schreiner

251

Men are what their mothers made them.
~Ralph Waldo Emerson

No matter how old a mother is, she watches her middle-aged children for signs of improvement.
~Florida Scott-Maxwell

Of all the rights of women, the greatest is to be a mother.
~Lin Yutang

Life began with waking up and loving my mother's face.
~George Eliot

Motivation

Be miserable. Or motivate yourself. Whatever has to be done, it's always your choice.
~Wayne Dyer

'Tis the motive exalts the action; 'tis the doing, and not the deed.
~Margaret Preston

The more I want to get something done the less I call it work.
~Richard Bach

Joys are our wings, sorrows our spurs.
~Jean Paul Richter

Ability is what you're capable of doing. Motivation determines what you do. Attitude determines how well you do it.
~Lou Holtz

If you know the why, you can live any how.
~Friedrich Nietsche

Success isn't a result of spontaneous combustion. You must set yourself on fire.
~Arnold H. Glasow

Don't simply retire from something; have something to retire to.
~Harry Emerson Fosdick

Music

One good thing about music, when it hits you, you feel no pain.
~Bob Marley

If music be the food of love, play on.
~William Shakespeare

Music washes away from the soul the dust of everyday life.
~Berthold Auerbach

Great music is that which penetrates the ear with facility and leaves the memory with difficulty. Magical music never leaves the memory.
~Thomas Beecham

One good thing about music, when it hits you, you feel no pain.
~Bob Marley

Take a music bath once or twice a week for a few seasons, and you will find that it is to the soul what the water bath is to the body.
~Oliver Wendell Holmes

Music is the only language in which you cannot say a mean or sarcastic thing.
~John Erskine

Nature

Nature has been for me, for as long as I remember, a source of solace, inspiration, adventure, and delight; a home, a teacher, a companion.
~Lorraine Anderson

There are no accidents, only nature throwing her weight around . . . nature will pick up the cards we have spilled, shuffle them, and begin her game again.
~Camille Paglia

If you watch how nature deals with adversity, continually renewing itself, you can't help but learn.
~Bernie Siegel

The sea is always the same: and yet the sea always changes.
~Carl Sandburg

Loveliest of trees, the cherry now is hung with bloom along the bough, and stands about the woodland ride wearing white for Eastertide.
~A. E. Housman

A longing pure and not to be described drove me to wander over woods and fields, and in a mist of hot abundant tears I felt a world arise and live for me.
~Johann Wolfgang von Goethe

Nature hath secret lore for those who lean Upon her breast, with leisure in their soul.
~Lydia Howard Sigourney

Sunlight is like the breath of life to the pomp of autumn.
~Nathaniel Hawthorne

Adopt the pace of nature: her secret is patience.
~Ralph Waldo Emerson

Needs

Don't deny your basic needs . . . Find ways to incorporate these necessary functions into even the busiest schedule.
~Stephanie Goddard Davidson

All I ever wanted . . . couldn't hold a candle to what I've been given. I've been given what I need.
~Michael McLean

We live in an age when unnecessary things are our only necessities.
~Oscar Wilde

New Day

With the new day comes new strength and new thoughts.
~Eleanor Roosevelt

I have always been delighted at the prospect of a new day, a fresh try, one more start, with perhaps a bit of magic waiting somewhere behind the morning.
~J. B. Priestley

Today a new sun rises for me; everything lives, everything is animated, everything seems to speak to me of my passion, everything invites me to cherish it.
~Anne de L'Enclos

New Year

The new year stands before us, like a chapter in a book, waiting to be written. We can help write that story by setting goals.
~Melody Beattie

And now we welcome the new year. Full of things that have never been.
~Rainer Maria Rilke

The best preparation for a better life next year is a full, complete, harmonious, joyous life this year.
~Thomas Dreier

Cheers to a new year and another chance for us to get it right.
~Oprah Winfrey

Normal

The only normal people are the ones you don't know very well.
~Alfred Adler

Normal is not something to aspire to, it's something to get away from.
~Jodie Foster

Nothing

Positive anything is better than negative nothing.
~Elbert Hubbard

Nothing is the worst thing that can happen to us.

~Richard Bach

Nothing will work unless you do.

~Maya Angelou

Oath

He who promises more than he is able to perform is false to himself, and he who does not perform what he has promised, is a traitor to his friend.

~George Shelley

It is not the oath that makes us believe the man, but the man the oath.

~Aeschylus

Obligation

Loyalty, friendship, family ties, the duty owed to an ideal—in our time, these obligations seem to have lost their force as motivators and connectors.

~Elizabeth Janeway

A man must not deny his manifest abilities, for that is to evade his obligations.

~William Feather

The more obligations we accept that are self-imposed, the freer we are.

~John C. Schroeder

Observation

The eye of a master will do more work than both his hands.
~Benjamin Franklin

Obstacles

Nothing will ever be attempted if all possible objections must first be overcome.

~Samuel Johnson

The greatest obstacle to discovery is not ignorance—it is the illusion of knowledge.

~Daniel J. Boorstin

If you believe it will work out, you'll see opportunities. If you believe it won't, you'll see obstacles.

~Wayne Dyer

Obstacles are those frightful things you see when you take your eyes off your goal.

~Henry Ford

Once you overcome seemingly insurmountable obstacles, other hurdles become less daunting.

~Howard Schultz

Obstacles don't have to stop you. If you run into a wall, don't turn around and give up. Figure out how to climb it, go through it, or work around it.

~Michael Jordan

Occupation

There is no more noble occupation in the world than to assist another human being—to help someone succeed.

~Alan Loy McGinnis

Choose a job you love, and you will never have to work a day in your life.

~Confucius

There is as much dignity in tilling a field as in writing a poem.
~Booker T. Washington

Money and title don't get you very far when you are miserable eight hours a day.

~Stephanie Goddard Davidson

Opinions

Public opinion is a weak tyrant compared with our own private opinion. What a man thinks of himself, that it is which determines, or rather indicates, his fate.

~Henry David Thoreau

I am not one of those who in expressing opinions confine them-selves to facts.

~Mark Twain

People do not seem to realize that their opinion of the world is also a confession of character.

~Ralph Waldo Emerson

The man who never alters his opinion is like standing water, and breeds reptiles of the mind.

~William Blake

It is a golden rule not to judge men by their opinions but rather by what their opinions make of them.

~Georg Christoph Lichtenberg

New opinions are always suspected, and usually opposed, without any other reason but because they are not already common.

~John Locke

Fight for your opinions, but do not believe that they contain the whole truth, or the only truth.

~Charles A. Dana

I think we ought always to entertain our opinions with some mea-sure of doubt. I shouldn't wish people dogmatically to believe any philosophy, not even mine.

~Bertrand Russell

I never make the mistake of arguing with people for whose opin-ions I have no respect.

~Edward Gibbon

Opportunity

Opportunity is missed by most people because it is dressed in over-alls and looks like work.

~Thomas Edison

If opportunity doesn't knock, build a door.

~Milton Berle

Sometimes opportunity knocks, but most of the time it sneaks up and then quietly steals away.

~Doug Larson

When a dog runs at you, whistle for him.

~Henry David Thoreau

The doors of Opportunity are marked "Push" and "Pull."

~Ethel Watts Mumford

Sometimes opportunities float right past your nose. Work hard, apply yourself, and be ready. When an opportunity comes you can grab it.

~Julie Andrews

The only way of catching a train I have ever discovered is to miss the train before.

~Gilbert K. Chesterton

Opportunities multiply as they are seized; they die when neglected. Life is a long line of opportunities.

~John Wicker

While we stop to think, we often miss our opportunity.

~Publilius Syrus

A wise man will make more opportunities than he finds.

~Francis Bacon

Problems can become opportunities when the right people come together.

~Robert Redford

Do not wait for ideal circumstances, nor the best opportunities; they will never come.

~Janet Erskine Stuart

Freedom means the opportunity to be what we never thought we would be.

~Daniel J. Boorstin

Follow your bliss and the universe will open doors where there were only walls.

~Joseph Campbell

If you believe it will work, you'll see opportunities. If you believe it won't, you'll see obstacles.

~Wayne Dyer

The secret of success in life is for a man to be ready for his opportunity when it comes.

~Benjamin Disraeli

Opportunities multiply as they are seized.

~Sun Tzu

We are all faced with a series of great opportunities brilliantly disguised as impossible situations.

~Charles R. Swindoll

When one door of happiness closes, another opens; but often we look so long at the closed door that we do not see the one which has been opened for us.

~Helen Keller

Watch out for emergencies. They are your big chance.

~Fritz Reiner

Opposition

Strong people are made by opposition like kites that go up against the wind.

~Frank Harris

Oppression

We must remember that any oppression, any injustice, any hatred, is a wedge designed to attack our civilization.

~Franklin D. Roosevelt

Singular indeed that the people should be writhing under oppression and injury, and yet not one among them to be found, to raise the voice of complaint.

~Abraham Lincoln

We cannot change anything unless we accept it. Condemnation does not liberate; it oppresses.

~Carl Jung

Being oppressed means the absence of choices.

~Bell Hooks

Optimism

My optimism wears heavy boots and is loud.

~Henry Rollins

The point of living, and of being an optimist, is to be foolish enough to believe the best is yet to come.

~Peter Ustinov

Optimism is essential to achievement and it is also the foundation of courage and true progress.

~Nicholas Murray Butler

A pessimist sees the difficulty in every opportunity; an optimist sees the opportunity in every difficulty.

~Winston Churchill

Never talk defeat. Use words like hope, belief, faith, victory.

~Norman Vincent Peale

Although the world is full of suffering, it is full also of the over-coming of it. My optimism, then, does not rest of the absence of evil, but on a glad belief in the preponderance of good and a willing effort always to cooperate with the good, that it may prevail.

~Helen Keller

Nothing is the worst thing that can happen to us.

~Richard Bach

Everyone take heart, it'll be a good year.

~Peter Breinholt

Form the habit of saying 'Yes' to your good ideas. Then write down all the reasons why they will work. There will always be plenty of people around to tell you why they won't work.

~Gil Atkinson

Do not anticipate trouble, or worry about what may never happen. Keep in the sunlight.

~Benjamin Franklin

One of the things I learned the hard way was that it doesn't pay to get discouraged. Keeping busy and making optimism a way of life can restore your faith in yourself.

~Lucille Ball

An optimist is the human personification of spring.

~Susan J. Bissonette

Action and reaction, ebb and flow, trial and error, change—this is the rhythm of living. Out of our over-confidence, fear; out of our fear, clearer vision, fresh hope. And out of hope, progress.

~Bruce Barton

For myself I am an optimist—it does not seem to be much use being anything else.

~Winston Churchill

Order

Each day, and the living of it, has to be a conscious creation in which discipline and order are relieved with some play and pure foolishness.

~May Sarton

The art of progress is to preserve order amid change and to preserve change amid order.

~Alfred North Whitehead

Don't agonize. Organize.

~Florynce Kennedy

How very much do they err who consider the absence of order and method as implying greater liberty or removing a sense of restraint!

~Charlotte Elizabeth Tonna

Ordinary

The difference between ordinary and extraordinary is that little extra.

~Jimmy Johnson

Revel in the ordinary.
~M. J. Ryan

The ordinary acts we practice every day at home are of more importance to the soul than their simplicity might suggest.
~Thomas Moore

Overwhelmed

When you reach the end of your rope, tie a knot in it and hang on.
~Franklin D. Roosevelt

I am convinced that there are times in everybody's experience when there is so much to be done, that the only way to do it, is to sit down and do nothing.
~Fanny Fern

I know of no higher fortitude than stubbornness in the face of overwhelming odds.
~Louis Nizer

If you aren't in over your head, how do you know how tall you are?
~T. S. Eliot

Pain

Human pain does not let go of its grip at one point in time. Rather, it works its way out of our consciousness over time. There is a season of sadness. A season of anger. A season of tranquility. A season of hope.
~Robert Veninga

Accept the pain, cherish the joys, resolve the regrets; then can come the best of benedictions — "If I had my life to live over, I'd do it all the same."
~Joan McIntosh

The chief pang of most trials is not so much the actual suffering itself as our own spirit of resistance to it.
~Jean Nicolas Grou

Humor is the instinct for taking pain playfully.
~Max Eastman

Take chances, make mistakes. That's how you grow. Pain nourishes your courage. You have to fail in order to practice being brave.
~Mary Tyler Moore

Parenting

Our children give us the opportunity to become the parents we always wished we'd had.
~Louise Hart

Men are what their mothers made them.
~Ralph Waldo Emerson

We cannot always build the future for our youth, but we can always build our youth for the future.
~Franklin D. Roosevelt

Where parents do too much for their children, the children will not do much for themselves.
~Elbert Hubbard

One of the greatest gifts parents can give their children is the assurance that Mom and Dad love them just as they are, apart from anything that they do.
~Max Lucado

Each day of our lives we make deposits in the memory banks of our children.
~Charles Swindoll

Passion

Life is a paradise for those who love many things with a passion.
~Leo Buscaglia

Great dancers are not great because of their technique; they are great because of their passion.
~Martha Graham

Find something you're passionate about and keep tremendously interested in it.
~Julia Child

Where passion is not found, no virtue ever dwelt.
~Maria Brooks

To control our passions we must govern our habits, and keep watch over ourselves in the small details of everyday life.
~Sir John Lubbock

Learn to be happy. And think of life as a terminal illness because if you do you will live it with joy and passion, as it ought to be lived.
~Anna Quindlen

Who is wise? He that learns from everyone. Who is powerful? He that governs his passions. Who is rich? He that is content.
~Benjamin Franklin

I am seeking, I am striving, I am in it with all my heart.
~Vincent van Gogh

Pursue your passion and live your dream.
~Katherine Logan

Passion persuades.
~Anita Roddick

The happiness of a man in this life does not consist in the absence but on the mastery of his passions.
~Alfred, Lord Tennyson

Without passion man is a mere latent force and possibility, like the flint which awaits the shock of the iron before it can give forth its spark.
~Henri-Frédéric Amiel

A man without a passion is like a vessel waiting for wind and not budging.
~Arsène Houssaye

Past

Things that are done, it is needless to speak about . . . that's that are past, it is needless to blame.
~Confucius

The time is now, the place is here. Stay in the present. You can do nothing to change the past, and the future will never come exactly as you plan or hope for.

~Dan Millman

The past is finished. There is nothing to be gained by going over it. Whatever it gave us in the experiences it brought us was something we had to know.

~Rebecca Beard

When the past no longer illuminates the future, the spirit walks in darkness.

~Alexis de Tocqueville

You can't have a better tomorrow if you are thinking about yesterday all the time.

~Charles F. Kettering

Remembering the past gives power to the present.

~Fae Myenne Ng

To look backward for a while is to refresh the eye, to restore it, and to render it the more fit for its prime function of looking forward.

~Margaret Fairless Barber

Isn't it amazing the way the future succeeds in creating an appropriate past?

~John Leonard

Let me remember lessons learned, and profit from the past, and may I build a bridge of dreams, that shall forever last.

~Grace E. Easley

Don't let yesterday take up too much of today.

~Will Rogers

Happy is the soul that has something to look backward to with pride, and something to look forward to with hope.

~Oliver G. Wilson

Don't cry because it's over, smile because it happened.

~Theodor Seuss Geisel (Dr. Seuss)

Nothing changes more constantly than the past; for the past that influences our lives does not consist of what actually happened, but of what men believe happened.
~Gerald W. Johnson

Patience

Time can but make it easier to be wise though now it seems impossible, and so all that you need is patience.
~William Butler Yeats

Adopt the pace of nature: her secret is patience.
~Ralph Waldo Emerson

Patience and goodness will ever in the end conciliate the goodwill of others.
~Josephine

Patience is the art of concealing your impatience.
~Guy Kawasaki

Patience serves as a protection against wrongs as clothes do against cold. For if you put on more clothes as the cold increases, it will have no power to hurt you.
~Leonardo da Vinci

Have patience. All things are difficult before they become easy.
~Saadi

Adjust the pace of nature: her secret is patience.
~Ralph Waldo Emerson

The two most powerful warriors are patience and time.
~Leo Tolstoy

Patience is a necessary ingredient of genius.
~Benjamin Disraeli

Genius is nothing but a greater aptitude for patience.
~Benjamin Franklin

You must grow in patience when you meet with great wrongs, and they will then be powerless to vex your mind.
~Leonardo da Vinci

Have patience with all things, but chiefly have patience with yourself. Do not lose courage in considering your own imperfections but instantly set about remedying them—every day begin the task anew.

~Francis de Sales

Patience is not simply the ability to wait—it's how we behave while we're waiting.

~Joyce Meyer

Patience is the best remedy for every trouble.

~Plautus

He that can have patience can have what he will.

~Benjamin Franklin

Every man must patiently bide his time. He must wait—not in listless idleness, . . . but in constant, steady, cheerful endeavors, always willing and fulfilling and accomplishing his task, that, when the occasion comes, he may be equal to the occasion.

~Henry Wadsworth Longfellow

It is not necessary for all men to be great in action. The greatest and sublimest power is often simple patience.

~Horace Bushnell

Patience serves as a protection against wrongs as clothes do against cold. For if you put on more clothes as the cold increases, it will have no power to hurt you.

~Leonardo da Vinci

Always remember that the future comes one day at a time.

~Dean Acheson

Patriotism

I only regret that I have but one life to lose for my country.

~Nathan Hale

This nation will remain the land of the free only so long as it is the home of the brave.

~Elmer Davis

The strength of a nation derives from the integrity of the home.
~Confucius

I have a great belief in the future of my people and my country.
~Marian Anderson

Our flag honors those who have fought to protect it, and is a reminder of the sacrifice of our nation's founders and heroes. As the ultimate icon of America's storied history, the Stars and Stripes represents the very best of this nation.
~Joe Barton

The American flag is the symbol of our freedom, national pride and history.
~Mike Fitzpatrick

The flag is the embodiment, not of sentiment, but of history.
~Woodrow Wilson

But the freedom that they fought for, and the country grand they wrought for, Is their monument to-day, and for aye.
~Thomas Dunn English

The American flag represents all of us and all the values we hold sacred.
~Adrian Cronauer

My fellow Americans, ask not what your country can do for you, ask what you can do for your country.
~John F. Kennedy

America is hope. It is compassion. It is excellence. It is valor.
~Paul Tsongas

Each President is the President not only of all who live, but, in a very real sense, of all those who have yet to live.
~John F. Kennedy

America was not built on fear. America was built on courage, on imagination and an unbeatable determination to do the job at hand.
~Harry S. Truman

Our flag honors those who have fought to protect it, and is a re-minder of the sacrifice of our nation's founders and heroes. As the ultimate icon of America's storied history, the Stars and Stripes represents the very best of this nation.
~Joe Barton

Where liberty dwells, there is my country.
~Benjamin Franklin

Freedom is never more than one generation away from extinction. We didn't pass it to our children in the bloodstream. It must be fought for, protected, and handed on for them to do the same.
~Ronald Reagan

I have long believed that sacrifice is the pinnacle of patriotism.
~Bob Riley

Peace

Nothing is more conducive to peace of mind than not having any opinions at all.
~Georg Christoph Lichtenberg

We shall find peace. We shall hear the angels, we shall see the sky sparkling with diamonds.
~Anton Chekhov

An ambitious man can never know peace.
~J. Krishnamurti

Peace is not absence of conflict, but the ability to cope with conflict by peaceful means.
~Ronald Reagan

An ounce of peace is worth more than a pound of victory.
~St. Robert Bellarmine

Peace of mind is that mental condition in which you have accepted the worst.
~Lin Yutang

Do not overrate what you have received, nor envy others. He who envies others does not obtain peace of mind.
~Buddha

We've got to recognize that we are not working (primarily) for a peaceful world. Peace will be a by-product of something else. We are working for a world of justice and rightness. Peace is a by-product of justice and mercy.

~Stanley High

If we have no peace, it is because we have forgotten that we belong to each other.

~Mother Teresa

Courage is the price that life exacts for granting peace.

~Amelia Earhart

If there is to be any peace it will come through being, not having.

~Henry Miller

Before me peaceful, behind me peaceful, under me peaceful, over me peaceful, all around me peaceful.

~Navajo Proverb

When peace has been broken anywhere, the peace of all countries everywhere is in danger.

~Franklin D. Roosevelt

Mirth is like a flash of lightning that breaks through a gloom of clouds and glitters for a moment. Cheerfulness keeps up a daylight in the mind, filling it with a steady and perpetual serenity.

~Samuel Johnson

Every goal, every action, every thought, every feeling one experiences, whether it be consciously or unconsciously known, is an attempt in increase one's level of peace of mind.

~Sydney Madwed

Perfection

Perfection is not attainable, but if we chase perfection we can catch excellence.

~Vince Lombardi

Perfection is achieved, not when there is nothing more to add, but when there is nothing left to take away.

~Antoine de Saint-Exupéry

To live is to change, and to be perfect is to have changed often.
~John Henry Newman

Living with a saint is more grueling than being one.
~Robert Neville

I am for everything starting into full-blown perfection at once.
~Susan Edmonstone Ferrier

Practice does not make perfect. Only perfect practice makes perfect.
~Vince Lombardi

The man with insight enough to admit his limitations comes nearest to perfection.
~Johann Wolfgang von Goethe

Perseverance

Most of the important things in the world have been accomplished by people who have kept on trying when there seemed to be no hope at all.
~Dale Carnegie

By prevailing over all obstacles and distractions, one may unfailingly arrive at his chosen goal or destination.
~Christopher Columbus

Success is not final, failure is not fatal: it is the courage to continue that counts.
~Winston Churchill

Nothing could be worse than the fear that one had given up too soon, and left one unexpended effort that might have saved the world.
~Jane Addams

Life is not easy for any of us. But what of that? We must have perseverance and, above all, confidence in ourselves. We must believe that we are gifted for something, and that this thing must be attained.
~Marie Curie

Sticking to it is the genius.

~Thomas Edison

I think a hero is an ordinary individual who finds the strength to persevere and endure in spite of overwhelming obstacles.
~Christopher Reeve

Ninety percent of all those who fail are not actually defeated. They simply quit.

~Paul J. Meyer

You do what you can for as long as you can, and when you finally can't you do the next best thing. You back up, but you don't give up.

~Chuck Yeager

Just don't give up trying to do what you really want to do.
~Ella Fitzgerald

When you reach the end of your rope, tie a knot in it and hang on.
~Franklin D. Roosevelt

Perseverance is not a long race; it is many short races one after another.
~Walter Elliott

Constant dripping hollows out a stone.

~Lucretius

Run with your head the first two thirds of a race and with your heart the final one third.
~Jack Daniels

Hope begins in the dark, the stubborn hope that if you just show up and try to do the right thing, the dawn will come. You wait and watch and work: you don't give up.
~Anne Lamott

If you really want something, and really work hard, take advantage of opportunities, and never give up, you will somehow find a way.
~Jane Goodall

Fall down seven times, stand up eight.

~Japanese Proverb

Remember, a person who wins success may have been counted out many times before. He wins because he refuses to give up.

~Kemmons Wilson

The greatest results in life are usually attained by simple means and the exercise of ordinary qualities. These may for the most part be summed in these two — common sense and perseverance.

~Owen Feltham

The question of life is not whether you get knocked down. You will. The question is, are you ready to get back up, are you willing to get back up and fight for what you believe in?

~Dan Quayle

Some people fold after making one timid request. They quit too soon. Keep asking until you find the answers. In sales, there are usually four or five "no's" before you get a "yes."

~Jack Canfield

Life ought to be a struggle of desire toward adventures whose nobility will fertilize the soul.

~Rebecca West

As I continued upward, I saw my life as a whole. . . . It was simply this: I was meant for a long, hard climb.

~Lance Armstrong

Effort only fully releases its reward after a person refuses to quit.

~Napoleon Hill

Big shots are only little shots who keep shooting.

~Christopher Morley

Successful people keep moving. They make mistakes, but they don't quit.

~Conrad Hilton

I have discovered there are ways of getting almost anywhere you want to go, if you really want to go.

~Langston Hughes

Obstacles don't have to stop you. If you run into a wall, don't turn around and give up. Figure out how to climb it, go through it, or work around it.

~Michael Jordan

They'll tell you, "Quit now, you'll never make it." If you disregard this advice, you'll be halfway there.

~David Zucker

There are no gold medals for the 95-yard dash.

~Max De Pree

Some minds seem almost to create themselves, springing up under every disadvantage and working their solitary but irresistible way through a thousand obstacles.

~Washington Irving

Courage and perseverance have a magical talisman, before which difficulties disappear and obstacles vanish into air.

~John Quincy Adams

Any change, any loss, does not make us victims. Others can shake you, surprise you, disappoint you, but they can't prevent you from acting, from taking the situation you're presented with and moving on.

~Blaine Lee

For every finish-line tape a runner breaks—complete with the cheers of the crowd and the clicking of hundreds of cameras—there are the hours of hard and often lonely work that rarely gets talked about.

~Grete Waitz

People often say that motivation doesn't last. Well neither does bathing—that's why we recommend it daily.

~Zig Ziglar

Do more than is required. What is the distance between someone who achieves their goals consistently and those who spend their lives and careers merely following? The extra mile.

~Gary Ryan Blair

Persistence

Vitality shows not only in the ability to persist, but in the ability to start over.

~F. Scott Fitzgerald

Energy and persistence conquer all things.

~Benjamin Franklin

We can do anything we want to do if we stick to it long enough.
~Helen Keller

I think and think for months and years. Ninety-nine times, the conclusion is false. The hundredth time I am right.

~Albert Einstein

I walk slowly, but I never walk backward.

~Abraham Lincoln

Perspective

Colors seen by candlelight will not look the same by day.
~Elizabeth Barrett Browning

We see things not as they are, but as we are.

~Anaïs Nin

Clouds come floating into my life, no longer to carry rain or usher storm, but to add color to my sunset sky.

~Rabindranath Tagore

All things are difficult before they are easy.

~Thomas Fuller

Stretching his hand up to reach the stars, too often man forgets the flowers at his feet.

~Jeremy Bentham

I like nonsense, it wakes up the brain cells. Fantasy is a necessary ingredient in living, it's a way of looking at life through the wrong end of a telescope. Which is what I do, and that enables you to laugh at life's realities.

~Theodor Seuss Geisel (Dr. Seuss)

Keep your face to the sunshine and you cannot see a shadow.
~Helen Keller

A little perspective, like a little humor, goes a long way.
~Allen Klein

Inside yourself or outside, you never have to change what you see, only the way you see it.
~Thaddeus Golas

I have not failed. I've just found 10,000 ways that won't work.
~Thomas A. Edison

Who looks outside, dreams; who looks inside, awakes.
~Carl Jung

Two men look out through the same bars; one sees the mud and one the stars.
~Frederick Langbridge

For those who have seen the Earth from space . . . the experience most certainly changes your perspective. The things that we share in our world are far more valuable than those which divide us.
~Donald E. Williams

One's destination is never a place but rather a new way of looking at things.
~Henry Miller

Nothing is the worst thing that can happen to us.
~Richard Bach

Don't cry because it's over, smile because it happened.
~Theodor Seuss Geisel (Dr. Seuss)

Please subdue the anguish of your soul. Nobody is destined only to happiness or to pain. The wheel of life takes one up and down by turn.
~Kālidāsa

What is a weed? A plant whose virtues have not yet been discovered.
~Ralph Waldo Emerson

Now here is the best of my days, but I don't really know it, yes.
~Peter Breinholt

'Tis distance lends enchantment to the view, and robes the mountain in its azure hue.
~Thomas Campbell

The optimist proclaims that we live in the best of all possible worlds; and the pessimist fears this is true.
~James Branch Cabell

When a man sits with a pretty girl for an hour, it seems like a minute. But let him sit on a hot stove for a minute and it's longer than any hour. That's relativity.
~Albert Einstein

A man sees in the world what he carries in his heart.
~Johann Wolfgang von Goethe

A single hand's turn given heartily to the world's great work helps one amazingly with one's own small tasks.
~Louisa May Alcott

The world is divided into two classes, those who believe the incredible, and those who do the improbable.
~Oscar Wilde

If what you did yesterday seems big, you haven't done anything today.
~Lou Holtz

In this life we will encounter hurts and trials that we will not be able to change; we are just going to have to allow them to change us.
~Ron Lee Davis

The only human beings I have thoroughly admired and respected in the world have been those who carried the load of the world with a smile, and who, in the face of anxieties that would have knocked me clean out, never showed a tremor.
~Henry Brooks Adams

Accept the pain, cherish the joys, resolve the regrets; then can come the best of benedictions — "If I had my life to live over, I'd do it all the same."

~Joan McIntosh

In 20 years, you'll look back at photos of yourself and recall in a way you can't grasp now how much possibility lay before you and how fabulous you really looked.

~Mary Schmich

Bein' optimistic after you've got ever'thing you want don't count.
~Kin Hubbard

Each of us makes his own weather, determines the color of the skies in the emotional universe which he inhabits.

~Fulton J. Sheen

Every new day begins with possibilities. It's up to us to fill it with the things that move us toward progress and peace.

~Ronald Reagan

A loving person lives in a loving world. A hostile person lives in a hostile world: everyone you meet is your mirror.

~Ken Keyes Jr.

Abundance is not something we acquire. It is something we tune into.

~Wayne Dyer

All things are possible for the one who believes.
~Mark 9:23 English Standard Version

Beloved, it is morn! A redder berry on the thorn, A deeper yellow on the corn, For this good day new-born!

~Emily Hickey

Any change, any loss, does not make us victims. Others can shake you, surprise you, disappoint you, but they can't prevent you from acting, from taking the situation you're presented with and moving on.

~Blaine Lee

It is almost impossible to throw dirt on someone without getting a little on yourself.

~Abigail Van Buren

We could never learn to be brave and patient, if there were only joy in the world.

~Helen Keller

If you're in a bad situation, don't worry it'll change. If you're in a good situation, don't worry it'll change.

~John A. Simone Sr.

If youth but knew: if age but could.

~Henri Estienne

Try, try, try, and keep on trying is the rule that must be followed to become an expert in anything.

~W. Clement Stone

Pessimism

A pessimist sees the difficulty in every opportunity; an optimist sees the opportunity in every difficulty.

~Winston Churchill

Philosophy

Philosophy is a battle against the bewitchment of our intelligence by means of language.

~Ludwig Wittgenstein

I have a new philosophy. I'm only going to dread one day at a time.

~Charles Schulz

One's philosophy is not best expressed in words; it is expressed in the choices one makes.

~Eleanor Roosevelt

Love as a principle, the order as a foundation, and progress as a goal.

~Auguste Comte

The point of philosophy is to start with something so simply as not to seem worth stating, and to end with something so paradoxical that no one will believe it.

~Bertrand Russell

Picture

A photograph is a secret about a secret, the more it tells you the less you know.

~Diane Arbus

Planning

I have never yet seen any plan which has not been mended by the observations of those who were much inferior in understanding to the person who took the lead in the business.

~Edmund Burke

When we are planning for posterity, we ought to remember that virtue is not hereditary.

~Thomas Paine

Make no little plans. They have no magic to stir men's blood . . . Make big plans, aim high in hope and work.

~Daniel H. Burnham

Always plan with the end result in mind . . . Be clear. Be specific.
~Stephanie Goddard Davidson

Even the best team, without a sound plan, can't score.

~Woody Hayes

As the wind blows, you must set your sail.

~Thomas Fuller

The success of a project will depend critically upon the effort, care, and skill you applied in its initial planning.

~Gerard M. Blair

The general who wins a battle makes many calculations . . . ere the battle is fought. The general who loses a battle makes but few calculations beforehand. Thus do many calculations lead to victory and few calculations to defeat.

~Sun Tzu

Always plan with the end result in mind . . . Be clear. Be specific.
~Stephanie Goddard Davidson

Strategy is not the consequence of planning, but the opposite: its starting point.

~Henry Mintzberg

Long-range planning does not deal with future decisions, but with the future of present decisions.

~Peter F. Drucker

Chance favors the prepared mind.

~Louis Pasteur

The only way of catching a train I have ever discovered is to miss the train before.

~Gilbert K. Chesterton

Just because something doesn't do what you planned it to do doesn't mean it's useless.

~Thomas Edison

Your present circumstances don't determine where you can go they merely determine where you start.

~Nido Qubein

A discovery is said to be an accident meeting a prepared mind.
~Albert Szent-Györgyi

Planning ahead is a measure of class.

~Gloria Steinem

The God who knows you best knows the best for you.
~Woodrow Kroll

Happy people plan actions, they don't plan results.
~Denis Waitley

It takes as much energy to wish as it does to plan.
~Eleanor Roosevelt

Whether or not it is clear to you, no doubt the universe is unfolding as it should.

~Desiderata

Every moment spent in planning saves three or four in execution.
~Crawford H. Greenewalt

Even a two-car parade gets fouled up when you don't decide ahead of time who's going to lead.

~Zig Ziglar

It wasn't raining when Noah built the ark.

~Howard Ruff

A goal without a plan is just a wish.

~Antoine de Saint-Exupéry

Playful

Each day, and the living of it, has to be a conscious creation in which discipline and order are relieved with some play and pure foolishness.

~May Sarton

Pleasure

You find yourself refreshed by the presence of cheerful people. Why not make an honest effort to confer that pleasure on others? Half the battle is gained if you never allow yourself to say anything gloomy.

~Lydia Marie Child

There is more pleasure in loving than in being beloved.
~Thomas Fuller

Most men pursue pleasure with such breathless haste that we hurry past it.

~Søren Kierkegaard

That man is the richest whose pleasures are the cheapest.
~Henry David Thoreau

The rule of my life is to make business a pleasure, and pleasure my business.

~Aaron Burr

Poor

I prefer the company of peasants because they have not been educated sufficiently to reason incorrectly.

~Michel de Montaigne

The only gift is giving to the poor; all else is exchange.

~Thiruvalluvar

Positivity

It is healthier to see the good points of others than to analyze our own bad ones.

~Françoise Sagan

Positive anything is better than negative nothing.

~Elbert Hubbard

Work hard, stay positive, and get up early. It's the best part of the day.

~George Allen

You cannot have a positive life and a negative mind.

~Joyce Meyer

A positive attitude is something everyone can work on, and everyone can learn how to employ it.

~Joan Lunden

Live life to the fullest, and focus on the positive.

~Matt Cameron

Keep your face always toward the sunshine—and shadows will fall behind you.

~Walt Whitman

These are the days of miracle and wonder.

~Paul Simon

This is the best day the world has ever seen; tomorrow will be better.

~R. A. Campbell

Possessions

Keep your old love letters. Throw away your old bank statements.
~Mary Schmich

It is possible to own too much. A man with one watch knows what time it is; a man with two watches is never quite sure.
~Lee Segall

An object in possession seldom retains the same charm that it had in pursuit.
~Pliny the Elder

It is not how much we have, but how much we enjoy, that makes happiness.
~Charles H. Spurgeon

See the things you want as already yours. Think of them as yours, as belonging to you, as already in your possession.
~Robert Collier

Everything in life is passing and whatever we possess cannot endure forever but ends in nothingness.
~Helen Steiner Rice

We are more, much more, than what we have.
~Don Wilson

It is possible to own too much. A man with one watch knows what time it is; a person with two watches is never quite sure.
~Lee Segall

They love their land because it is their own, And scorn to give aught other reason why.
~Fitz-Greene Halleck

Possibility

So long as we think dugout canoes are the only possibility—all that is real or can be real—we will never see the ship, we will never feel the free wind blow.
~Sonia Johnson

I strive for the best and I do the possible.
~Lyndon B. Johnson

What we find is that if you have a goal that is very, very far out, and you approach it in little steps, you start to get there faster. Your mind opens up to the possibilities.
~Mae Jemison

The future belongs to people who see possibilities before they become obvious.
~John Sculley

Every new day begins with possibilities. It's up to us to fill it with the things that move us toward progress and peace.
~Ronald Reagan

Nothing is impossible to a willing heart.
~John Heywood

You ask me how I want to be remembered, what I want on my tombstone? "Si se puede—It can be done."
~Dolores Huerta

The only thing that can stop you from fulfilling your dreams is you.
~Tom Bradley

When nothing is sure, everything is possible.
~Margaret Drabble

I start with the idea that nothing is impossible and everything can be done in the end.
~Alberta Ferretti

I am looking for a lot of people who have an infinite capacity to now know what can't be done.
~Henry Ford

Over, under, around, or through, there's always a way.
~Sherrilyn Kenyon

The Wright brothers flew right through the smoke screen of impossibility.
~Charles F. Kettering

Possibilities do not add up. They multiply.
~Paul M. Romer

Never ask yourself, "Can I do this?" Ask instead, "How can I do this?"
~Dan Zadra

Impossible is just an opinion.
~Gil Atkinson

Nothing is impossible, the word itself says, "I'm possible!"
~Audrey Hepburn

Potential

The greatest crime in the world is to not develop your potential.
~Roger Williams

We must make the choices that enable us to fulfill the deepest capacities of our real selves.
~Thomas Merton

We know what we are, but know not what we may become.
~William Shakespeare

Every great dream begins with a dreamer. Always remember, you have within you the strength, the patience, and the passion to reach for the stars to change the world.
~Harriet Tubman

You never will be the person you can be if pressure, tension and discipline are taken out of your life.
~James G. Bilkey

Each child has . . . an equal opportunity, not to become equal, but to become different—to realize whatever unique potential of body, mind and spirit he or she possesses.
~John Fischer

No bird soars too high, if he soars with his own wings.
~William Blake

Successful and unsuccessful people do not vary greatly in their abilities. They vary in their desires to reach their potential.

~John C. Maxwell

We all have the extraordinary coded within us, waiting to be released.

~J. L. Houston

If things come naturally, you may not bother to work at improving them, and you can fall short of your potential.

~Bob Pettit

Power

When there is hope in the future, there is power in the present.

~Zig Ziglar

The great charm of all power is modesty.

~Louisa May Alcott

My doctrine is this, that if we see cruelty or wrong that we have the power to stop, and do nothing, we make ourselves sharers in the guilt.

~Anna Sewell

We have learned that power is a positive force if it is used for positive purposes.

~Elizabeth Dole

If there is no struggle there is no progress . . . Power concedes nothing without a demand. It never did and it never will.

~Frederick Douglass

Who is wise? He that learns from everyone. Who is powerful? He that governs his passions. Who is rich? He that is content.

~Benjamin Franklin

Knowledge will give you power, but character respect.

~Bruce Lee

Do not pray for tasks equal to your powers. Pray for powers equal to your tasks.

~Phillips Brooks

Words are nothing but words; power lies in deeds. Be a person of action.

~Mali Oriot Mamadu Konyate

Power is the ability to do good things for others.

~Brooke Astor

The greatest power that a person possesses is the power to choose.

~J. Martin Kohe

It is said that power corrupts, but actually it's more true that power attracts the corruptible. The sane are usually attracted by other things than power.

~David Brin

Let not thy will roar, when thy power can but whisper.

~Thomas Fuller

Praise

Everyone needs recognition for his accomplishments but few people make the need known quite as clearly as the little boy who said to his father: "Let's play darts. I'll throw and you say 'Wonderful!'"

~Arthur Lenehan

Praise, like gold and diamonds, owes its value only to its scarcity.

~Samuel Johnson

Prayer

Do not pray for tasks equal to your powers. Pray for powers equal to your tasks.

~Phillips Brooks

Prejudice

It is never too late to give up our prejudices.

~Henry David Thoreau

Everyone is a prisoner of his own experiences. No one can eliminate prejudices —just recognize them.

~Edward R. Murrow

Preparation

By failing to prepare, you are preparing to fail.

~Benjamin Franklin

Humor is the instinct for taking pain playfully.

~Max Eastman

Sometimes opportunities float right past your nose. Work hard, apply yourself, and be ready. When an opportunity comes you can grab it.

~Julie Andrews

This is the precept by which I have lived: Prepare for the worst; expect the best; and take what comes.

~Hannah Arendt

The best preparation for tomorrow is doing your best today.

~H. Jackson Brown Jr.

To stay ahead, you must have your next idea waiting in the wings.

~Rosabeth Moss Kanter

Whoever is first in the field and awaits the coming of the enemy, will be fresh for the fight; whoever is second in the field and has to hasten to battle will arrive exhausted.

~Sun Tzu

He who would leap high must take a long run.

~Danish Proverb

If we are prepared, we have the edge. If we have the edge, we succeed.

~Jeanelle Anderson

Getting ready is the secret to success.

~Henry Ford

Prepare. The time to win your battle is before it starts.
~Frederick W. Lewis

Chance favors the prepared mind.

~Louis Pasteur

Present

*We have only this moment, sparkling like a star in our hand . . .
and melting like a snowflake. Let us use it before it is too late.*
~Marie Beyon Ray

*The time is now, the place is here. Stay in the present. You can do
nothing to change the past, and the future will never come exactly
as you plan or hope for.*
~Dan Millman

*The more I give myself permission to live in the moment and enjoy
it without feeling guilty or judgmental about any other time, the
better I feel about the quality of my work.*
~Wayne Dyer

*Today, this hour, this minute is the day, the hour, the minute for
each of us to sense the fact that life is good, with all of its trials and
troubles, and perhaps more interesting because of them.*
~Robert R. Updegraff

Real generosity toward the future lies in giving all to the present.
~Albert Camus

Remembering the past gives power to the present.
~Fae Myenne Ng

*We can experience nothing but the present moment, live in no oth-
er second of time, and to understand this is as close as we can get
to eternal life.*
~P. D. James

Seize the moment before it's gone, for another day begins at dawn.
~Clay Harrison

It is only possible to live happily ever after on a daily basis.
~Margaret Bonanno

Don't let yesterday take up too much of today.

~Will Rogers

We are here, and it is now. What else is there?

~Kobi Yamada

The present time has one advantage over every other—it is our own.

~Charles Colton

Mark but the hist'ry of a modern day, Composed of nonsense, foppery, and play.

~Ann Murry

Pride

Never be haughty to the humble; never be humble to the haughty.
~Jefferson Davis

The charity that hastens to proclaim its good deeds, ceases to be charity, and is only pride and ostentation.

~William Hutton

Principles

It is easier to fight for one's principles than to live up to them.
~Alfred Adler

A people that values its privileges above its principles soon loses both.

~Dwight D. Eisenhower

'Tis the business of little minds to shrink; but he whose heart is firm, and whose conscience approves his conduct, will pursue his principles unto death.

~Thomas Paine

Nature imitates herself. A grain thrown into good ground brings forth fruit; a principle thrown into a good mind brings forth fruit.
~Blaise Pascal

Honest hearts produce honest actions.

~Brigham Young

Do what you feel in your heart to be right—for you'll be criticized anyway. You'll be damned if you do, and damned if you don't.
~Eleanor Roosevelt

The easiest thing to be in the world is you. The most difficult thing to be is what other people want you to be. Don't let them put you in that position.
~Leo Buscaglia

To stand upon the ramparts and die for our principles is heroic, but to sally forth to battle and win for our principles is something more than heroic.
~Franklin D. Roosevelt

Principles, like troops of the line, are undisturbed, and stand fast.
~John Paul Richter

Priorities

Never let the urgent crowd out the important.
~Kelly Catlin Walker

In the absence of clearly-defined goals, we become strangely loyal to performing daily trivia until ultimately we become enslaved by it.
~Robert Heinlein

Problems

Each problem that I solved became a rule, which served afterwards to solve other problems.
~René Descartes

Whatever creativity is, it is in part a solution to a problem.
~Brian Aldiss

The best years of your life are the ones in which you decide your problems are your own. You don't blame them on your mother, the ecology, or the president. You realize that you control your own destiny.
~Albert Ellis

A clever person solves a problem. A wise person avoids it.
~Albert Einstein

Problems can become opportunities when the right people come together.
~Robert Redford

Most people spend more time and energy going around problems than in trying to solve them.
~Henry Ford

The man who is forever disturbed about the condition of humanity either has no problems of his own or has refused to face them.
~Henry Miller

Believe it is possible to solve your problem. Tremendous things happen to the believer. So believe the answer will come. It will.
~Norman Vincent Peale

Intellectuals solve problems; geniuses prevent them.
~Albert Einstein

You can't solve a problem on the same level that it was created. You have to rise above it to the next level.
~Albert Einstein

All problems boil down to limited choices, and the choice we often forget is love.
~Tom Daly

Don't dwell on what went wrong. Instead, focus on what to do next. Spend your energies on moving forward toward finding the answer.
~Denis Waitley

It is characteristic of all deep human problems that they are not to be approached without some humor and some bewilderment.
~Freeman Dyson

Procrastination

Procrastination is the art of keeping up with yesterday.
~Don Marquis

Far from being a thief of Time, procrastination is the king of it.
~Ogden Nash

Those who wait till evening for sunrise . . . will find that they have lost the day.
~Elizabeth Hamilton

Know the true value of time; snatch, seize, and enjoy every moment of it. No idleness, no laziness, no procrastination: never put off till tomorrow what you can do today.
~Philip Stanhope

Progress

The exact measure of the progress of civilization is the degree in which the intelligence of the common mind has prevailed over wealth and brute force.
~George Bancroft

Emergencies have always been necessary to progress. It was darkness which produced the lamp . . . . Fog that produced the compass . . . . Hunger that drove us to exploration. And it took a depression to teach us the real value of a job.
~Victor Hugo

Choose your rut carefully; you'll be in it for the next ten miles.
~Road sign in upstate New York

The art of progress is to preserve order amid change and to preserve change amid order.
~Alfred North Whitehead

If you're walking down the right path and you're willing to keep walking, eventually you'll make progress.
~Barack Obama

Progress is not created by contented people.
~Frank Tyger

I walk slowly, but I never walk backward.
~Abraham Lincoln

A workable measure of your progress is how fast you can get free when you are stuck and how many ways you know to get free.

~Kathleen Hendricks

Promise

He who promises more than he is able to perform is false to himself, and he who does not perform what he has promised, is a traitor to his friend.

~George Shelley

It is not the oath that makes us believe the man, but the man the oath.

~Aeschylus

Prosperity

Prosperity proves the fortunate, adversity the great.

~Rose Kennedy

If you count all your assets, you always show a profit.

~Wilson Mizner

Prosperity is only an instrument to be used, not a deity to be worshipped.

~Calvin Coolidge

If we had no winter, the spring would not be so pleasant: if we did not sometimes taste of adversity, prosperity would not be so welcome.

~Anne Bradstreet

Prosperity doth best discover vice, but adversity doth best discover virtue.

~Francis Bacon

Let me remember lessons learned, And profit from the past, And may I build a bridge of dreams, That shall forever last.

~Grace E. Easley

Purpose

In a world as empirical as ours, a youngster who does not know what he is good at will not be sure what he is good for.
~Edgar Z. Friedenberg

I began to have an idea of my life, not as the slow shaping of achievement to fit my preconceived purposes, but as the gradual discovery and growth of a purpose which I did not know.
~Marion Milner

A day of unselfish purpose is always a day of confident hope.
~Woodrow Wilson

Let how you live your life stand for something, no matter how small and incidental it may seem.
~Jodie Foster

Life is beautiful. He who reads that As in the window of some distant, speeding train Knows what he wants, and what will befall.
~John Ashbery

The purpose of our lives is to give birth to the best which is within us.
~Marianne Williamson

You are only as strong as your purpose, therefore let us choose reasons to act that are big, bold, righteous, and eternal.
~Barry Munro

If there is a purpose in life at all, there must be a purpose in suffering and in dying. But no man can tell another what this purpose is. . . . If he succeeds he will continue to grow in spite of all indignities.
~Gordon W. Allport

A rock pile ceases to be a rock pile the moment a single man contemplates it, bearing within him the image of a cathedral.
~Antoine de Saint-Exupéry

Give me matter, and I will construct a world out of it!
~Immanuel Kant

Nothing contributes so much to tranquilize the mind as a steady purpose—a point on which the soul may fix its intellectual eye.
~Mary Shelley

The idea is to seek a vision that gives you purpose in life and then to implement that vision.
~Lewis P. Johnson

It isn't common ground that bonds people together, it's higher ground.
~Tom Brown

We all need to believe in what we are doing.
~Allan D. Gilmour

I am not afraid. . . . I was born to do this.
~Joan of Arc

Those who wander are not necessarily lost.
~Joseph Stein

Down deep in every human heart is a hidden longing, impulse, and ambition to do something fine and enduring.
~Grenville Kleiser

Don't be pushed by your problems. Be led by your dreams.
~Ralph Waldo Emerson

The two most important days in your life are the day you are born and the day you find out why.
~Mark Twain

Living with purpose is more a question of what we put in than what we take out.
~Howard Barnes

It is not enough to be busy; so are the ants. The question is: What are we busy about?
~Henry David Thoreau

Whenever I get to a low point, I go back to the basics. I ask myself, "Why am I doing this?" It comes down to passion.
~Lyn St. James

To love what you are doing. To believe in what you are doing. To know what you are doing. These are the three essentials.

~Steve Musseau

Here's a test to find whether your mission on Earth is finished: If you're alive, it isn't.

~Richard Bach

Be ashamed to die until you have won some victory for humanity.

~Horace Mann

There is a place here that only you can fill.

~Michael McLean

As I continued upward, I saw my life as a whole. . . . It was simply this: I was meant for a long, hard climb.

~Lance Armstrong

Continuity of purpose is one of the most essential ingredients of happiness in the long run, and for most men this comes chiefly through their work.

~Bertrand Russell

The happiest excitement in life is to be convinced that one is fighting for all one is worth on behalf of some clearly seen and deeply felt good.

~Ruth Benedict

What's the subject of life—to get rich? All of those fellows out there getting rich could be dancing around the real subject of life.

~Paul A. Volcker

Act as if what you do makes a difference. It does.

~William James

You were placed on this earth to create, not to compete.

~Robert Anthony

Pursuit

An object in possession seldom retains the same charm that it had in pursuit.

~Pliny the Elder

Quality

Quality is never an accident. It is always the result of intelligent effort.

~John Ruskin

It is quality rather than quantity that matters.
~Lucius Annaeus Seneca

Quality begins on the inside . . . then works its way out.
~Bob Moawad

The secret of success is to do the common things uncommonly well.
~John D. Rockefeller Jr.

Quality never goes out of style.

~Levi Strauss

Quantity

It is quality rather than quantity that matters.
~Lucius Annaeus Seneca

Question

The only questions that really matter are the ones you ask yourself.
~Ursula K. Le Guin

Judge a man by his questions rather than his answers.

~Voltaire

The common question that gets asked in business is, "Why?" That's a good question, but an equally valid question is, "Why not?"

~Jeff Bezos

Never be afraid to ask a question, especially of yourself. Discovery is the mission of life.

~Brian Kates

Quiet

To create you must quiet your mind. You need a quiet mind so that ideas will have a chance of connecting.

~Eric Maisel

Blessed is the man who, having nothing to say, abstains from giving us wordy evidence of the fact.

~George Eliot

There is no greater agony than bearing an untold story inside you.
~Maya Angelou

Quitting

Don't give up. Don't lose hope. Don't sell out.

~Christopher Reeve

Nothing could be worse than the fear that one had given up too soon, and left one unexpended effort that might have saved the world.

~Jane Addams

Our greatest weakness lies in giving up. The most certain way to succeed is always to try just one more time.

~Thomas A. Edison

Being defeated is often a temporary condition. Giving up is what makes it permanent.

~Marilyn vos Savant

You do what you can for as long as you can, and when you finally can't you do the next best thing. You back up, but you don't give up.

~Chuck Yeager

If you fell down yesterday, stand up today.

~H. G. Wells

A man is not finished when he is defeated. He is finished when he quits.

~Richard M. Nixon

Ninety percent of all those who fail are not actually defeated. They simply quit.

~Paul J. Meyer

Reaction

It's not what happens to you, but how you react to it that matters.

~Epictetus

Reading

That is a good book which is opened with expectation and closed with delight and profit.

~Amos Bronson Alcott

I read my eyes out and can't read half enough . . . the more one reads, the more one sees we have to read.

~John Adams

When I read a book I seem to read it with my eyes only, but now and then I come across a passage, perhaps only a phrase, which has a meaning for me, and it becomes part of me.

~W. Somerset Maugham

There is a great deal of difference between an eager man who wants to read a book and the tired man who wants a book to read.

~G. K. Chesterton

Employ your time in improving yourself by other men's writings so that you shall gain easily by what others have labored hard for.

~Socrates

The man who does not read good books has no advantage over the man who cannot read them.

~Mark Twain

We read to train the mind, to fill the mind, to rest the mind, to recreate the mind, or to escape the mind.

~Holbrook Jackson

Since it is so likely that [children] will meet cruel enemies, let them at least have heard of brave knights and heroic courage. Otherwise you are making their destiny not brighter but darker.

~C. S. Lewis

Much reading is like much eating—wholly useless without diges-tion.

~Robert South

Reality

Reality is that which, when you stop believing in it, doesn't go away.

~Philip K. Dick

Realism . . . has no more to do with reality than anything else.
~Hob Broun

Grasp at the shadow and lose the substance.

~Aesop

You can avoid reality, but you cannot avoid the consequences of avoiding reality.

~Ayn Rand

Dream passionate dreams. Design their reality.
~Candis Fancher

Keep your eyes on the stars, and your feet on the ground.
~Theodore Roosevelt

Reality was such a jungle—with no signposts, landmarks, or boundaries.

~Helen Hayes

My dreams have become puny with the reality my life has become.
~Imelda Marcos

If you understand, things are just as they are; if you do not under-stand, things are just as they are.

~Zen Proverb

Reality is something you rise above.

~Liza Minelli

The difference between fiction and reality? Fiction has to make sense.

~Tom Clancy

Set up as an ideal the facing of reality as honestly and as cheerfully as possible.

~Karl Menninger

When you jump for joy, beware that no one moves the ground from beneath your feet.

~Stanisław Jerzy Lec

Receive

There is a very real relationship, both quantitatively and qualitatively, between what you contribute and what you get out of this world.

~Oscar Hammerstein II

Refinement

There is nothing so catching as refinement.

~Emily Eden

Reflection

A loving person lives in a loving world. A hostile person lives in a hostile world: everyone you meet is your mirror.

~Ken Keyes Jr.

Reflection is the beginning of reform.

~Mark Twain

Regret

Accept the pain, cherish the joys, resolve the regrets; then can come the best of benedictions — "If I had my life to live over, I'd do it all the same."

~Joan McIntosh

I'd rather regret the things I've done than regret the things I haven't done.

~Lucille Ball

A year from now you will wish you had started today.

~Karen Lamb

We might have been — these are but common words, and yet they make the sum of life's bewailing.

~Letitia Landon

Regret for the things we did can be tempered by time; it is regret for the things we did not do that is inconsolable.

~Sydney J. Harris

Relationships

Coming together is a beginning. Keeping together is progress. Working together is success.

~Henry Ford

I look upon every day to be lost, in which I do not make a new acquaintance.

~Samuel Johnson

The best thing to hold onto in life is each other.

~Audrey Hepburn

You cannot shake hands with a clenched fist.

~Indira Gandhi

Associate yourself with men of good quality, if you esteem your own reputation; for 'tis better to be alone than in bad company.

~George Washington

I love mankind — it's people I can't stand.

~Charles Schulz

When we seek for connection, we restore the world to wholeness. Our seemingly separate lives become meaningful as we discover how truly necessary we are to each other.

~Margaret Wheatley

In many ways the saying "Know thyself" is lacking. Better to know other people.

~Menander

The acceptance of the truth that joy and sorrow, laughter and tears are not confined to any particular time, place or people, but are universally distributed, should make us more tolerant of and more interested in the lives of others.

~William M. Peck

Get a life in which you are not alone. Find people you love, and who love you. And remember that love is not leisure, it is work.

~Anna Quindlen

There are people who take the heart out of you, and there are people who put it back.

~Elizabeth David

I have found out that there ain't no surer way to find out whether you like people or hate them than to travel with them.

~Mark Twain

Too often we underestimate the power of a touch, a smile, a kind word, a listening ear, an honest compliment, or the smallest act of caring, all of which have the potential to turn a life around.

~Leo Buscaglia

Those who are not looking for happiness are the most likely to find it, because those who are searching forget that the surest way to be happy is to seek happiness for others.

~Martin Luther King Jr.

Things are temporary, relationships last forever. Nothing can re-place the time we spend investing in the life of another.

~Roy Lessin

Be who you are and say what you feel, because those who mind don't matter, and those who matter don't mind.

~Bernard Baruch

Really listening and suspending one's own judgment is necessary in order to understand other people on their own terms. . . . This is a process that requires trust and builds trust.

~Mary Field Belenky

I don't believe an accident of birth makes people sisters or brothers. It makes them siblings, gives them mutuality of parentage. Sisterhood and brotherhood is a condition people have to work at.

~Maya Angelou

If you make it plain you like people, it's hard for them to resist liking you back.

~Lois McMaster Bujold

When you make a commitment to a relationship, you invest your attention and energy in it more profoundly because you now experience ownership of that relationship.

~Barbara De Angelis

One of the most time-consuming things is to have an enemy.

~E. B. White

The most perfect expression of human behavior is a string quartet.

~Jeffrey Tate

The only normal people are the ones you don't know very well.

~Alfred Adler

The eyes of other people are the eyes that ruin us. If all but myself were blind, I should want neither fine clothes, fine houses, nor fine furniture.

~Benjamin Franklin

The human heart, at whatever age, opens only to the heart that opens in return.

~Maria Edgeworth

Loyalty, friendship, family ties, the duty owed to an ideal—in our time, these obligations seem to have lost their force as motivators and connectors.

~Elizabeth Janeway

The royal road to a man's heart is to talk to him about the things he treasures most.

~Dale Carnegie

To understand the true quality of people, you must look into their minds, and examine their pursuits and aversions.

~Marcus Aurelius

Relaxation

People would have more leisure time if it weren't for all the leisure-time activities that use it up.

~Peg Bracken

Man is so made that he can only find relaxation from one kind of labor by taking up another.

~Anatole France

A day's work is a day's work, neither more nor less, and the man who does it needs a day's sustenance, a night's repose, and due leisure, whether he be painter or ploughman.

~George Bernard Shaw

Remember

May I forget what ought to be forgotten; and recall, unfailing, all that ought to be recalled, each kindly thing, forgetting what might sting.

~Mary Caroline Davies

We do not remember days, we remember moments.

~Cesare Pavese

If you tell the truth, you don't have to remember anything.

~Mark Twain

How we remember, what we remember, and why we remember form the most personal map of our individuality.

~Christina Baldwin

In the end, we will remember not the words of our enemies, but the silence of our friends.

~Martin Luther King Jr.

Reputation

Begin somewhere; you cannot build a reputation on what you intend to do.

~Liz Smith

Associate yourself with men of good quality, if you esteem your own reputation; for 'tis better to be alone than in bad company.

~George Washington

Your net worth to the world is usually determined by what remains after your bad habits are subtracted from your good ones.

~Benjamin Franklin

Resistance

The chief pang of most trials is not so much the actual suffering itself as our own spirit of resistance to it.

~Jean Nicolas Grou

Reputation is what other people know about you. Honor is what you know about yourself.

~Lois McMaster Bujold

Resolute

Never grow a wishbone, daughter, where your backbone ought to be.

~Clementine Paddleford

If they don't stand for something, they will fall for anything.

~Gordon A. Eadie

Respect

Respect yourself if you would have others respect you.

~Baltasar Gracián y Morales

Be modest, be respectful of others, try to understand.

~Lakhdar Brahimi

He removes the greatest ornament of friendship who takes away from it respect.

~Marcus Tullius Cicero

Everyone should be respected as an individual, but no one idolized.
~Albert Einstein

I got a simple rule about everybody. If you don't treat me right—shame on you!

~Louis Armstrong

Knowledge will give you power, but character respect.
~Bruce Lee

One of the most sincere forms of respect is actually listening to what another has to say.
~Bryant H. McGill

Silence may be golden, but can you think of a better way to entertain someone than to listen to him?
~Brigham Young

The basic difference between being assertive and being aggressive is how our words and behavior affect the rights and well-being of others.
~Sharon Anthony Bower

Responsibility

You are responsible for your life. You can't keep blaming somebody else for your dysfunction. Life is really about moving on.
~Oprah Winfrey

What I must do is all that concerns me, not what the people think.
~Ralph Waldo Emerson

Things turn out for the best for those who make the best of the way things turn out.
~John Wooden

Each of us must work for his own improvement, and at the same time share a general responsibility for all humanity.
~Marie Curie

Perhaps it is better to be irresponsible and right, than to be responsible and wrong.
~Winston Churchill

There's an old saying that victory has 100 fathers and defeat is an orphan.

~John F. Kennedy

If you are to be, you must begin by assuming responsibility. You alone are responsible for every moment of your life, for every one of your acts.

~Antoine de Saint-Exupéry

One's philosophy is not best expressed in words; it is expressed in the choices one makes. In the long run, we shape our lives, and we shape ourselves. The process never ends until we die. And the choices we make are ultimately our own responsibility.

~Eleanor Roosevelt

Having family responsibilities and concerns just has to make you a more understanding person.

~Sandra Day O'Connor

Responsibility is the price of freedom.

~Elbert Hubbard

Seven national crimes: 1. I don't think. 2. I don't know. 3. I don't care. 4. I am too busy. 5. I leave well enough alone. 6. I have no time to read and find out. 7. I am not interested.

~William J. H. Boetcker

An individual without information can't take responsibility. An individual with information can't help but take responsibility.

~Jan Carlzon

There is always room for those who can be relied upon to deliver the goods when they say they will.

~Napoleon Hill

Rest

A day's work is a day's work, neither more nor less, and the man who does it needs a day's sustenance, a night's repose, and due leisure, whether he be painter or ploughman.

~George Bernard Shaw

Take rest; a field that has rested gives a bountiful crop.

~Ovid

Slowing down is sometimes the best way to speed up.
~Mike Vance

If the pace and the push, the noise and the crowds are getting to you, it's time to stop the nonsense and find a place of solace to refresh your spirit.

~Charles Swindoll

True silence is the rest of the mind; and is to the spirit what sleep is to the body, nourishment and refreshment.

~William Penn

Results

Happy people plan actions, they don't plan results.
~Denis Waitley

The greatest results in life are usually attained by simple means and the exercise of ordinary qualities. These may for the most part be summed in these two—common sense and perseverance.
~Owen Feltham

Results! Why man, I have gotten a lot of results. I know several thousand things that won't work.

~Thomas Edison

Retirement

Don't simply retire from something; have something to retire to.
~Harry Emerson Fosdick

Revenge

Never does the human soul appear so strong and noble as when it forgoes revenge, and dares to forgive an injury.
~Edwin Hubbell Chapin

Retribution often means that we eventually do to ourselves what we have done unto others.

~Eric Hoffer

Reward

Believe me, the reward is not so great without the struggle.

~Wilma Rudolph

The highest reward for man's toil is not what he gets for it but what he becomes by it.

~John Ruskin

Right

To see what is right and not to do it is want of courage, or of principle.

~Confucius

I have to be wrong a certain number of times in order to be right a certain number of times. However, in order to be either, I must first make a decision.

~Frank N. Giampietro

The truth of the matter is that you always know the right thing to do. The hard part is doing it.

~Norman Schwarzkopf

Love all, trust a few, do wrong to none.

~William Shakespeare

We must use time creatively—and forever realize that the time is always hope to do right.

~Martin Luther King Jr.

Sometimes things can go right only by first going very wrong.

~Edward Tenner

Whoever claims a right for himself must respect the like right in another.

~James Bryce

Always do right. This will gratify some people, and astonish the rest.

~Mark Twain

Management is doing things right; leadership is doing the right things.

~Peter Drucker

You cannot make yourself feel something you do not feel, but you can make yourself do right in spite of your feelings.

~Pearl S. Buck

As a family, we had a code, which was to do the right thing, do it the best we could, never complain and never take advantage.

~Margaret Truman

Perhaps it is better to be irresponsible and right, than to be responsible and wrong.

~Winston Churchill

Stand with anybody that stands right. Stand with him while he is right and part with him when he goes wrong.

~Abraham Lincoln

The difference between the almost right word and the right word is really a large matter. 'Tis the difference between lightning bug and the lightning.

~Mark Twain

What is right to be done cannot be done too soon.

~Jane Austen

What's right is what's left if you do everything else wrong.

~Robin Williams

Risk

Behold the turtle. He makes progress only when he sticks his neck out.

~James B. Conant

To conquer without risk is to triumph without glory.

~Pierre Corneille

Be brave. Take risks. Nothing can substitute experience.

~Paulo Coelho

What you risk reveals what you value.
~Jeanette Winterson

Jump, and you will find out how to unfold your wings as you fall.
~Ray Bradbury

You've got to go out on a limb sometimes because that's where the fruit is.
~Will Rogers

There's no such thing as "zero risk."
~William Driver

Romance

Is not this the true romantic feeling; not to desire to escape life, but to prevent life from escaping you.
~Thomas Wolfe

In a great romance, each person basically plays a part that the other one really likes.
~Elizabeth Ashley

Roots

It isn't where you come from; it's where you're going that counts.
~Ella Fitzgerald

Routine

We are often imprisoned in the cage of our own abilities and routines, which provides us with a sense of security.
~Alice Miller

Because of the routines we follow, we often forget that life is an ongoing adventure.
~Maya Angelou

Rules

The young man knows the rules but the old man knows the exceptions.

~Oliver Wendell Holmes

Sacrifice

To gain that which is worth having, it may be necessary to lose everything else.

~Bernadette Devlin

In order to live free and happily you must sacrifice boredom. It is not always an easy sacrifice.

~Richard Bach

In this life we get only those things for which we hunt, for which we strive, and for which we are willing to sacrifice.

~George Matthew Adams

The important thing is this: to be able at any moment to sacrifice what we are for what we could become.

~Charles Du Bos

Sadness

Human pain does not let go of its grip at one point in time. Rather, it works its way out of our consciousness over time. There is a season of sadness. A season of anger. A season of tranquility. A season of hope.

~Robert Veninga

The soul would have no rainbow, had the eyes no tears.
~John Vance Cheney

One must not let oneself be overwhelmed by sadness.
~Jackie Kennedy

A face that cannot smile is like a bud that cannot blossom and dries up in the stalk.

~Henry Ward Beecher

Safety

A harbor, even if it is a little harbor, is a good thing . . . it takes something from the world, and has something to give in return.
~Sarah Orne Jewett

Avoiding danger is no safer in the long run than outright exposure. The fearful are caught as often as the bold.
~Helen Keller

Satisfaction

You can never get enough of what you don't need, because what you don't need won't satisfy you.
~Dallin H. Oaks

If I have a thousand ideas and only one turns out to be good, I am satisfied.
~Alfred Nobel

The amount of satisfaction you get from life depends largely on your own ingenuity, self-sufficiency, and resourcefulness. People who wait around for life to supply their satisfaction usually find boredom instead.
~William Menninger

Happiness does not come from doing easy work but from the afterglow of satisfaction that comes after the achievement of a difficult task that demanded our best.
~Theodore Isaac Rubin

Search

Often the search proves more profitable than the goal.
~E. L. Konigsburg

Secrets

Everything secret degenerates, even the administration of justice; nothing is safe that does not show how it can bear discussion and publicity.
~John Emerich Edward Dalberg-Acton

A photograph is a secret about a secret, the more it tells you the less you know.

~Diane Arbus

Three may keep a secret, if two of them are dead.

~Benjamin Franklin

Security

We are often imprisoned in the cage of our own abilities and routines, which provides us with a sense of security.

~Alice Miller

Security represents your sense of worth, your identity, your emotional anchorage, your self-esteem, your basic personal strength or lack of it.

~Stephen Covey

Self

There's only one corner of the universe you can be certain of improving, and that's your own self.

~Aldous Huxley

We are all apt to believe what the world believes about us.

~George Eliot

Employ your time in improving yourself by other men's writings so that you shall gain easily by what others have labored hard for.

~Socrates

Be faithful to that which exists nowhere but in yourself.

~André Gide

We must not allow other people's limited perceptions to define us.

~Virginia Satir

Everybody must learn this lesson somewhere—that it cost something to be what you are.

~Shirley Abbott

Be who you are and say what you feel, because those who mind don't matter, and those who matter don't mind.

~Bernard Baruch

We can be sure that the greatest hope for maintaining equilibrium in the face of any situation rests within ourselves.
~Francis J. Braceland

We are often imprisoned in the cage of our own abilities and routines, which provides us with a sense of security.
~Alice Miller

We are cups, constantly and quietly being filled. The trick is, knowing how to tip ourselves over and let the beautiful stuff out.
~Ray Bradbury

Self-Care

Don't deny your basic needs . . . Find ways to incorporate these necessary functions into even the busiest schedule.
~Stephanie Goddard Davidson

The key is to keep company only with people who uplift you, whose presence calls forth your best.
~Epictetus

Self-Centered

It is the individual who is not interested in his fellow men who has the greatest difficulties in life and provides the greatest injury to others. It is from among such individuals that all human failures spring.
~Alfred Adler

What we have done for ourselves alone dies with us; what we have done for others and the world remains and is immortal.
~Albert Pike

I looked always outside of myself to see what I could make the world give me instead of looking within myself to see what was there.
~Belle Livingstone

Self-Confidence

It is unwise to be too sure of one's own wisdom. It is healthy to be reminded that the strongest might weaken and the wisest might err.

~Mohandas K. Gandhi

Better to be despised for too anxious apprehensions, than ruined by too confident security.

~Edmund Burke

Belief in oneself is one of the most important bricks in building any successful venture.

~Lydia Maria Child

Getting ahead in a difficult profession requires avid faith in yourself. That is why some people with mediocre talent, but with a great inner drive, go much farther than people with vastly superior talent.

~Sophia Loren

Have confidence that if you have done a little thing well, you can do a bigger thing well, too.

~David Storey

No one can make you feel inferior without your consent.

~Eleanor Roosevelt

One important key to success is self-confidence. An important key to self-confidence is preparation.

~Arthur Ashe

Never explain—your friends do not need it and your enemies will not believe you anyway.

~Elbert Hubbard

Trust your hunches. They're usually based on facts filed away just below the conscious level.

~Joyce Brothers

To live a creative life, we must lose our fear of being wrong.

~Joseph Chilton Pearce

Self-Conscious

We would worry less about what others think of us, if we realized how seldom they do.

~Ethel Barrett

Did you ever see an unhappy horse? Did you ever see a bird that had the blues? One reason why birds and horses are not unhappy is because they are not trying to impress other birds and horses.

~Dale Carnegie

I envy paranoids; they actually feel people are paying attention to them.

~Susan Sontag

Self-Control

Man seems to be capable of great virtues but not of small virtues; capable of defying his torturer but not of keeping his temper.

~G. K. Chesterton

To control our passions we must govern our habits, and keep watch over ourselves in the small details of everyday life.

~Sir John Lubbock

He that hath no rule over his own spirit is like a city that is broken down and without walls.

~Taylor Caldwell

Rule your mind or it will rule you.

~Horace

Silence is the great teacher, and to learn its lessons you must pay attention to it. There is no substitute for the creative inspiration, knowledge, and stability that come from knowing how to contact your core of inner silence.

~Deepak Chopra

Good temper, like a sunny day, sheds a brightness over everything; it is the sweetener of toil and the soother of disquietude.

~Washington Irving

If we are not responsible for the thoughts that pass our doors, we are at least responsible for those we admit and entertain.
~Charles B. Newcomb

To be elated at success and disappointed at failure is to be the child of circumstances; how can such a one be called master of himself?
~Chinese Proverb

There are more quarrels smothered by just shutting your mouth, and holding it shut, than by all the wisdom in the world.
~Henry Ward Beecher

Nothing gives one person so much advantage over another as to remain always cool and unruffled under all circumstances.
~Thomas Jefferson

The tongue is the only instrument that gets sharper with use.
~Washington Irving

Self-Discipline

Character contributes to beauty. It fortifies a woman as her youth fades. A mode of conduct, a standard of courage, discipline, fortitude, and integrity can do a great deal to make a woman beautiful.
~Jacqueline Bisset

Each day, and the living of it, has to be a conscious creation in which discipline and order are relieved with some play and pure foolishness.
~May Sarton

Be vigilant; guard your mind against negative thoughts.
~Buddha

Class is an aura of confidence that is being sure without being cocky. Class has nothing to do with money. Class never runs scared. It is self-discipline and self-knowledge. It's the sure-footedness that comes with having proved you can meet life.
~Ann Landers

Self-Discovery

The secret of concentration is the secret of self-discovery. You reach inside yourself to discover your personal resources, and what it takes to match them to the challenge.

~Arnold Palmer

Day after day, we discover our own lives. Because we never know what we will find, every discovery is an unexpected gift we give to ourselves.

~Barbara J. Esbensen

The greatest thing is, at any moment, to be willing to give up who we are in order to become all that we can become.

~Max De Pree

I was always looking outside myself for strength and confidence, but it comes from within. It is there all the time.

~Anna Freud

No one can really predict to what heights you might soar. Even you will not know until you spread your wings.

~Gil Atkinson

We all have many gifts that we've never opened. It's time to open some of yours. Find your wings.

~Dan Zadra

Every one of us has in himself a continent of undiscovered character. Happy is he who acts the Columbus to his own soul.

~Sir J. Stevens

You have got to discover you, what you do, and trust it.

~Barbra Streisand

Self-Esteem

Outstanding leaders go out of the way to boost the self-esteem of their personnel. If people believe in themselves, it's amazing what they can accomplish.

~Sam Walton

The only way to get positive feelings about yourself is to take positive actions. Man does not live as he thinks, he thinks as he lives.
~Vaughan Quinn

Self-Examination

Open your eyes, look within. Are you satisfied with the life you're living?
~Bob Marley

Look within, for within is the wellspring of virtue, which will not cease flowing, if you cease not from digging.
~Marcus Aurelius

Don't be humble. You're not that great.
~Golda Meir

Re-examine all that you have been told . . . dismiss that which insults your own soul.
~Walt Whitman

If one is out of touch with oneself, then one cannot touch others.
~Anne Morrow Lindbergh

The self-explorer, whether he wants to or not, becomes the explorer of everything else.
~Elias Canetti

The aim of life is self-development. To realize one's nature perfectly—that is what each of us is here for.
~Oscar Wilde

Self-Image

Our self-image and our habits tend to go together. Change one and you will automatically change the other.
~Maxwell Maltz

A strong, positive self-image is the best possible preparation for success.
~Joyce Brothers

The kinds of people who can go on to greater emotional maturity are those who really like themselves, even if the world seems to turn against them.
~Theodore Irwin

What you think of yourself is much more important than what others think of you.
~Lucius Annaeus Seneca

It's not what you are that holds us back, it's what you think you are not.
~Denis Waitley

I believe it is in my nature to dance by virtue of the beat of my heart, the pulse of my blood, and the music in my mind.
~Robert Fulghum

No man is happy who does not think himself so.
~Marcus Aurelius

The ablest man I ever met is the man you think you are.
~Franklin D. Roosevelt

Never be bullied into silence. Never allow yourself to be made a victim. Accept no one's definition of your life, but define yourself.
~Harvey Fierstein

Self-Knowledge

The highest purpose of intellectual cultivation is to give a man a perfect knowledge and mastery of his own inner self.
~Novalis

There is more inside you than you dare think.
~David Brower

The more faithfully you listen to the voices within you, the better you will hear what is sounding outside.
~Dag Hammarskjöld

Once we know our weaknesses they cease to do us any harm.
~Georg Christoph Lichtenberg

Go to your bosom; Knock there, and ask your heart what it doth know.

~William Shakespeare

Curious things, habits. People themselves never knew they had them.

~Agatha Christie

This above all: to thine own self be true, And it must follow, as the night the day, Thou canst not then be false to any man.

~William Shakespeare

One should always act from one's inner sense of rhythm.

~Rosamond Lehmann

The man with insight enough to admit his limitations comes nearest to perfection.

~Johann Wolfgang von Goethe

Self-Love

It is man's foremost duty to awaken the understanding of the inner Self and to know his own real inner greatness. Once he knows his true worth, he can know the worth of others.

~Swami Muktananda

Self-Pity

There ain't no free lunches in this country. And don't go spending your whole life commiserating that you got raw deals. You've got to say, "I think that if I keep working at this and want it bad enough I can have it."

~Lee Iacocca

No one who cannot rejoice in the discovery of his own mistakes deserves to be called a scholar.

~Donald Foster

Self-Sufficiency

Don't expect anyone else to support you. Maybe you have a trust fund. Maybe you'll have a wealthy spouse. But you never know when either one might run out.

~Mary Schmich

Self-Talk

Make it a point to rid your speech and thoughts of all forms of negative self-talk.

~Karl Albrecht

Self-Worth

He who undervalues himself is justly undervalued by others.
~William Hazlitt

There has never been another you.

~Dan Zadra

Realize how good you really are.

~Og Mandino

To have that sense of one's intrinsic worth which constitutes self-respect is potentially to have everything.

~Joan Didion

The best thing you have to offer the world is yourself. You don't have to copy anyone else. If you do, you're second best. To achieve success is to be first, and that's being yourself.

~John Denver

Security represents your sense of worth, your identity, your emotional anchorage, your self-esteem, your basic personal strength or lack of it.

~Stephen Covey

One of the things I learned the hard way was that it doesn't pay to get discouraged. Keeping busy and making optimism a way of life can restore your faith in yourself.

~Lucille Ball

Selfish

I looked always outside of myself to see what I could make the world give me instead of looking within myself to see what was there.
~Belle Livingstone

Selfishness is not living as one wishes to live, it is asking others to live as one wishes to live.

~Oscar Wilde

I think we have one foot in heaven and the other on the banana peel of self-interest.

~Lawrence W. Bash

Servanthood

To serve is beautiful, but only if it is done with joy and a whole heart and a free mind.

~Pearl S. Buck

Only those who have learned the power of sincere and selfless contribution experience life's deepest joy: true fulfillment.

~Tony Robbins

Life's most persistent and urgent question is, "What are you doing for others?"

~Martin Luther King Jr.

The more you learn what to do with yourself, and the more you do for others, the more you will learn to enjoy the abundant life.

~William Boetcker

Provision for others is a fundamental responsibility of human life.

~Woodrow Wilson

It is one of the most beautiful compensations of this life that no man can sincerely try to help another without helping himself.

~Ralph Waldo Emerson

What we have done for ourselves alone dies with us; what we have done for others and the world remains and is immortal.

~Albert Pike

Dedicate some of your life to others. Your dedication will not be a sacrifice. It will be an exhilarating experience because it is intense effort applied toward a meaningful end.

~Thomas Dooley

It is high time that the ideal of success should be replaced with the ideal of service.

~Albert Einstein

If we all tried to make other people's paths easy, our own feet would have a smooth even place to walk on.

~Myrtle Reed

Make finding a solution and improving your service a higher priority than placing blame.

~Cathy Harrington

The essential difference in service is not machines or things. The essential difference is minds, hearts, spirits, and souls.

~Herb Kelleher

One of the things I keep learning is that the secret to being happy is doing things for other people.

~Dick Gregory

The greatest comfort of my old age, . . . is the pleasing remembrance of the many benefits and friendly offices I have done to others.

~Marcus Cato

Unless we think of others and do something for them, we miss one of the greatest sources of happiness.

~Ray Lyman Wilbur

Sow good services: sweet remembrances will grow from them.

~Madame de Staël

The pleasure we derive from doing favors is party in the feeling it gives us that we are not altogether worthless. It is a pleasant surprise to ourselves.

~Eric Hoffer

Do not wait for leaders; do it alone, person to person.

~Mother Teresa

You begin saving the world by saving one man at a time; all else is grandiose romanticism or politics.

~Charles Bukowski

Our work-a-day lives are filled with opportunities to bless others. The power of a single glance or an encouraging smile must never be underestimated.

~G. Richard Rieger

It is literally true that you can succeed best and quickest by helping others to succeed.

~Napoleon Hill

Shame

Be ashamed to die until you have won some victory for humanity.
~Horace Mann

Shelter

A harbor, even if it is a little harbor, is a good thing . . . it takes something from the world, and has something to give in return.
~Sarah Orne Jewett

Shortcuts

There are no shortcuts to any place worth going.

~Beverly Sills

Silence

The temple of our purest thoughts is silence.
~Sarah Josepha Hale

There are more quarrels smothered by just shutting your mouth, and holding it shut, than by all the wisdom in the world.
~Henry Ward Beecher

Think twice before you speak, because your words and influence will plant the seed of either success or failure in the mind of another.

~Napoleon Hill

Well-timed silence hath more eloquence than speech.
~Martin Farquhar Tupper

There are times when silence has the loudest voice.
~Leroy Brownlow

Not merely an absence of noise, Real Silence begins when a reasonable being withdraws from the noise in order to find peace and order in his inner sanctuary.
~Peter Minard

True silence is the rest of the mind; and is to the spirit what sleep is to the body, nourishment and refreshment.
~William Penn

Simplicity

Simplicity is the ultimate sophistication.
~Leonardo da Vinci

It is the sweet, simple things of life which are the real ones after all.
~Laura Ingalls Wilder

The ability to simplify means to eliminate the unnecessary so that the necessary may speak.
~Hans Hoffman

The ordinary acts we practice every day at home are of more importance to the soul than their simplicity might suggest.
~Thomas Moore

Fishing is much more than fish. It is the great occasion when we may return to the fine simplicity of our forefathers.
~Herbert Hoover

The greatest truths are the simplest; and so are the greatest men.
~Julius C. Hare

Sin

I will write of him who fights and vanquishes his sins, who struggles on through weary years against himself . . . and wins.
~Caroline Begelow LeRow

Sincerity

The most exhausting thing in life is being insincere.
~Anne Morrow Lindbergh

It is one of the most beautiful compensations of this life that no man can sincerely try to help another without helping himself.
~Ralph Waldo Emerson

Civility is not a sign of weakness, and sincerity is always subject to proof.
~John F. Kennedy

It's amazing how much you can learn if your intentions are truly earnest.
~Chuck Berry

If you have sincerity, all other things will be added to you.
~A. S. Neill

No man can produce great things who is not thoroughly sincere in dealing with himself.
~James Russell Lowell

Sincerity is impossible, unless it pervades the whole being, and the pretence of it saps the very foundation of character.
~James Russell Lowell

Sincerity makes the very least person to be of more value than the most talented hypocrite.
~Charles H. Spurgeon

Sincerity is like traveling on a plain, beaten road, which commonly brings a man sooner to his journey's end than byways, in which men often lose themselves.
~John Tillotson

Sing

Those who wish to sing always find a song.
~Swedish Proverb

Sleep

One hour's sleep before midnight is worth three after.
~George Herbert

There will be enough sleeping in the grave.
~Benjamin Franklin

Smile

I think that anybody that smiles automatically looks better.
~Diane Lane

If you're not using your smile, you're like a man with a million dollars in the bank and no checkbook.
~Les Giblin

A smile is happiness you'll find right under your nose.
~Tom Wilson

If the world's a vale of tears, Smile, till rainbows span it.
~Lucy Larcom

A warm smile is the universal language of kindness.
~William Arthur Ward

Let us always meet each other with smile, for the smile is the beginning of love.
~Mother Teresa

Because of your smile, you make life more beautiful.
~Thich Nhat Hanh

What's the use of worrying? It never was worthwhile, so, pack up your troubles in your kit-bag and smile, smile, smile.
~George Henry Powell

Society

Where the habits are simple, and the mind truly elevated, then is society in the best state.
~Mary Martha Sherwood

If a free society cannot help the many who are poor, it cannot save the few who are rich.

~John F. Kennedy

No one can be perfectly free till all are free; no one can be perfectly moral till all are moral; no one can be perfectly happy till all are happy.

~Herbert Spencer

We've got to recognize that we are not working (primarily) for a peaceful world. Peace will be a by-product of something else. We are working for a world of justice and rightness. Peace is a by-product of justice and mercy.

~Stanley High

Injustice anywhere is a threat to justice everywhere.

~Martin Luther King Jr.

A people that values its privileges above its principles soon loses both.

~Dwight D. Eisenhower

Among a people generally corrupt, liberty cannot long exist.

~Edmund Burke

A society grows great when old men plant trees whose shade they know they shall never sit in.

~Greek Proverb

Society produces technology and technology produces society in an endless mesh of action and interaction.

~Kenneth E. Boulding

The fountains are with the rich, but they are no better than a stagnant pool till they flow in streams to the labouring people.

~Catharine Maria Sedgwick

The superior man is easy to serve, but difficult to please. . . . The inferior man is, on the other hand, difficult to serve, but easy to please.

~Confucius

The progression or emancipation of any class usually, if not always, takes place through the efforts of individuals of that class.

~Harriet Martineau

So long as little children are allowed to suffer, there is no true love in this world.
~Isadora Duncan

A society can be no better than the men and women who compose it.
~Adlai E. Stevenson

Whoever claims a right for himself must respect the like right in another.
~James Bryce

There is no such thing as "them and us." In a world this size there can only be "we" — all of us working together.
~Don Ward

I look upon every day to be lost, in which I do not make a new acquaintance.
~Samuel Johnson

Injustice anywhere is a threat to justice everywhere.
~Martin Luther King Jr.

It is the dull man who is always sure, and the sure man who is always dull.
~H. L. Mencken

We cannot live only for ourselves. A thousand fibers connect us with our fellow man.
~Herman Melville

[Only by] the good influence of our conduct may we bring salvation in human affairs.
~Desiderius Erasmus

Provision for others is a fundamental responsibility of human life.
~Woodrow Wilson

It is easy in the world to live after the world's opinion; it is easy in solitude to live after our own; but the great man is he who in the midst of the crowd keeps with perfect sweetness the independence of solitude.
~Ralph Waldo Emerson

The saddest aspect of life right now is that science gathers knowledge faster than society gathers wisdom.

~Isaac Asimov

All that is necessary for the triumph of evil is that good men do nothing.

~Edmund Burke

Solitude

I lived in solitude in the country and noticed how the monotony of a quiet life stimulates the creative mind.

~Albert Einstein

Solitude is as needful to the imagination as society is wholesome for the character.

~James Russell Lowell

Sorrow

Cast away care, he that loves sorrow lengthens not a day, nor can buy tomorrow.

~Thomas Dekker

At night, when heavenly peace is flying Above the world that sorrow mars, Ah, think not of my grave with sighing! For then I greet you from the stars.

~Annette von Droste-Hülshoff

There's no such thing as old age, there is only sorrow.

~Edith Wharton

The soul would have no rainbow, had the eyes no tears.

~John Vance Cheney

This is my last message to you: in sorrow seek happiness.

~Fyodor Dostoyevsky

Joys are our wings, sorrows our spurs.

~Jean Paul Richter

Speech

Be generous with kindly words, especially about those who are absent.

~Johann Wolfgang von Goethe

Be true to your work and your word.

~Ben Morrow

The superior man is modest in his speech, but exceeds in his actions.

~Confucius

I have never been hurt by what I have not said.

~Calvin Coolidge

There are more quarrels smothered by just shutting your mouth, and holding it shut, than by all the wisdom in the world.

~Henry Ward Beecher

Think twice before you speak, because your words and influence will plant the seed of either success or failure in the mind of another.

~Napoleon Hill

Your words create what you speak about. Learn to speak positively.
~Sanaya Roman

Make it a point to rid your speech and thoughts of all forms of negative self-talk.

~Karl Albrecht

You can preach a better sermon with your life than with your lips.
~Oliver Goldsmith

Language most shews a man: Speak, that I may see thee.
~Ben Jonson

Be true to your work, your word, and your friend.
~John Boyle O'Reilly

Say what you know, do what you must, come what may.
~Sofia Kovalevskaya

In times like the present, men should utter nothing for which they would not willingly be responsible through time and eternity.
~Abraham Lincoln

The whole art of life is knowing the right time to say things.
~Maeve Binchy

Nature has given us two ears but only one mouth.
~Benjamin Disraeli

If you must speak ill of another, do not speak it, write it in the sand near the water's edge.
~Napoleon Hill

Nothing in this world is harder than speaking the truth, nothing easier than flattery.
~Fyodor Dostoyevsky

A speech is a solemn responsibility. The man who makes a bad thirty-minute speech to two hundred people wastes only a half hour of his own time. But he wastes one hundred hours of the audience's time—more than four days—which should be a hanging offense.
~Jenkin Lloyd Jones

Blessed is the man who, having nothing to say, abstains from giving us wordy evidence of the fact.
~George Eliot

Well-timed silence hath more eloquence than speech.
~Martin Farquhar Tupper

Long and curious speeches are as fit for dispatch as a robe, or mantle, with a long train, is for a race.
~Francis Bacon

The tongue is the only instrument that gets sharper with use.
~Washington Irving

The ability to express an idea is well nigh as important as the idea itself.
~Bernard Baruch

Kind words can be short and easy to speak, but their echoes are truly endless.

~Mother Teresa

Perhaps you will forget tomorrow the kind words you say today, but the recipient may cherish them over a lifetime.

~Dale Carnegie

Spiritual

The spiritual life does not remove us from the world but leads us deeper into it.

~Henri J. M. Nouwen

The body is the instrument of the soul.

~Gary Zukav

You don't have a soul, Doctor. You are a soul. You have a body, temporarily.

~Walter M. Miller Jr.

Starting

Start where you are. Use what you have. Do what you can.
~Arthur Ashe

The way to get started is to quit talking and begin doing.
~Walt Disney

Vitality shows not only in the ability to persist, but in the ability to start over.

~F. Scott Fitzgerald

Begin somewhere; you cannot build a reputation on what you intend to do.

~Liz Smith

Your present circumstances don't determine where you can go they merely determine where you start.

~Nido Qubein

How wonderful it is that nobody need wait a single moment before starting to improve the world.

~Anne Frank

The starting point of all achievement is desire.

~Napoleon Hill

Nothing will ever be attempted if all possible objections must first be overcome.

~Samuel Johnson

We should be taught not to wait for inspiration to start a thing. Action always generates inspiration. Inspiration seldom generates action.

~Frank Tibolt

The secret of getting ahead is getting started.

~Mark Twain

Strength

Men are made stronger on realization that the helping hand they need is at the end of their own arm.

~Sidney J. Phillips

With the new day comes new strength and new thoughts.

~Eleanor Roosevelt

In order to feel anything, you need strength.

~Anna Maria Ortese

You're braver than you believe, stronger than you seem, and smarter than you think.

~A. A. Milne

Strong people are made by opposition like kites that go up against the wind.

~Frank Harris

Our real problem, then, is not our strength today; it is the vital necessity of action today to ensure our strength tomorrow.

~Dwight D. Eisenhower

There is nothing stronger in this world than gentleness.
~Han Suyin

I have discovered an inner strength, I knew not I possessed, a quiet peace that flutters, like a dove within my breast.
~Grace E. Easley

You are only as strong as your purpose, therefore let us choose reasons to act that are big, bold, righteous, and eternal.
~Barry Munro

Fire is the test of gold; adversity, of strong men.
~Lucius Annaeus Seneca

To keep our faces toward change and behave like free spirits in the presence of fate is strength undefeatable.
~Helen Keller

For the strength of the Pack is the Wolf, and the strength of the Wolf is the Pack.
~Rudyard Kipling

Strength and wisdom are not opposing values.
~William J. Clinton

Life only demands from you the strength you possess.
~Dag Hammarskjöld

Stress

When you reach the end of your rope, tie a knot in it and hang on.
~Franklin D. Roosevelt

You never will be the person you can be if pressure, tension and discipline are taken out of your life.
~James G. Bilkey

Stress is an ignorant state. It believes that everything is an emergency. Nothing is that important.
~Natalie Goldberg

The perfect no-stress environment is the grave. When we change our perception we gain control.
~Greg Anderson

The stress becomes a challenge, not a threat. When we commit to action, to actually doing something rather than feeling trapped by events, the stress in our life becomes manageable.
~Greg Anderson

Struggle

I will write of him who fights and vanquishes his sins, who struggles on through weary years against himself . . . and wins.
~Caroline Begelow LeRow

If there is no struggle there is no progress . . . Power concedes nothing without a demand. It never did and it never will.
~Frederick Douglass

Believe me, the reward is not so great without the struggle.
~Wilma Rudolph

Stubbornness

I know of no higher fortitude than stubbornness in the face of overwhelming odds.
~Louis Nizer

Time has a way of demonstrating the most stubborn are the most intelligent.
~Yevgeny Yevtushenko

Obstinacy in a bad cause is but constancy in a good.
~Thomas Browne

Success

I couldn't wait for success, so I went ahead without it.
~Jonathan Winters

Success is simple. Do what's right, the right way, at the right time.
~Arnold H. Glasow

Our greatest weakness lies in giving up. The most certain way to succeed is always to try just one more time.
~Thomas A. Edison

Success is not final, failure is not fatal: it is the courage to continue that counts.

~Winston Churchill

In order to succeed, we must first believe that we can.

~Nikos Kazantzakis

Getting along with others is the essence of getting ahead, success being linked with cooperation.

~William Feather

A successful individual typically sets his next goal somewhat but not too much above his last achievement. In this way he steadily raises his level of aspiration.

~Kurt Lewin

Success is blocked by concentrating on it and planning for it. . . . Success is shy—it won't come out while you're watching.

~Tennessee Williams

Successful people keep moving. They make mistakes, but they don't quit.

~Conrad Hilton

Think twice before you speak, because your words and influence will plant the seed of either success or failure in the mind of another.

~Napoleon Hill

I don't believe in failure. It is not failure if you enjoyed the process.
~Oprah Winfrey

It's fine to celebrate success but it is more important to heed the lessons of failure.

~Bill Gates

Success is never final. Failure is never fatal. It's courage that counts.

~Winston Churchill

No one who achieves success does so without acknowledging the help of others.

~Alfred North Whitehead

A strong, positive self-image is the best possible preparation for success.
~Joyce Brothers

The real secret of success is enthusiasm.
~Walter P. Chrysler

The dictionary is the only place where success comes before work.
~Vince Lombardi

What great thing would you attempt if you knew you could not fail?
~Robert H. Schuller

Put your heart, mind, and soul into even your smallest acts. This is the secret of success.
~Swami Sivananda

It takes time to succeed because success is merely the natural reward of taking time to do anything well.
~Joseph Ross

There is only one success . . . to be able to spend your life in your own way, and not to give others absurd maddening claims upon it.
~Christopher Morley

Success does not consist in never making mistakes but in never making the same one a second time.
~George Bernard Shaw

Many of life's failures are people who did not realize how close they were to success when they gave up.
~Thomas Edison

Failure will never overtake me if my determination to succeed is strong enough.
~Og Mandino

Success makes us intolerant of failure and failure makes us intolerant of success.
~William Feather

Be of good cheer. Do not think of today's failures, but of the success that may come tomorrow.

~Helen Keller

Nothing succeeds like success.

~Alexandre Dumas

Your best shot at happiness, self-worth and personal satisfaction — the things that constitute real success — is not in earning as much as you can but in performing as well as you can something that you consider worthwhile.

~William Raspberry

Nobody has things just as he would like them. The thing to do is to make a success with what material I have. It is a sheer waste of time and soul-power to imagine what I would do if things were different. They are not different.

~Frank Crane

It is wise to keep in mind that neither success nor failure is ever final.

~Roger Babson

Success is often the result of taking a misstep in the right direction.
~Al Bernstein

The secret of success is to do the common things uncommonly well.
~John D. Rockefeller Jr.

Belief in oneself is one of the most important bricks in building any successful venture.

~Lydia Maria Child

Success is a little like wrestling a gorilla. You don't quit when you're tired — you quit when the gorilla is tired.

~Robert Strauss

If A is a success in life, then A equals x plus y plus z. Work is x; y is play; and z is keeping your mouth shut.

~Albert Einstein

It is high time that the ideal of success should be replaced with the ideal of service.

~Albert Einstein

The secret of success in life is for a man to be ready for his opportunity when it comes.

~Benjamin Disraeli

Failure is the foundation of success: success is the lurking place of failure.

~Lao Tzu

The conduct of a successful business merely consists in doing things in a very simple way, doing them regularly, and never neglecting to do them.

~William Hesketh Lever

The success of a project will depend critically upon the effort, care, and skill you applied in its initial planning.

~Gerard M. Blair

I cannot give you the formula for success, but I can give you the formula for failure—which is: Try to please everybody.

~Herbert Bayard Swope

If you wish success in life, make perseverance your bosom friend, experience your wise counselor, caution your elder brother and hope your guardian genius.

~Joseph Addison

Remember, a person who wins success may have been counted out many times before. He wins because he refuses to give up.

~Kemmons Wilson

Successful and unsuccessful people do not vary greatly in their abilities. They vary in their desires to reach their potential.

~John C. Maxwell

It is possible to fail in many ways . . . while to succeed is possible only in one way.

~Aristotle

The successful person has unusual skill at dealing with conflict and ensuring the best outcome for all.

~Sun Tzu

Picture yourself vividly as winning, and that alone will contribute immeasurably to success.

~Harry Emerson Fosdick

Advancement only comes with habitually doing more than you are asked.

~Gary Ryan Blair

Success requires three bones—wishbone, backbone, and funny-bone.

~Kobi Yamada

If we are prepared, we have the edge. If we have the edge, we succeed.

~Jeanelle Anderson

Half of success is thinking that what we are doing has got to be done the best anybody ever did it.

~Helen Gurley Brown

Success is an inside job.

~Ralph Ford

Some succeed because they are destined to, but most succeed because they are determined to.

~Henry Van Dyke

People rarely success unless they have fun in what they are doing.
~Dale Carnegie

To be believable is the only way that you could be successful.
~Tanya Tucker

The talent of success is nothing more than doing what you can do well and doing well whatever you do.

~Henry Wadsworth Longfellow

Success is a science; if you have the conditions, you get the results.
~Oscar Wilde

It isn't success after all, is it, if it isn't an expression of your deepest energies?

~Marilyn French

Success is to be measured not so much by the position that one has reached in life as by the obstacles which he has overcome.

~Booker T. Washington

The successful man will profit from his mistakes and try again in a different way.

~Dale Carnegie

Far better it is to dare mighty things, to win glorious triumphs, even though checkered by failure, than to rank with those poor spirits who neither enjoy nor suffer much because they live in the gray twilight that knows neither victory nor defeat.

~Theodore Roosevelt

Coming together is a beginning. Keeping together is progress. Working together is success.

~Henry Ford

Success usually comes to those who are too busy to be looking for it.

~Henry David Thoreau

Most great people have attained their greatest success just one step beyond their greatest failure.

~Napoleon Hill

A minute's success pays the failure of years.

~Robert Browning

Success is how high you bounce when you hit bottom.

~George S. Patton Jr.

Self-trust is the first secret of success.

~Ralph Waldo Emerson

If one advances confidently in the direction of his dreams, and endeavors to live the life which he has imagined, he will meet with a success unexpected in common hours.

~Henry David Thoreau

Suffering

If suffer we must, let's suffer on the heights.

~Victor Hugo

The chief pang of most trials is not so much the actual suffering itself as our own spirit of resistance to it.

~Jean Nicolas Grou

Those who have suffered understand suffering and therefore extend their hand.

~Patti Smith

The truth that many people never understand, until it is too late, is that the more you try to avoid suffering, the more you suffer, because smaller and more insignificant things begin to torture you, in proportion to your fear of being hurt.

~Thomas Merton

Sunshine

Give me the splendid silent sun with all his beams full-dazzling.

~Walt Whitman

Support

Those whom we support hold us up in life.

~Marie von Ebner-Eschenbach

Don't expect anyone else to support you. Maybe you have a trust fund. Maybe you'll have a wealthy spouse. But you never know when either one might run out.

~Mary Schmich

Surrender

He is no fool who gives what he cannot keep to gain that which he cannot lose.

~Jim Elliott

Talent

If you have great talents, industry will improve them: if you have but moderate abilities, industry will supply their deficiency.

~Sir Joshua Reynolds

It takes people a long time to learn the difference between talent and genius, especially ambitious young men and women.
~Louisa May Alcott

Talent wins games, but teamwork and intelligence win championships.
~Michael Jordan

Everyone has talent. What is rare is the courage to follow the talent to the dark place where it leads.
~Erica Jong

Talent does what it can: genius does what it must.
~Edward G. Bulwer-Lytton

Hide not your talents. They for use were made. What's a sundial in the shade?
~Benjamin Franklin

Too many companies believe people are interchangeable. Truly gifted people never are. They have unique talents. Such people cannot be forced into roles they are not suited for, nor should they be.
~Warren G. Bennis

One machine can do the work of fifty ordinary men. No machine can do the work of one extraordinary man.
~Elbert Hubbard

You can judge the height of someone's talent by what he aspires to. Only a great thing can satisfy a great talent.
~Baltasar Gracián y Morales

If things come naturally, you may not bother to work at improving them, and you can fall short of your potential.
~Bob Pettit

Talent is like electricity. We don't understand electricity. We use it.
~Maya Angelou

If you have a talent, use it in every which way possible. Don't hoard it. Don't dole it out like a miser. Spend it lavishly like a millionaire intent on going broke.
~Brendan Francis Behan

Talking

The way to get started is to quit talking and begin doing.
~Walt Disney

One advantage of talking to yourself is that you know at least somebody's listening.
~Franklin P. Jones

Talk happiness. The world is sad enough without your woe. No path is wholly rough.
~Ella Wheeler Wilcox

We seldom regret talking too little, but very often talking too much. This is a well-known maxim which everybody knows and nobody practices.
~La Bruyère

Nature hath bestowed upon us two ears, and two eyes, yet but one tongue, which is an emblem unto us that though we hear and see much, yet out we to speak but little.
~Mary Tattlewell

The deepest rivers flow with the least sound.
~Quintus Curtius Rufus

Every man is bound to leave a story better than he found it.
~Mary Augusta Ward

Taxes

The income tax has made more liars out of the American people than golf has.
~Will Rogers

There's just one thing I can't figure out. My income tax!
~Nat King Cole

Teaching

We cannot teach people anything; we can only help them discover it within themselves.
~Galileo Galilei

It is the supreme art of the teacher to awaken joy in creative expression and knowledge.

~Albert Einstein

Life ought to be a struggle of desire toward adventures whose nobility will fertilize the soul.

~Rebecca West

A master can tell you what he expects of you. A teacher, though, awakens your own expectations.

~Patricia Neal

If you would thoroughly know anything, teach it to others.

~Tryon Edwards

Teamwork

Talent wins games, but teamwork and intelligence win championships.

~Michael Jordan

There is no such thing as "them and us." In a world this size there can only be "we" —all of us working together.

~Don Ward

Great men are rarely isolated mountain peaks; they are the summits of ranges.

~Thomas Wentworth Higginson

Great discoveries and improvement invariably involve the cooperation of many minds. I may be given credit for having blazed the trail, but when I look at the subsequent developments I feel the credit is due to others rather than to myself.

~Alexander Graham Bell

Women and men have to fight together to change society—and both will benefit . . . . Partnership, not dependence, is the real romance in marriage.

~Muriel Fox

No one can whistle a symphony. It takes an orchestra to play it.

~H. E. Luccock

A good team is a great place to be, exciting, stimulating, supportive, successful. A bad team is horrible, a sort of human prison.
~Charles Handy

The ultimate power of a successful general staff lies, not in the brilliance of its individual members, but in the cross-fertilization of its collective abilities.
~Reg Revans

Teamwork is a constant balancing act between self-interest and group interest.
~Susan Campbell

A team is not a bunch of people with job titles, but a congregation of individuals, each of whom has a role that is understood by other members.
~Meredith Belbin

For the strength of the Pack is the Wolf, and the strength of the Wolf is the Pack.
~Rudyard Kipling

No one who achieves success does so without acknowledging the help of others.
~Alfred North Whitehead

Two men working as a team will produce more than three men working as individuals.
~Charles P. McCormick

Tears

The soul would have no rainbow, had the eyes no tears.
~John Vance Cheney

Technology

Society produces technology and technology produces society in an endless mesh of action and interaction.
~Kenneth E. Boulding

Temper

Man seems to be capable of great virtues but not of small virtues; capable of defying his torturer but not of keeping his temper.
~G. K. Chesterton

Temptations

There is not any memory with less satisfaction than the memory of some temptation we resisted.
~James Branch Cabell

Why comes temptation, but for man to meet and master and make crouch beneath his foot, and so be pedestaled in triumph?
~Robert Browning

Temptations, like misfortunes, are sent to test our moral strength.
~Margaret of Valois

Thankfulness

Thanks . . . Small word . . . Big meaning.
~Barbara Bartocci

If the only prayer you say in your whole life is thank you, that would suffice.
~Meister Eckhart

The thankful receiver bears a plentiful harvest.
~William Blake

A thankful heart is . . . the parent of all other virtues.
~Marcus Tullius Cicero

Thoughts

I have always thought the actions of men the best interpreters of their thoughts.
~John Locke

With the new day comes new strength and new thoughts.
~Eleanor Roosevelt

The temple of our purest thoughts is silence.
~Sarah Josepha Hale

The highest possible stage in moral culture is when we recognize that we ought to control our thoughts.
~Charles Darwin

Make it a point to rid your speech and thoughts of all forms of negative self-talk.
~Karl Albrecht

The thoughts you think will irradiate you as though you are a transparent vase.
~Maurice Maeterlinck

Thoughts are energy, and you can make your world or break your world by your thinking.
~Susan L. Taylor

A thought which does not result in an action is nothing much, and an action which does not proceed from a thought is nothing at all.
~Georges Bernanos

As you think, you travel, and as you love, you attract. You are to-day where your thoughts have brought you; you will be tomorrow where your thoughts take you.
~James Lane Allen

When you rule your mind you rule your world. When you choose your thoughts you choose results.
~Imelda Shanklin

So long as we think dugout canoes are the only possibility—all that is real or can be real—we will never see the ship, we will never feel the free wind blow.
~Sonia Johnson

You know more than you think you know.
~Oscar Wilde

The most courageous act is still to think for yourself. Aloud.
~Coco Chanel

There is nothing either good or bad, but thinking makes it so.
~William Shakespeare

If we are not responsible for the thoughts that pass our doors, we are at least responsible for those we admit and entertain.
~Charles B. Newcomb

The soul becomes dyed with the color of its thoughts.
~Marcus Aurelius

Great thoughts speak only to the thoughtful mind, but great actions speak to all mankind.
~Theodore Roosevelt

I know for sure that what we dwell on is who we become.
~Oprah Winfrey

Life is not long, and too much of it must not pass in idle deliberation how it shall be spent.
~Samuel Johnson

Very little is needed to make a happy life; it is all within yourself, in your way of thinking.
~Marcus Aurelius

You can't have a better tomorrow if you are thinking about yesterday all the time.
~Charles F. Kettering

Play with your ideas; thinking should be fun.
~Harold R. McAlindon

What we have to do is to be forever curiously testing new opinions and courting new impressions.
~Walter Pater

Think positively and masterfully, with confidence and faith, and life becomes more secure, more fraught with action, richer in achievement and experience.
~Swami Sivananda

There is nothing wrong with taking time to just sit and think.
~Stephanie Goddard Davidson

While we stop to think, we often miss our opportunity.
~Publilius Syrus

I must have something to engross my thoughts, some object in life which will fill this vacuum and prevent this sad wearing away of the heart.
~Elizabeth Blackwell

You cannot always control your circumstances. But you can control your own thoughts.
~Charles E. Popplestone

The only reason some people get lost in thought is because it's unfamiliar territory.
~Paul Fix

We know what a person thinks not when he tells us what he thinks, but by his actions.
~Isaac Bashevis Singer

Clear thinking requires courage rather than intelligence.
~Thomas Szasz

Freedom means the opportunity to be what we never thought we would be.
~Daniel J. Boorstin

Diversity: the art of thinking independently together.
~Malcolm Forbes

The mind ought sometimes to be diverted that it may return to better thinking.
~Phaedrus

Often you get the best insights by considering extremes — by thinking of the opposite of that with which you are directly concerned.
~C. Wright Mills

By your thoughts you are daily, even hourly, building your life; you are carving your destiny.
~Ruth Barrick Golden

Reason itself is fallible, and this fallibility must find a place in our logic.

~Nicola Abbagnano

Half of our mistakes in life arise from feeling where we ought to think, and thinking where we ought to feel.

~John Churton Collins

We do not live to think, but, on the contrary, we think in order that we may succeed in surviving.

~José Ortega y Gasset

They can because they think they can.

~Virgil

Think twice before you speak, because your words and influence will plant the seed of either success or failure in the mind of another.

~Napoleon Hill

What you think, you become.

~Buddha

It's time to start thinking with the heart.

~Beverley Wilson

There is a sacred realm of privacy for every man and woman where he makes his choices and decisions—a realm of his own essential rights and liberties into which the law, generally speaking, must not intrude.

~Geoffrey Fisher

Be vigilant; guard your mind against negative thoughts.

~Buddha

Change your thoughts and you change your world.

~Norman Vincent Peale

A little thought in life is like salt upon rice.

~Rudyard Kipling

Remember, happiness doesn't depend upon who you are or what you have, it depends solely upon what you think.

~Dale Carnegie

Look at all the sentences which seem true and question them.
~David Reisman

Whatever comes from the brain carries the hue of the place it came from, and whatever comes from the heart carries the heat and color of its birthplace.
~Oliver Wendell Holmes Sr.

Our minds become magnetized with the dominating thoughts which we hold in our minds, and . . . these "magnets" attract to us the forces, the people, the circumstances of life which harmonize with the nature of our domination thoughts.
~Napoleon Hill

People are usually more convinced by reasons they discovered themselves than by those found out by others.
~Blaise Pascal

Time

It is so easy to waste our lives: our days, our hours, our minutes . . . It is so easy to exist instead of live.
~Anna Quindlen

All that really belongs to us is time; even he who has nothing else has that.
~Baltasar Gracián y Morales

The years teach much that the days never know.
~Ralph Waldo Emerson

Death is a commingling of eternity with time; in the death of a good man, eternity is seen looking through time.
~Johann Wolfgang von Goethe

An unhurried sense of time is in itself a form of wealth.
~Bonnie Friedman

Time can but make it easier to be wise though now it seems impossible, and so all that you need is patience.
~William Butler Yeats

It is astonishing how short a time it can take for very wonderful things to happen.

~Frances Burnett

Remember that time is money.

~Benjamin Franklin

The only reason for time is so that everything doesn't happen at once.

~Albert Einstein

To reconstruct is to collaborate with time gone by, penetrating or modifying its spirit, and carrying it toward a longer future.

~Marguerite Yourcenar

I would rather have 30 minutes of "wonderful" than a lifetime of nothing special.

~Julia Roberts

We must use time creatively—and forever realize that the time is always hope to do right.

~Martin Luther King Jr.

Do not delay: the golden moments fly!

~Henry Wadsworth Longfellow

Time is my greatest enemy.

~Evita Perón

Don't let the fear of the time it will take to accomplish something stand in the way of your doing it.

~Earl Nightingale

It takes time to succeed because success is merely the natural reward of taking time to do anything well.

~Joseph Ross

Time is the most valuable thing a man can spend.

~Theophrastus

The two most powerful warriors are patience and time.

~Leo Tolstoy

The whole art of life is knowing the right time to say things.

~Maeve Binchy

Do not wait: the time will never be "just right."

~Napoleon Hill

People would have more leisure time if it weren't for all the leisure-time activities that use it up.

~Peg Bracken

Rightly conceived, time is the friend of all who are in any way in adversity, for its mazy road winds in and out of the shadows sooner or later into sunshine, and when one is at its darkest point one can be certain that presently it will grow brighter.

~Arthur Bryant

My own experience has taught me this: if you wait for the perfect moment when all is safe and assured it may never arrive.

~Maurice Chevalier

I live what most people call the good life. I was happy, but deep inside I always felt that, with the short amount of time we are given to live and love in this world, we spend too much time loving things instead of people.

~Mother Antonia

If time be of all things most precious, wasting time must be the greatest prodigality, since lost time is never found again.

~Benjamin Franklin

Time as he grows old teaches all things.

~Aeschylus

Time is the coin of your life. It is the only coin you have, and only you can determine how it will be spent. Be careful lest you let other people spend it for you.

~Carl Sandburg

Sometimes being a friend means mastering the art of timing. There is a time for silence. A time to let go and allow people to hurl themselves into their own destiny. And a time to prepare to pick up the pieces when it's all over.

~Gloria Naylor

Far from being a thief of Time, procrastination is the king of it.
~Ogden Nash

Money and time are the heaviest burdens of life, and . . . the un-happiest of all mortals are those who have more of either than they know how to use.
~Samuel Johnson

The present is the ever moving shadow that divides yesterday from tomorrow. In that lies hope.
~Frank Lloyd Wright

A speech is a solemn responsibility. The man who makes a bad thir-ty-minute speech to two hundred people wastes only a half hour of his own time. But he wastes one hundred hours of the audience's time—more than four days—which should be a hanging offense.
~Jenkin Lloyd Jones

The proper function of man is to live, not to exist. I shall not waste my days in trying to prolong them. I shall use my time.
~Jack London

Tomorrow hopes we have learned something from yesterday.
~John Wayne

If you haven't got the time to do it right, when will you find the time to do it over?
~Jeffery J. Mayer

Time is the substance from which I am made.
~Jorge Luis Borges

How pleasant it is at the end of the day, no follies to repent, but reflect on the past and be able to say, My time has been properly spent!
~Ann and Jane Taylor

People find life entirely too time-consuming.
~Stanisław Jerzy Lec

I recommend you to take care of the minutes, for hours will take care of themselves.
~Philip Dormer Stanhope

And of all glad words of prose or rhyme, The gladdest are Act while there is yet time.
~Franklin P. Adams

Waste your money and you're only out of money, but waste your time and you've lost a part of your life.
~Michael LeBoeuf

Clocks slay time . . . time is dead as long as it is being clicked off by little wheels; only when the clock stops does time come to life.
~William Faulkner

Much may be done in those little shreds and patches of time which every day produces, and which most men throw away.
~Charles Caleb Colton

Today

What you do today can improve all your tomorrows.
~Ralph Marston

Today always goes better in the light of God's tomorrow.
~David Jeremiah

Today is the only day. Yesterday is gone.
~John Wooden

Every day is a miracle.
~James Gould Cozzens

The only limit to our realization of tomorrow will be our doubts of today. Let us move forward with strong and active faith.
~Franklin D. Roosevelt

Today, this hour, this minute is the day, the hour, the minute for each of us to sense the fact that life is good, with all of its trials and troubles, and perhaps more interesting because of them.
~Robert R. Updegraff

The most wasted of all days is one without laughter.
~E. E. Cummings

I have learned to live each day as it comes, and not to borrow trouble by dreading tomorrow. It is the dark menace of the future that makes cowards of us.

~Dorothy Dix

Every day is my best day; this is my life. I'm not going to have this moment again.

~Bernie Siegel

Today is the day in which to express your noblest qualities of mind and heart, to do at least one worthy thing which you have long postponed.

~Grenville Kleiser

The best preparation for tomorrow is doing your best today.
~H. Jackson Brown Jr.

But today is ours to live its treasures now to use, and it can be our best day we alone can choose.

~Helen Gleason

This is the best day the world has ever seen; tomorrow will be better.

~R. A. Campbell

I feel very happy to see the sun come up every day. I feel happy to be around . . . I like to take this day—any day—and go to town with it.

~James Dickey

Don't let yesterday take up too much of today.

~Will Rogers

Today is a new day. You will get out of it just what you put into it.
~Mary Pickford

So here hath been dawning another blue day: Think, wilt thou let it Slip useless away?

~Thomas Carlyle

I have a new philosophy. I'm only going to dread one day at a time.
~Charles Schulz

You have to count on living every single day in a way you believe will make you feel good about your life—so that if it were over tomorrow you'd be content with yourself.

~Jane Seymour

Tolerance

Blessed is the man who has a skin of the right thickness. He can work happily in spite of enemies and friends.

~Henry T. Bailey

The acceptance of the truth that joy and sorrow, laughter and tears are not confined to any particular time, place or people, but are universally distributed, should make us more tolerant of and more interested in the lives of others.

~William M. Peck

I've learned to be more tolerant, With others and myself, And that one cannot truly give . . . Until one gives himself.

~Grace E. Easley

Tomorrow

The only limit to our realization of tomorrow will be our doubts of today. Let us move forward with strong and active faith.

~Franklin D. Roosevelt

I have learned to live each day as it comes, and not to borrow trouble by dreading tomorrow. It is the dark menace of the future that makes cowards of us.

~Dorothy Dix

You can't have a better tomorrow if you are thinking about yesterday all the time.

~Charles F. Kettering

The best preparation for tomorrow is doing your best today.

~H. Jackson Brown Jr.

Yesterday is not ours to recover, but tomorrow is ours to win or lose.

~Lyndon B. Johnson

Life lived for tomorrow will always be just a day away from being realized.

~Leo Buscaglia

Tradition

What custom hath endeared; we part with sadly, tho we prize it not.

~Joanna Baillie

Tradition is a guide and not a jailer.

~W. Somerset Maugham

Tradition does not form us automatically: we have to work to understand it.

~Thomas Merton

Tradition is what you resort to when you don't have the time or the money to do it right.

~Kurt Herbert Adler

If you have always done it that way, it is probably wrong.

~Charles F. Kettering

"Tradition" is very often an excuse word for people who don't want to change.

~Red Barber

Tranquility

Human pain does not let go of its grip at one point in time. Rather, it works its way out of our consciousness over time. There is a season of sadness. A season of anger. A season of tranquility. A season of hope.

~Robert Veninga

When we are unable to find tranquility within ourselves, it is useless to seek it elsewhere.

~François de La Rochefoucauld

Transformation

The most powerful agent of growth and transformation is something much more basic than any technique: a change of heart.

~John Welwood

Transparency

No man can produce great things who is not thoroughly sincere in dealing with himself.

~James Russell Lowell

Travel

We travel, some of us forever, to seek other states, other lives, other souls.

~Anaïs Nin

I have found out that there ain't no surer way to find out whether you like people or hate them than to travel with them.

~Mark Twain

Treasure

Your diamonds are not in far distant mountains or in yonder seas; they are in your own backyard, if you but dig for them.

~Russell H. Conwell

Troubles

Bad times have a scientific value. These are occasions a good learner would not miss.

~Ralph Waldo Emerson

I have come to realize that all my trouble with living has come from fear and smallness within me.

~Angela L. Wozniak

It is characteristic of all deep human problems that they are not to be approached without some humor and some bewilderment.

~Freeman Dyson

Incident piled on incident no more makes life than brick piled on brick makes a house.

~Edith Ronald Mirrielees

Expect trouble as an inevitable part of life, and when it comes, hold your head high, look it squarely in the eye and say, "I will be bigger than you. You cannot defeat me."

~Ann Landers

Today, this hour, this minute is the day, the hour, the minute for each of us to sense the fact that life is good, with all of its trials and troubles, and perhaps more interesting because of them.

~Robert R. Updegraff

The chief pang of most trials is not so much the actual suffering itself as our own spirit of resistance to it.

~Jean Nicolas Grou

I'm not afraid of storms, for I'm learning how to sail my ship.

~Louisa May Alcott

If a man could have half his wishes, he would double his troubles.

~Benjamin Franklin

Troubles come in every shape, and tend to make one frown—but just cheer up, and never let your troubles get you down.

~Miriam Barker

After a storm comes a calm.

~Matthew Henry

Storms make oaks take deeper root.

~George Herbert

When you reach the end of your rope, tie a knot in it and hang on.

~Franklin D. Roosevelt

Life, misfortunes, isolation, abandonment, poverty, are battlefields that have their heroes; obscure heroes, sometimes greater than illustrious heroes.

~Victor Hugo

It is a pity that our tears on account of our troubles should so blind our eyes that we should not see our mercies.

~John Flavel

The true way to soften one's troubles is to solace those of others.

~Françoise d'Aubigné

When we become aware that we do not have to escape our pains, but that we can mobilize them into a common search for life, those very pains are transformed from expressions of despair into signs of hope.

~Henri J. M. Nouwen

If everything were perfect in this life, we would never learn anything new. We would not be able to elevate our spirits through the events that happen to us.

~Lynn V. Andrews

The question of life is not whether you get knocked down. You will. The question is, are you ready to get back up, are you willing to get back up and fight for what you believe in?

~Dan Quayle

Our achievements speak for themselves. What we have to keep track of are our failures, discouragements, and doubts. We tend to forget the past difficulties, the many false starts, and the painful groping.

~Eric Hoffer

When in doubt, mumble; when in trouble, delegate; when in charge, ponder.

~James H. Boren

In this life we will encounter hurts and trials that we will not be able to change; we are just going to have to allow them to change us.

~Ron Lee Davis

Trust

Love all, trust a few, do wrong to none.

~William Shakespeare

Trust your own instinct. Your mistakes might as well be your own, instead of someone else's.

~Billy Wilder

If we really want to be full and generous in spirit, we have no choice by to trust at some level.

~Rita Dove

Trust is a treasured item.

~Mary Augustine

The chief lesson I have learned in a long life is that the only way to make a man trustworthy is to trust him; and the surest way to make him untrustworthy is to distrust him and show your distrust.

~Henry L. Stimson

Truth

Truth will ultimately prevail where there is pains to bring it to light.

~George Washington

If you look for the truth outside yourself, it gets farther and farther away.

~Tung-Shan

All truth, in the long run, is only common sense clarified.
~Thomas Henry Huxley

The truth of the matter is that you always know the right thing to do. The hard part is doing it.

~Norman Schwarzkopf

Be true to your work, your word, and your friend.
~John Boyle O'Reilly

Truth is like the sun. You can shut it out for a time, but it ain't goin' away.

~Elvis Presley

If you tell the truth, you don't have to remember anything.
~Mark Twain

If you do not tell the truth about yourself you cannot tell it about other people.

~Virginia Woolf

When a thing is true, there is no need to use any arguments to substantiate it.

~Vinoba Bhave

You never find yourself until you face the truth.

~Pearl Bailey

If we live truly, we shall see truly.

~Ralph Waldo Emerson

The fewer the voices on the side of truth, the more distinct and strong must be your own.

~William Ellery Channing

Man has no nobler function than to defend the truth.

~Ruth McKenney

This above all: to thine own self be true, and it must follow, as the night the day, thou canst not then be false to any man.

~William Shakespeare

Truth burns up error.

~Sojourner Truth

It takes two to speak the truth—one to speak and another to hear.

~Henry David Thoreau

Truth indeed rather alleviates than hurts, and will always bear up against falsehood, as oil does above water.

~Miguel de Cervantes

Truth is tough. It will not break, like a bubble, at a touch; nay, you may kick it about all day like a football, and it will be found and full at evening.

~Oliver Wendell Holmes Sr.

In the province of the mind, what one believes to be true either is true or becomes true.

~John Lilly

When in doubt tell the truth.

~Mark Twain

There is nothing so powerful as truth; and often nothing so strange.
~Daniel Webster

Nothing in this world is harder than speaking the truth, nothing easier than flattery.

~Fyodor Dostoyevsky

The greatest friend of truth is Time, her greatest enemy is Prejudice, and her constant companion is Humility.
~Charles Caleb Colton

Honest hearts produce honest actions.

~Brigham Young

All truth passes through three stages. First, it is ridiculed. Second, it is violently opposed. Third, it is accepted as being self-evident.
~Arthur S. Schopenhauer

Even in literature and art, no man who bothers about originality will ever be original: whereas if you simply try to tell the truth (without caring twopence how often it has been told before) you will, nine times out of ten, become original without ever having noticed it.

~C. S. Lewis

For my part, whatever anguish of spirit it may cost, I am willing to know the whole truth—to know the worst and provide for it.
~Patrick Henry

The truth is incontrovertible. Malice may attack it, ignorance may deride it, but in the end, there it is.

~Winston Churchill

It makes all the difference in the world whether we put truth in the first place, or in the second place.

~John Morley

Everything secret degenerates, even the administration of justice; nothing is safe that does not show how it can bear discussion and publicity.

~John Emerich Edward Dalberg-Acton

We know the truth, not only by the reason, but also by the heart.
~Blaise Pascal

The deepest truths are best read between the lines, and, for the most part, refuse to be written.
~Amos Bronson Alcott

Truth is impossible to be soiled by any outward touch as the sunbeam.
~John Milton

An epigram is a flashlight of a truth; a witticism, truth laughing at itself.
~Minna Antrim

Fight for your opinions, but do not believe that they contain the whole truth, or the only truth.
~Charles A. Dana

Try

Defeat is not the worst of failure. Not to have tried is the true failure.
~George E. Woodberry

Nothing is too small to know, and nothing is too big to attempt.
~William Van Horne

It is common sense to take a method and try it; if it fails, admit it frankly and try another. But above all, try something.
~Franklin D. Roosevelt

Ever tried. Ever failed. No matter. Try again. Fail again. Fail better.
~Samuel Beckett

There is no failure except in no longer trying.
~Elbert Hubbard

A person who has never made a mistake never tried anything new.
~Albert Einstein

You may be disappointed if you fail, but you are doomed if you don't try.

~Beverly Sills

What would life be if we had no courage to attempt anything?
~Vincent van Gogh

Tyranny

Concepts such as truth, justice, and compassion . . . are often the only bulwarks which stand against ruthless power.

~Aung San Suu Kyi

Understanding

Be modest, be respectful of others, try to understand.
~Lakhdar Brahimi

Mystery creates wonder and wonder is the basis of man's desire to understand.

~Neil Armstrong

Nothing in life is to be feared, it is only to be understood. Now is the time to understand more, so that we may fear less.
~Marie Curie

The more and more you listen, the more and more you will hear. The more you hear, the more and more deeply you will understand.
~Khyentse Rinpohe

One of the most beautiful qualities of true friendship is to understand and to be understood.

~Lucius Annaeus Seneca

The more you learn what to do with yourself, and the more you do for others, the more you will learn to enjoy the abundant life.
~William Boetcker

There is much satisfaction in work well done . . . but there can be no happiness equal to the joy of finding a heart that understands.
~Victor Robinson

In a world as empirical as ours, a youngster who does not know what he is good at will not be sure what he is good for.
~Edgar Z. Friedenberg

Every man hears only what they understand.
~Johann Wolfgang von Goethe

Unhappiness

Unhappiness is not knowing what we want and killing ourselves to get it.
~Don Herold

Uniqueness

Every man is more than just himself; he also represents the unique, the very special and always significant and remarkable point at which the world's phenomena intersect, only once in this way, and never again.
~Herman Hesse

There has never been another you.
~Dan Zadra

Not all horses were born equal. A few were born to win.
~Mark Twain

Each human is uniquely different. Like snowflakes, the human pattern is never cast twice.
~Alice Childress

In order to be irreplaceable one must always be different.
~Coco Chanel

There is a place here that only you can fill.
~Michael McLean

You are an unrepeatable miracle.
~Diane Roger

Everybody is talented, original, and has something important to say.
~Brenda Ueland

Each mind has its own method.

~Ralph Waldo Emerson

Unity

One for all, or all for one.

~William Shakespeare

We must learn to live together as brothers or perish together as fools.

~Martin Luther King Jr.

Value

What we obtain too cheap, we esteem too lightly.

~Thomas Paine

I think people don't place a high enough value on how much they are nurtured by doing whatever it is that totally absorbs them.

~Jean Shinoda Bolen

We never know the worth of water till the well is dry.

~Thomas Fuller

I was brought up to believe that the only thing worth doing was to add to the sum of accurate information in the world.

~Margaret Mead

A people that values its privileges above its principles soon loses both.

~Dwight D. Eisenhower

An object in possession seldom retains the same charm that it had in pursuit.

~Pliny the Elder

Open your arms to change, but don't let go of your values.

~Dalai Lama

What you risk reveals what you value.

~Jeanette Winterson

Our problem is not to find better values but to be faithful to those we profess.

~John W. Gardner

When your values are clear to you, making decisions becomes easier.

~Roy Disney

Sometimes you will never know the value of a moment until it becomes a memory.

~Theodor Seuss Geisel (Dr. Seuss)

Everything in life is passing and whatever we possess cannot endure forever but ends in nothingness.

~Helen Steiner Rice

Men are more important than tools. If you don't believe so, put a good tool into the hands of a poor workman.

~John J. Bernet

Too many companies believe people are interchangeable. Truly gifted people never are. They have unique talents. Such people cannot be forced into roles they are not suited for, nor should they be.

~Warren G. Bennis

Every true man, sir, who is a little above the level of the beasts and plants . . . lives so as to give a meaning and a value to his own to life.

~Luigi Pirandello

You are a child of the universe, no less than the trees and the stars; you have a right to be here.

~Max Ehrmann

Nature never made a nobody.

~Melvin Chapman

You are one of the forces of nature.

~Jules Michelet

We are more, much more, than what we have.

~Don Wilson

You are an unrepeatable miracle.
~Diane Roger

It's important that people should know what you stand for. It is equally important that they know what you won't stand for.
~Mary Waldrin

Keep your old love letters. Throw away your old bank statements.
~Mary Schmich

The little things? The little moments? They aren't little.
~Jon Kabat-Zinn

Everything is nothing 'Til you make it something more . . . For everything is special If you only make it so!
~Beverly Enderby Kimzey

What is a cynic? A man who knows the price of everything and the value of nothing.
~Oscar Wilde

There is nothing so catching as refinement.
~Emily Eden

Veterans

But the freedom that they fought for, and the country grand they wrought for, Is their monument to-day, and for aye.
~Thomas Dunn English

Victory

A mind troubled by doubt cannot focus on the course to victory.
~Arthur Golden

I came, I saw, I conquered.
~Julius Caesar

I will write of him who fights and vanquishes his sins, who struggles on through weary years against himself . . . and wins.
~Caroline Begelow LeRow

Be ashamed to die until you have won some victory for humanity.
~Horace Mann

If you believe in yourself and have dedication and pride—and never quit, you'll be a winner. The price of victory is high but so are the rewards.

~Bear Bryant

An ounce of peace is worth more than a pound of victory.
~St. Robert Bellarmine

Accept the challenges so that you can feel the exhilaration of victory.

~George S. Patton

A victory without danger is a triumph without glory.
~Pierre Corneille

The people who remained victorious were less like conquerors than conquered.

~Augustine

There are only two forces in the world: the sword and the spirit. In the long run the sword will always be conquered by the spirit.
~Napoleon Bonaparte

Violence

The practice of violence, like all action, changes the world, but the most probable change is a more violent world.

~Hannah Arendt

Violence is the last refuge of the incompetent.

~Isaac Asimov

Virtue

Virtue is bold, and goodness never fearful.

~William Shakespeare

Who sows virtue reaps honor.

~Leonardo da Vinci

The power of a man's virtue should not be measured by his special efforts, but by his ordinary doing.

~Blaise Pascal

Man seems to be capable of great virtues but not of small virtues; capable of defying his torturer but not of keeping his temper.
~G. K. Chesterton

When we are planning for posterity, we ought to remember that virtue is not hereditary.
~Thomas Paine

Elegance is inferior to virtue.
~Mary Wollstonecraft

Virtue is more clearly shown in the performance of fine actions than in the non-performance of base ones.
~Aristotle

The very spring and root of honesty and virtue lie in good education.
~Plutarch

All the world is searching for joy and happiness, but these cannot be purchased for any price in any market place, because they are virtues that come from within.
~Lucille R. Taylor

Kindness is the sunshine in which virtue grows.
~Robert G. Ingersoll

The truth of the matter is that you always know the right thing to do. The hard part is doing it.
~Norman Schwarzkopf

One's outlook is a part of his virtue.
~Amos Bronson Alcott

The man of virtue makes the difficulty to be overcome his first business, and success only a subsequent consideration.
~Confucius

Vision

They who see only what they wish to see in those around them are very fortunate.
~Marie Bashkirtseff

In forming a bridge between body and mind, dreams may be used as a springboard from which man can leap to new realms of experience lying outside his normal state of consciousness and enlarge his vision.

~Ann Faraday

So long as we think dugout canoes are the only possibility—all that is real or can be real—we will never see the ship, we will never feel the free wind blow.

~Sonia Johnson

See the things you want as already yours. Think of them as yours, as belonging to you, as already in your possession.

~Robert Collier

Where there is no vision, there is no hope.

~George Washington Carver

Our vision controls the way we think and, therefore, the way we act. . . . The vision we have of our job determines what we do and the opportunities we see or don't see.

~Charles Koch

Vitality

Vitality shows not only in the ability to persist, but in the ability to start over.

~F. Scott Fitzgerald

Vows

He who promises more than he is able to perform is false to himself, and he who does not perform what he has promised, is a traitor to his friend.

~George Shelley

It is not the oath that makes us believe the man, but the man the oath.

~Aeschylus

Vulnerable

When we were children, we used to think that when we were grown-up, we would no longer be vulnerable. But to grow up is to accept vulnerability . . . To be alive is to be vulnerable.
~Madeleine L'Engle

Waiting

My own experience has taught me this: if you wait for the perfect moment when all is safe and assured it may never arrive.
~Maurice Chevalier

Do not wait: the time will never be "just right."
~Napoleon Hill

Patience is not simply the ability to wait—it's how we behave while we're waiting.
~Joyce Meyer

Wander

As the rolling stone gathers no moss, so the roving heart gathers no affections.
~Anna Brownell Jameson

War

But the freedom that they fought for, and the country grand they wrought for, Is their monument to-day, and for aye.
~Thomas Dunn English

War is a beastly business, it is true, but one proof we are human is our ability to learn, even from it, how better to exist.
~M. F. K. Fisher

Warning

One thorn of experience is worth a whole wilderness of warning.
~James Russell Lowell

There are two types of people who will tell you that you cannot make a difference in this world: those who are afraid to try and those who are afraid you will succeed.

~Ray Goforth

If you can't be a good example, then you'll just have to be a horrible warning.

~Catherine Aird

Weakness

Our greatest weakness lies in giving up. The most certain way to succeed is always to try just one more time.

~Thomas A. Edison

Wealth

An unhurried sense of time is in itself a form of wealth.

~Bonnie Friedman

Who is wise? He that learns from everyone. Who is powerful? He that governs his passions. Who is rich? He that is content.

~Benjamin Franklin

Wealth consists not in having great possessions, but in having few wants.

~Epictetus

No man can become rich without himself enriching others.

~Andrew Carnegie

There is no fixed road to wealth, and goods do not stay with the same master forever.

~Sima Qian

Money is only a tool. It will take you wherever you wish, but it will not replace you as the driver.

~Ayn Rand

It is only by following your deepest instinct that you can lead a rich life, and if you let your fear of consequence prevent you from following your deepest instinct, then your life will be safe, expedient and thin.

~Katharine Butler Hathaway

There is no wealth but life.

~John Ruskin

If we command our wealth, we shall be rich and free; if our wealth commands us, we are poor indeed.

~Edmund Burke

Weeds

What is a weed? A plant whose virtues have not yet been discovered.

~Ralph Waldo Emerson

Weep

I have wept to see thee weep.

~Mary Robinson

A good laugh is good for the spirits it's true, but a good cry is good for the soul.

~Bette Midler

Will

Great things are not something accidental, but must certainly be willed.

~Vincent Van Gogh

It is energy—the central element of which is will—that produces the miracles of enthusiasm in all ages. Everywhere it is the mainspring of what is called force of character, and the sustaining power of all great action.

~Samuel Smiles

Winning

Winning is only half of it. Having fun is the other half.
~Bum Phillips

Sooner or later, those who win are those who think they can.
~Richard Bach

I will write of him who fights and vanquishes his sins, who struggles on through weary years against himself . . . and wins.
~Caroline Begelow LeRow

If you believe in yourself and have dedication and pride—and never quit, you'll be a winner. The price of victory is high but so are the rewards.
~Bear Bryant

Unless both sides win, no agreement can be permanent.
~Jimmy Carter

If we win, nobody will care. If we lose, there will be nobody to care.
~Winston Churchill

Winning isn't everything—but wanting to win is.
~Vince Lombardi

Before you can win, you have to believe you are worthy.
~Mike Ditka

You don't win games on optimism. You win games with preparation.
~Monte Clark

I would rather lose in a cause that will someday win, than win in a cause that will someday lose!
~Woodrow Wilson

Winning is a habit. Unfortunately so is losing.
~Vince Lombardi

Wisdom

The only true wisdom is in knowing you know nothing.
~Socrates

It is good even for old men to learn wisdom.
~Aeschylus

Those who wish to appear wise among fools, among the wise seem foolish.
~Quintilian

Knowledge comes, but wisdom lingers.

~Alfred, Lord Tennyson

Like an ability or a muscle, hearing your inner wisdom is strengthened by doing it.

~Robbie Gass

Never mistake knowledge for wisdom. One helps you make a living; the other helps you make a life.

~Eleanor Roosevelt

The man with insight enough to admit his limitations comes nearest to perfection.

~Johann Wolfgang von Goethe

The wisest of the men I've talked to mostly have said the same things: talk to your father and mother, talk to your wife, talk to your kids . . . be there for the small moments, appreciate yourself, don't be afraid to be too happy.

~Bill Scanlon

A clever person solves a problem. A wise person avoids it.

~Albert Einstein

Knowing yourself is the beginning of all wisdom.

~Aristotle

Authority without wisdom is like a heavy axe without an edge, fitter to bruise than polish.

~Anne Bradstreet

They must often change who would remain constant in happiness or wisdom.

~Confucius

Undoubtedly the greatest wisdom is not to be too wise.

~Catherine Willoughby

A loving heart is the truest wisdom.

~Charles Dickens

It is far easier to be wise for others than to be so for oneself.

~François Due de La Rochefoucauld

A wise man will make more opportunities than he finds.
~Francis Bacon

No man is wise enough by himself.
~Titus Maccius Plautus

Throughout life, one does not miss any chance to hold onto the things that are really precious, if one is truly wise.
~Ed Greenwood

Who is wise? He that learns from everyone. Who is powerful? He that governs his passions. Who is rich? He that is content.
~Benjamin Franklin

It is wise to keep in mind that neither success nor failure is ever final.
~Roger Babson

The best-informed man is not necessarily the wisest.
~Dietrich Bonhoeffer

We cannot change the cards we are dealt, just how we play the hand.
~Randy Pausch

What wisdom can you find that is greater than kindness.
~Jean Jacques Rousseau

The older I grow the more I distrust the familiar doctrine that age brings wisdom.
~H. L. Mencken

Strength and wisdom are not opposing values.
~William J. Clinton

Misfortune seldom intrudes upon the wise man; his greatest and highest interests are directed by reason throughout the course of life.
~Epicurus

If you must speak ill of another, do not speak it, write it in the sand near the water's edge.
~Napoleon Hill

The wise does at once what the fool does at last.
~Baltasar Gracián y Morales

There are two types of people—those who come into a room and say, "Well, here I am!" and those who come in and say, "Ah, there you are!"
~Frederick L. Collins

The only medicine for suffering, crime, and all the other woes of mankind, is wisdom.
~Thomas Henry Huxley

Wisdom is ofttimes nearer when we stoop than when we soar.
~William Wordsworth

A man begins cutting his wisdom teeth the first time he bites off more than he can chew.
~Herb Caen

The fool doth think he is wise, but the wise man knows himself to be a fool.
~William Shakespeare

Life cannot be administered by definite rules and regulations; that wisdom to deal with a man's difficulties comes only through some knowledge of his life and habits as a whole.
~Jane Addams

The saddest aspect of life right now is that science gathers knowledge faster than society gathers wisdom.
~Isaac Asimov

Besides the noble art of getting things done, there is the noble art of leaving things undone. The wisdom of life consists in the elimination of non-essentials.
~Lin Yutang

Seize the moment of excited curiosity on any subject to solve your doubts; for if you let it pass, the desire may never return, and you may remain in ignorance.
~William Wirt

Every man builds his world in his own image; he has the power to choose, but no power to escape the necessity of choice.
~Ayn Rand

Reduce your plan to writing. The moment you complete this, you will have definitely given concrete form to the intangible desire.
~Napoleon Hill

Your intellect may be confused, but your emotions will never lie to you.
~Roger Ebert

Whenever you find yourself on the side of the majority, it is time to pause and reflect.
~Mark Twain

We learn wisdom from failure much more than from success. We often discover what will do by finding out what will not do; and probably he who never made a mistake never made a discovery.
~Samuel Smiles

Wishes

If a man could have half his wishes, he would double his troubles.
~Benjamin Franklin

Woman

Most of us have trouble juggling. The woman who says she doesn't is someone whom I admire but have never met.
~Barbara Walters

I would venture to guess that Anon, who wrote so many poems without signing them, was often a woman.
~Virginia Woolf

Wonder

The larger the island of knowledge, the longer the shoreline of wonder.
~Ralph W. Sockman

The world will never starve for want of wonders, but only for want of wonder.
~G. K. Chesterton

Mystery creates wonder and wonder is the basis of man's desire to understand.

~Neil Armstrong

The man who cannot wonder . . . is but a pair of spectacles behind which there is not eye.

~Thomas Carlyle

Nobody can conceive or imagine all the wonders there are unseen and unseeable in the world.

~Francis P. Church

Words

There's a great power in words, if you don't hitch too many of them together.

~Josh Billings

Be true to your work and your word.

~Ben Morrow

Think twice before you speak, because your words and influence will plant the seed of either success or failure in the mind of another.

~Napoleon Hill

Your words create what you speak about. Learn to speak positively.
~Sanaya Roman

Be true to your work, your word, and your friend.
~John Boyle O'Reilly

Good words are worth much, and cost little.

~George Herbert

It is with words as with sunbeams—the more they are condensed, the deeper they burn.

~Robert Southey

Handle them carefully, for words have more power than atom bombs.

~Pearl Strachan Hurd

Whatever words we utter should be chosen with care for people will hear them and be influenced by them for good or ill.

~Buddha

No matter what people tell you, words and ideas can change the world.

~Robin Williams

Words are nothing but words; power lies in deeds. Be a person of action.

~Mali Oriot Mamadu Konyate

An intellectual is a man who takes more words than necessary to tell more than he knows.

~Dwight D. Eisenhower

The great enemy of clear language is insincerity. Where there is a gap between one's real and one's declared aims, one turns, as it were, instinctively to long words and exhausted idioms, like a cuttlefish squirting out ink.

~George Orwell

Some men's words I remember so well that I must often use them to express my thought. Yes, because I perceive that we have heard the same truth, but they have heard it better.

~Ralph Waldo Emerson

Style is a simple way of saying complicated things.

~Jean Cocteau

In the end, we will remember not the words of our enemies, but the silence of our friends.

~Martin Luther King Jr.

Work

Nothing will work unless you do.

~Maya Angelou

The days you work are the best days.

~Georgia O'Keeffe

The highest reward for man's toil is not what he gets for it but what he becomes by it.

~John Ruskin

Continuous effort — not strength or intelligence — is the key to unlocking our potential.

~Winston Churchill

Men are more important than tools. If you don't believe so, put a good tool into the hands of a poor workman.

~John Bernet

Work like you don't need the money. Dance like no one is watching. And love like you've never been hurt.

~Mark Twain

Men, for the sake of getting a living, forget to live.

~Margaret Fuller

Be true to your work and your word.

~Ben Morrow

If you want someone to do a good job, ask a busy person.

~Benjamin Franklin

The importance of laughter and humor in the workplace can't be emphasized enough.

~Mike Vance and Diane Deacon

When your work speaks for itself, don't interrupt.

~Henry J. Kaiser

Opportunity is missed by most people because it is dressed in overalls and looks like work.

~Thomas Edison

The best things in life must come by effort from within, not by gifts from the outside.

~Fred Corson

The more I want to get something done the less I call it work.

~Richard Bach

In this life we get only those things for which we hunt, for which we strive, and for which we are willing to sacrifice.
~George Matthew Adams

The more I give myself permission to live in the moment and enjoy it without feeling guilty or judgmental about any other time, the better I feel about the quality of my work.
~Wayne Dyer

If you have great talents, industry will improve them: if you have but moderate abilities, industry will supply their deficiency.
~Sir Joshua Reynolds

Work is not always required . . . there is such a thing as sacred idleness, the cultivation of which is now fearfully neglected.
~George MacDonald

In an industrial society which confuses work and productivity, the necessity of producing has always been an enemy of the desire to create.
~Raoul Vaneigem

Be true to your work, your word, and your friend.
~John Boyle O'Reilly

Work hard, stay positive, and get up early. It's the best part of the day.
~George Allen

Laziness may appear attractive, but work gives satisfaction.
~Anne Frank

There is no substitute for hard work.
~Thomas A. Edison

The dictionary is the only place where success comes before work.
~Vince Lombardi

Sometimes opportunities float right past your nose. Work hard, apply yourself, and be ready. When an opportunity comes you can grab it.
~Julie Andrews

Make no little plans. They have no magic to stir men's blood . . .
Make big plans, aim high in hope and work.

~Daniel H. Burnham

Happiness, I have discovered, is nearly always a rebound from
hard work.

~David Grayson

Don't ever confuse the two, your life and your work . . . The second
is only part of the first.

~Anna Quindlen

The trick is in what one emphasizes. We either make ourselves mis-
erable, or we make ourselves happy. The amount of work is the
same.

~Carlos Castaneda

You cannot be really first-rate at your work if your work is all you
are.

~Anna Quindlen

If he works for you, you work for him.

~Japanese Proverb

I am a great believer in luck, and I find the harder I work the more
I have of it.

~Stephen Leacock

A day's work is a day's work, neither more nor less, and the man
who does it needs a day's sustenance, a night's repose, and due
leisure, whether he be painter or ploughman.

~George Bernard Shaw

Derive happiness in oneself from a good day's work from illumi-
nating the fog that surrounds us.

~Henri Matisse

There ain't no free lunches in this country. And don't go spend-
ing your whole life commiserating that you got raw deals. You've
got to say, "I think that if I keep working at this and want it bad
enough I can have it."

~Lee Iacocca

One must not always think so much about what one should do, but rather what one should be. Our works do not ennoble us; but we must ennoble our works.

~Meister Eckhart

Nothing ever comes to one, that is worth having, except as a result of hard work.

~Booker T. Washington

I learned the value of hard work by working hard.

~Margaret Mead

Luck is the dividend of sweat. The more you sweat, the luckier you get.

~Ray Kroc

Stop wearing your wishbone where your backbone ought to be.

~Elizabeth Gilbert

Get a life in which you are not alone. Find people you love, and who love you. And remember that love is not leisure, it is work.

~Anna Quindlen

Choose a job you love, and you will never have to work a day in your life.

~Confucius

Man needs, for his happiness, not only the enjoyment of this or that, but hope and enterprise and change.

~Bertrand Russell

Work keeps us from three great evils: boredom, vice, and poverty.

~Voltaire

The most important motive for work in school and in life is pleasure in work, pleasure in its result, and the knowledge of the value of the result to the community.

~Albert Einstein

The secret joy in work is contained in one word—excellence. To know how to do something well is to enjoy it.

~Pearl S. Buck

Our vision controls the way we think and, therefore, the way we act. . . . The vision we have of our job determines what we do and the opportunities we see or don't see.

~Charles Koch

He that labors in any great or laudable undertaking has his fatigues first supported by hope, and afterwards rewarded by joy.

~Samuel Johnson

Pleasure in the job puts perfection in the work.

~Aristotle

If you haven't got the time to do it right, when will you find the time to do it over?

~Jeffery J. Mayer

Make your passion your profession.

~Carl Holmes

Your work is to discover your work and then with all your heart to give yourself to it.

~Buddha

Industry is the handmaid of good fortune.

~Martha Wilson

Making a living is only part of life.

~Cecil Andrus

If you have a job without aggravation, you don't have a job.

~Malcolm Forbes

By working faithfully eight hours a day, you may eventually get to be boss and work twelve hours a day.

~Robert Frost

Blessed is the man who has some congenial work, some occupation in which he can put his heart.

~John Burroughs

There is much satisfaction in work well done . . . but there can be no happiness equal to the joy of finding a heart that understands.

~Victor Robinson

Being busy does not always mean real work. The object of all work is production or accomplishment and to either of these ends there must be forethought, system, planning, intelligence, and honest purpose, as well as perspiration. Seeming to do is not doing.
~Thomas Edison

The hope, and not the fact, of advancement, is the spur to industry.
~Henry Taylor

The man who does more than he is paid for will soon be paid for more than he does.
~Napoleon Hill

World

The world ages us too fast. We grow up too quickly, we stop dreaming too early, and we develop the ability to worry at far too young an age.
~Doug Wecker

The more the wonders of the world become inaccessible, the more intensely do its curiosities affect us.
~Colette

Worry

Worry is nothing less than the misuse of your imagination.
~Ed Foreman

We would worry less about what others think of us, if we realized how seldom they do.
~Ethel Barrett

What worries you masters you.
~Haddon W. Robinson

Don't hurry. Don't worry.
~Walter Hagan

What's the use of worrying? It never was worthwhile, so, pack up your troubles in your kit-bag and smile, smile, smile.
~George Henry Powell

What creates despair is the imagination, which . . . insists on predicting millions of moments, thousands of days, and so drains you that you cannot live the moment at hand.

~Andre Dubus

Do not anticipate trouble, or worry about what may never happen. Keep in the sunlight.

~Benjamin Franklin

Worry a little bit every day and in a lifetime you will lose a couple of years. If something is wrong, fix it if you can. But train yourself not to worry. Worry never fixes anything.

~Ernest Hemingway

Worry affects the circulation, the heart and the glands, the whole nervous system, and profoundly affects the heart. I have never known a man who died from overwork, but many who died from doubt.

~Charles W. Mayo

If you can't sleep, then get up and do something instead of lying there and worrying. It's the worry that gets you, not the loss of sleep.

~Dale Carnegie

Worth

I was brought up to believe that the only thing worth doing was to add to the sum of accurate information in the world.

~Margaret Mead

What we obtain too cheap, we esteem too lightly.

~Thomas Paine

I think people don't place a high enough value on how much they are nurtured by doing whatever it is that totally absorbs them.

~Jean Shinoda Bolen

We never know the worth of water till the well is dry.

~Thomas Fuller

Learn to value yourself, which means: fight for your happiness.

~Ayn Rand

A man's worth is no greater than his ambitions.

~Marcus Aurelius

Why not spend some time in determining what is worthwhile for us, and then go after that?

~William Ross

Everything in life is passing and whatever we possess cannot endure forever but ends in nothingness.

~Helen Steiner Rice

Men are more important than tools. If you don't believe so, put a good tool into the hands of a poor workman.

~John J. Bernet

It is not what he has, or even what he does which expresses the worth of a man, but what he is.

~Henri-Frédéric Amiel

Too many companies believe people are interchangeable. Truly gifted people never are. They have unique talents. Such people cannot be forced into roles they are not suited for, nor should they be.

~Warren G. Bennis

Writing

Let other pens dwell on guilt and misery.

~Jane Austen

A No. 2 pencil and a dream can take you anywhere.

~Joyce A. Myers

You don't write because you want to say something; you write because you have something to say.

~F. Scott Fitzgerald

Wrong

I have to be wrong a certain number of times in order to be right a certain number of times. However, in order to be either, I must first make a decision.

~Frank N. Giampietro

Sometimes things can go right only by first going very wrong.
~Edward Tenner

My doctrine is this, that if we see cruelty or wrong that we have the power to stop, and do nothing, we make ourselves sharers in the guilt.

~Anna Sewell

To live a creative life, we must lose our fear of being wrong.
~Joseph Chilton Pearce

Perhaps it is better to be irresponsible and right, than to be responsible and wrong.

~Winston Churchill

Yesterday

Yesterday is not ours to recover, but tomorrow is ours to win or lose.

~Lyndon B. Johnson

Don't let yesterday take up too much of today.
~Will Rogers

Youth

Youth is a circumstance you can't do anything about. The trick is to grow up without getting old.

~Frank Lloyd Wright

Never suffer youth to be an excuse for inadequacy, nor age and fame to be an excuse for indolence.

~Benjamin Hayden

When I was young, my ambition was to be one of the people who made a difference in this world.

~Jim Henson

Youth is the gift of nature, but age is a work of art.
~Stanisław Jerzy Lec

Unthinking, idle, wild, and young, I laugh'd and danc'd and talk'd and sung.

~Princess Amelia

The deepest definition of youth is life as yet untouched by tragedy.
~Alfred North Whitehead

ACKNOWLEDGMENTS

Thank you to my daughter Elizabeth who was the first to step up and help organize this many quotations into some kind of inspirational format.

Thank you to my friend Julia Ripa who spent hours of typing the many pages and making the table of contents with an organizational approach to what I believe is a lifelong reference book.

Thank you to Rebekah Hakes for plugging away with hours of typing and spell checking to get to the finished product. I know many times your plate was full serving so many others. I admire your serving heart.

INDEX